UNDERSTANDING IMMIGRATION AND REFUGEE POLICY

Other titles in the series

Understanding the finance of welfare
What welfare costs and how to pay for it
Howard Glennerster, Department of Social Administration,
London School of Economics and Political Science
"... a brilliant and lively textbook that students will enjoy."
Ian Shaw, School of Sociology and Social Policy, University of Nottingham
PB £17.99 (US$26.95) ISBN-10 1 86134 405 8 ISBN-13 978 1 86134 405 2
HB £50.00 (US$59.95) ISBN-10 1 86134 406 6 ISBN-13 978 1 86134 406 9
240 x 172mm 256 pages May 2003

Understanding social security
Issues for policy and practice
Jane Millar, Department of Social and Policy Sciences, University of Bath
"This first-class text provides students with the most up-to-date review and analysis of social security issues. It will fast become the definitive guide to the subject." **Jonathan Bradshaw, Department of Social Policy and Social Work, University of York**
PB £17.99 (US$26.95) ISBN-10 1 86134 419 8 ISBN-13 978 1 86134 419 9
HB £50.00 (US$59.95) ISBN-10 1 86134 420 1 ISBN-13 978 1 86134 421 2
240 x 172mm 360 pages May 2003

Understanding social citizenship
Themes and perspectives for policy and practice
Peter Dwyer, Department of Sociology and Social Policy,
University of Leeds
"An excellent introduction to current debates about citizenship and the only general social policy text on the subject. Highly recommended. Students will certainly benefit from reading this book."
Nick Ellison, Department of Sociology and Social Policy, University of Durham
PB £17.99 (US$28.95) ISBN-10 1 86134 415 5 ISBN-13 978 1 86134 415 1
HB £50.00 (US$75.00) ISBN-10 1 86134 416 3 ISBN-13 978 1 86134 416 8
240 x 172mm 240 pages May 2004

Understanding the policy process
Analysing welfare policy and practice
John Hudson and **Stuart Lowe**, Department of Social Policy
and Social Work, University of York
"Hudson and Lowe's book provides an excellent review of the issues about the policy process in a changing society and a changing world." **Michael Hill, Visiting Professor in the Health and Social Policy Research Centre, University of Brighton**
PB £17.99 (US$28.95) ISBN-10 1 86134 540 2 ISBN-13 978 1 86134 540 0
HB £50.00 (US$75.00) ISBN-10 1 86134 539 9 ISBN-13 978 1 86134 539 4
240 x 172mm 304 pages June 2004

Forthcoming
Understanding health policy
Rob Baggott
PB £18.99 (US$34.95) ISBN 978 1 86134 630 8
HB £60.00 (US$80.00) ISBN 978 1 86134 631 5
240 x 172mm 296 pages June 2007
Understanding health and social care
Jon Glasby
PB £18.99 (US$34.95) ISBN 978 1 86134 910 1
HB £60.00 (US$80.00) ISBN 978 1 86134 911 8
240 x 172mm 216 pages June 2007

If you are interested in submitting a proposal for the series, please contact
The Policy Press
e-mail tpp-info@bristol.ac.uk
tel +44 (0)117 331 4054
fax +44 (0)117 331 4093

INSPECTION COPIES AND ORDERS AVAILABLE FROM:
Marston Book Services
PO Box 269 • Abingdon • Oxon
OX14 4YN UK
INSPECTION COPIES
Tel: +44 (0) 1235 465500
Fax: +44 (0) 1235 465556
Email: inspections@marston.co.uk
ORDERS
Tel: +44 (0) 1235 465500
Fax: +44 (0) 1235 465556
Email: direct.orders@marston.co.uk

www.policypress.org.uk

UNDERSTANDING IMMIGRATION AND REFUGEE POLICY

Contradictions and continuities

Rosemary Sales

First published in Great Britain in 2007 by

The Policy Press
University of Bristol
Fourth Floor, Beacon House
Queen's Road
Bristol BS8 1QU
UK

Tel +44 (0)117 331 4054
Fax +44 (0)117 331 4093
e-mail tpp-info@bristol.ac.uk
www.policypress.org.uk

British Library Cataloguing in Publication Data
A catalogue record for this book is available from the British Library

Library of Congress Cataloging-in-Publication Data
A catalog record for this book has been requested

ISBN 978 1 86134 451 9 paperback
ISBN 978 1 86134 452 6 hardcover

Rosemary Sales is Professor of Social Policy at Middlesex University

Cover design by Qube Design Associates, Bristol.
Front cover: photograph kindly supplied by Getty Images.
Printed and bound in Great Britain by Hobbs the Printers Ltd, Southampton.

To my son Joel Lichman and to the memory of my son
Sean Lawless

Contents

Detailed contents

List of boxes and tables

Boxes

Table

Acknowledgements

This book is based partly on several research projects, some of which are continuing, in which I have been engaged for the past decade. I would like to thank all those colleagues and former colleagues at Middlesex and elsewhere who have worked on these projects with me and whose ideas have helped in the development of the arguments in this book, especially: Brad Blitz, Alessio D'Angelo, Panos Hatziprokopiou, Lesley Hoggart, Tricia Hynes, Eleonore Kofman, Tom Lam, Xia Lin, Lisa Marzano, Veena Meetoo, Nicola Montagna, Louise Ryan, Bernadetta Siara and Mary Tilki. I would also like to thank the interviewees quoted, many of whom must remain anonymous. These projects have been funded by a variety of bodies, including the Economic and Social Research Council, the European Union, Refugee Action, the Big Lottery Fund and Middlesex University.

Thanks are also due to Emily Watt at The Policy Press for being so helpful and flexible during the process of writing this book.

Finally I would like to thank my husband, Keith Lichman, for his unfailing practical and emotional support, which made it possible to complete this book.

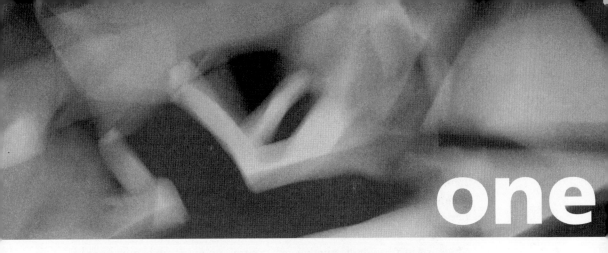

one

Introduction: immigration policy in the twenty-first century

Introduction

On 6 July 2005, it was announced that London had won the competition to host the 2012 Olympic Games. This unexpected decision was widely attributed to London's multiculturalism, which was featured prominently in the campaign to win the Games. The next day, four young British-born Muslims blew themselves up on the London transport network, killing a total of 52 people. This incident, which in the language adopted following the attacks of 11 September (9/11), has become known as 7/7, shattered London's celebration and sense of ease with itself.

This event exacerbated anxieties associated with immigration and ethnic diversity and raised questions about what it means to be a British citizen. These young men were born in Britain, but their acts suggested a rejection in the most deadly fashion of the society in which they lived and had been brought up. Statham, writing earlier, had suggested that the 'assault by the radical right on ... the failures of multiculturalism has effectively linked the anti-immigration debate to questions about the loyalty of groups of migrants who are in many cases already citizens, but ones of Muslim faith' (Statham, 2003: 165–6). This demand for loyalty was taken a stage further by Prime Minister Tony Blair on the first anniversary of the bombings. He demanded that Muslim leaders: 'do more to attack not just the extremists' methods, but their false sense of grievance about the West. Too many Muslim leaders give the impression that they understand and sympathise with the grievances, an attitude that ensures the extremists will never be defeated.'[1]

The main cause of this 'false sense of grievance' was the invasion of Iraq, but the prime minister has refused to acknowledge that this had any part in the motives of the bombers. In the statement above, opposition to the war became tantamount to disloyalty, making British Muslims a suspect community. The bombings thus threatened the long-standing tradition in British policy making of making a sharp distinction between immigration and race relations, which has involved increasingly harsh controls on entry while pursuing anti-discrimination policies and measures to incorporate those who had migrated earlier. This dualistic attitude reflects the ambivalent historical attitude to immigration.

Two weeks later, four other Muslims, all of whom had migrated to Britain, failed in an attempt to reproduce the carnage. Their intervention introduced another dimension; one of the suspects entered Britain as an unaccompanied minor and had been granted asylum. This rekindled the association between asylum and terrorism that had been at the fore, particularly in the wake of the 11 September attacks. The 2001 Anti-terrorism, Crime and Security Act introduced measures to speed up the asylum process for suspected terrorists, excluding substantive consideration of asylum claims where the secretary of state certified that their removal would be 'conducive to the public good'. Just before the July bombings, the government had been criticised in a 'scathing' report by the European commissioner for human rights for its anti-terror laws and its treatment of asylum seekers.[2] In fighting this new form of terrorism within its own borders, the government called for security to be placed above human rights, and sought a derogation from the European Convention on Human Rights to allow expulsions to countries with poor human rights records. Rejecting UN criticism of these planned expulsions, the home secretary claimed that 'the human rights of those people who were blown up on the tube in London on 7 July are, to be quite frank, more important than the human rights of the people who committed those acts'.[3] The government attempted unsuccessfully to introduce a measure allowing terrorist suspects to be detained without charge for three months, a period considerably longer than allowed in any other European country.

Another issue that featured prominently in the reporting of the failed bombing was indignation that one suspect had received welfare benefits while a refugee. With asylum policy increasingly aimed at separating the 'undeserving' majority from the 'deserving' few, this man represented the ultimate undeserving.

The issues raised by these events are central to this book. Immigration policy is now high on the political agenda of Britain and most other western states. This reflects the insecurities brought about by globalisation and the 'war on terror' that in July 2005 'came home' to one of its key instigators. This chapter introduces some of the issues that will be developed further in the rest of the book. The first section raises some general questions concerning immigration policy, challenging the contemporary 'common sense' that controls are inevitable or ethically justifiable. The next section discusses the politicisation of immigration, particularly the preoccupation with asylum that has become conflated with immigration, and sometimes race, in much popular discourse. The following section introduces some aspects of immigration policy that distinguish it from other policy areas, and the next outlines some alternative views about immigration policy. The final section describes the scope of the book and outlines the chapters that follow.

What is at stake in immigration policy?

Immigration policy is essentially concerned with exclusion and inclusion, defining 'insiders' and 'outsiders' in relation to entry to the nation state and the access of non-citizens to rights within that state. It also governs the process by which non-citizens may acquire citizenship.

In an era of globalisation of trade, investment, culture and communications, which undermines the powers of the nation state in many areas, immigration policy remains primarily determined at national level. Indeed, the ability to control national borders has a powerful ideological significance at a time of declining national power. Immigration policy, in determining who may belong to the nation state, is central to constructions of national identity.

Much contemporary rhetoric about immigration policy presupposes an unchanging national homeland around which borders are constructed. The notion of a national state gives legitimacy to government policy carried out in the name of the 'national interest'. In reality, the boundaries around who is included and who is excluded have not been static, but have shifted continually, and encompass both changing geographical borders and changing social divisions in which some groups have been privileged over others. The history of Britain's post-war immigration policy, for example, was one of gradual separation between the rights of different categories of British citizen. The first post-war immigration Act, the 1962 Commonwealth Immigrants Act, ended free entry to Britain for colonial subjects and citizens of the Commonwealth. With the introduction of the notion of 'patrial', which distinguished between citizens of the New (predominantly black) and Old (predominantly white) Commonwealth, this difference became based on ethnicity.

European Union integration has also involved many changes in relation to who are deemed 'insiders'. The development of EU citizenship, which gave the right of free movement within the EU to citizens of member states, was accompanied by stronger controls around the external borders in order to exclude outsiders – 'third country nationals' in EU-speak. Citizens from Eastern Europe have been both insiders and outsiders at different stages. Welcomed as refugees from communism during the Cold War, they became unwanted economic migrants when the collapse of these regimes brought thousands to the West in search of economic survival. Whereas they had been prevented from leaving by the old regimes, when free to emigrate they were met with increasing restrictions on entry to western states. With the restructuring of the EU's borders, and the accession of eight new members from Eastern Europe in 2004, their nationals became EU citizens themselves, although a transitional period prevented them from gaining immediate rights to work in most member states. The British government was one of three that opened its doors and its Five Year Strategy for Asylum and Immigration, produced in 2005, envisaged that workers from these new EU states would replace unskilled migrants from outside Europe (Home Office, 2005a: 13). As Europeans – and from states that are predominantly Christian – these migrants are considered to be more easily assimilated than migrants from outside Europe. They now occupy an ambiguous position in British society; like Irish migrants, they are both 'insiders' as new EU citizens but remain 'outsiders' in the face of economic and social exclusion. Furthermore, as part of the price for free movement within the EU, their governments have been required to pour money into placing borders around their own states (Cohen, 2003).

The current 'common sense' attitude towards immigration policy is that states have an incontrovertible right to control entry, and those who question this right tend to be seen as extremists. In fact, controls are relatively recent and those who campaigned for them were also initially dismissed as extremist (Hayter, 2000: 1). Britain first introduced control on entry just a century ago, with the 1905 Aliens Act, in response to agitation from a variety of sources, aimed particularly at Jewish immigrants fleeing persecution in Russia and Eastern Europe (Cohen, 2002). This was also the period when popular citizenship was developing based on the expansion of the franchise and the development of welfare and employment rights. While earlier in the nineteenth century, the exile had been 'free to land upon our shores, and free to perish of hunger beneath our inclement skies' (Harney, cited in Miller, 2004: 1), citizenship now represented something worth defending and also involved excluding others.

Until this period, state policy had been more concerned with emigration than with immigration. Countries often tried to discourage departure during the mercantilist period, since people – and their labour – were seen as necessary for the development of the nation, politically and economically (Castles, 2004a: 855). Britain encouraged emigration to the colonies as part of empire building, or the construction of the wider nation, a concern that continued up to the post-war period (Paul, 1997). Only fascist states and the authoritarian regimes of the old communist bloc have attempted to control emigration in the modern world. It remains a concern for poorer states, where the 'brain drain' robs them of their most dynamic and productive citizens. The rich states have, however, increasingly exercised their power to control entry in the name of protecting the national interest.

Banting identifies three main policy responses to immigrants: incorporation of new migrants; support for existing migrants but curbs on further migration; and exclusion through the curtailment of welfare to those in the country (Banting (2000), quoted in Bloch and Schuster, 2002: 305). In spite of their different traditions of migration, most major countries of immigration had moved towards the second of these by the 1970s. They have placed strict controls on entry but the settlement of immigrants and the development of minority ethnic communities including second and subsequent generations forced them to develop policies to incorporate those living within the state, and to develop paths towards citizenship. Contemporary policy, however, has shifted towards the third response. The economic benefits of migration are increasingly acknowledged but policies have been increasingly selective in terms of entry and the rights accorded to different groups. Charles Clarke, then British home secretary, spelt this out in 2005 in the foreword to the Five Year Strategy for Asylum and Immigration:

> We will continue to allow a small proportion of those who come here to settle permanently *where there is a clear economic benefit and where they are prepared to integrate socially.* We will tighten our conditions to reflect this by requiring those who want to settle to pass tests on English language and knowledge of the UK, *restricting settlement for economic migrants to skilled workers only.* (Home Office, 2005a: 10, my emphasis)

This selectivity has involved restrictions on the rights to welfare of migrants who have temporary residence status, particularly asylum seekers (those whose applications for refugee status are awaiting a decision). All major states are signatories to the Geneva Convention on Refugees. This recognises a humanitarian motive for entry that is at variance with the economic self-interest that governs most immigration policy in increasingly explicit terms. The definition of a refugee, however, is being interpreted more narrowly, with a declining proportion of applicants granted recognition. Governments argue that the high failure rate is due to an increasing proportion of unfounded claims, while critics suggest that it reflects the poor quality of official decision making on asylum claims (Flynn, 2005: 481) and diverging practices towards particular national groups (Somerville, 2006). 'Asylum seekers' have been increasingly separated – in legal and policy terms – from mainstream society.

In Australia, they are routinely detained while their application is processed. In other states, including Britain, separate support systems operate, aimed at inhibiting contact with local people and the ability to settle.

New global and national hierarchies are developing in relation to citizenship and the right to mobility. Trade and investment has brought virtually the whole world into the global market, but this has been experienced unequally between regions and groups of people, enriching some while others are impoverished and may lose the means to survive. This has created the conditions for migration from the poor to the rich countries, while the developed countries are raising ever-greater barriers in an effort to prevent the importation of the poverty it creates (Hirst and Thompson, 1999: 75). Immigration policy increasingly differentiates in its treatment of different groups and in relation to area of origin. Citizens of western states are broadly free to travel throughout the world for pleasure and employment. The 'club class' with skills and managerial expertise, though relatively small, is 'the most obvious manifestation of this inequity in long-term migratory opportunities' (Hirst and Thompson, 1999: 31). The children of the well-off are encouraged to spend 'gap' years backpacking around the world, seeking work wherever they find a place they want to stay for a few weeks or months, and returning after their exotic experiences to their real lives at home. Citizens of underdeveloped countries are not able to enjoy this free and casual international mobility. Those with desirable skills are able to penetrate the borders of the developed nations, and a minority are able to make an unanswerable case for refugee status. The majority who want to migrate in order to seek a better life, or to survive economically, face restrictions, and increasingly resort to smugglers to help them negotiate borders.

In enforcing ever-greater controls against those deemed 'undesirable', governments justify their policies in the name of the 'national interest'. This notion conceals the socially constructed nature of the nation, as well as the conflicting interests within the nation in relation to immigration policy. It also counterposes universal principles based on a common humanity against narrow economic interests that exclude people on the basis of arbitrary characteristics such as their place of birth. Underlying these issues are some key questions that are raised implicitly throughout the book and discussed more explicitly in Chapter Nine:

- Can immigration controls be rational, fair and ethically justified?
- Whose interests should immigration policy take into account?
- How could citizenship rights be allocated if there were no barriers to entering and working in nation states?
- Is it possible to reconcile tensions between the universality of citizenship and the particularity of national membership?

The politicisation of immigration and asylum

Immigration policy was at the forefront of the mainstream political agenda in the run-up to the British general election in May 2005. Numerous analyses showed that immigration and asylum, which were often confused, were high on voters' lists of concerns (Lewis, 2005). The opposition Conservative Party attempted to take advantage of this populist current, making immigration a major theme of its campaign with the insidious slogan 'is it racist to question immigration?'. This contrasted with immigration's relatively low profile in most previous elections. It is generally seen as too dangerous and unpredictable to be a major election issue, and a bi-partisan policy has kept debate within narrow bounds. In 2005, the Conservatives made little headway using this issue, but the right-wing British National Party, campaigning on an explicitly anti-immigration platform, made significant gains in electoral support while other anti-immigrant parties also gained votes in some areas, particularly on the outskirts of East London. Nevertheless, the new home secretary, John Reid, took up the Conservative phrase, when, announcing a new policy initiative on immigration in August 2006, he suggested that 'We have to get away from this daft so-called politically correct notion that anybody who wants to talk about immigration is somehow a racist.'[4]

Increased attention to immigration has been evident in other western states. In the French presidential elections of 2002 the anti-immigrant Front National (FN) came second to the eventual winner in the first round of voting, forcing parties of the left to combine with the right-wing party of Chirac in order to defeat the FN. In the Netherlands, conflict over immigration figured strongly in the election of 2002 with the intervention of Pym Fortuyn. In Australia, the Liberal Party of John Howard won an unexpected victory over Labour in 2004 after promising tough measures to deter asylum seekers.

An 'immigration crisis'?

It has become a truism repeated in sections of the mass media and among policy makers that there is an 'immigration crisis' and that immigration policy is out of control. The number of migrants in the world more than doubled in the 30 years between 1970 and 2000 (IOM, 2005: 397). In spite of this significant absolute and relative increase, however, it is worth remembering that the overwhelming majority of people remained in their home countries. There has been increased long-distance migration with 60% of international migrants now living in developed countries, where one in 10 people is a migrant, compared to only one in 70 in a developing country (IOM, 2005: 380). Hirst and Thompson (1999: 2) suggest that the scale of recent migration is by no means unprecedented and that immigration in the nineteenth century was higher than current rates. Most developed economies now have stable or falling populations as a result of low birth rates and emigration. Migrants in the nineteenth century, however, were able to move freely and went predominantly to the so-called 'empty lands', states such as the United States and Australia settled by Europeans, where they were absorbed into expanding agricultural or industrial production. Today's migrants face a world in which inequalities of power and wealth have been entrenched, and where the rich countries reject the poor, whose mobility is forced by these same unequal global relations.

Castles (2003: 5) argues that if there is a migration crisis, 'it is an ideological and political one'. The globalisation of trade and investment and the spread of a global culture through multinational corporations and global media such as television and the internet, together with the perceived loss of political sovereignty to global and regional institutions such as the European Union, have reduced the sense of national control over policy. Control over the national borders represents one area for the assertion of state sovereignty. States have often responded to globalisation by dismantling the welfare state (Jessop, 1990) and implementing social policies that have exacerbated inequalities (Hills et al, 2001). Immigrants, as the most visible sign of globalisation, can become a focus of resentment and a target of hostility. This may be increased by policy measures that have made migrants, particularly asylum seekers, more visible. Compulsory dispersal to areas where there are few ethnic minority communities, for example, makes them obvious as different and restrictions on their employment enforce idleness and dependence on welfare.

Reporting asylum

The media focus on asylum seekers indicates that the 'migration crisis' is generally perceived as one of forced migration (Castles, 2003: 4). Several studies on the reporting of asylum in Britain have shown that negative images predominate. Of 1,509 articles on asylum and immigration issues in national newspapers in the six months up to February 2005, most could be described as 'vitriolic, sensationalist and alarmist, spreading fear and generating hysterical and bigoted views among readers' (Ouseley, 2005). Trevor Phillips, chair of the Commission for Race Equality, in the foreword to a report on attitudes to asylum by the think tank Institute for Public Policy Research (Ippr), stated that 'the recent general election showed that vilifying and degrading asylum seekers is popular with some of the public and some sections of the media' (Phillips, 2005: v). Reporting of asylum by UK newspapers is regularly cited by organisations supporting refugees as one of the biggest problems affecting the quality of life of refugees and asylum seekers in the UK (ICAR, 2004: 1).

The language used about asylum seekers has become increasingly harsh. Although other forms of racism are becoming socially as well as legally unacceptable, there is 'no social sanction against expressing extremely prejudiced and racist views about asylum seekers' (Lewis, 2005: 44–5). Lewis found that many people used the term 'asylum seeker' to describe groups of black British citizens who behaved in ways they found unacceptable. Hostility towards asylum seekers thus has had a wider impact in legitimising the expression of racist attitudes. Racist parties are able to use it as a code word for other racialised groups. The widespread assumption in some parts of the country that any non-white or obviously non-British person is an asylum seeker means that the asylum issue has been absorbed into a wider discussion abut race (Lewis, 2005: 36).

According to Hewitt (2005: 156), the treatment of the issue by the UK press 'frequently amounts to an incitement to backlash'. Reporting focuses on negative images, perpetuating notions of asylum seekers as a threat, as taking 'our' jobs and a burden on society. The term 'asylum seeker' tends to be mentioned in relation to reports of crimes where it may be irrelevant (ICAR, 2004), but the bracketing of 'asylum seeker' with negative events serves to reinforce public prejudice.

Lewis (2005) found that negative attitudes were based on ignorance, particularly in relation to estimates of numbers, which were often wildly exaggerated. A common preconception was that asylum seekers who had entered the country clandestinely were themselves 'illegal'. Asylum seekers are often forced to use illegal means to enter because of lack of documentation (UNHCR, 2004) and often rely on smugglers to assist them (Morrison, 2000). This includes those subsequently deemed to meet the Geneva Convention definition of a refugee (see Chapter Four).

Concern about asylum is often highest in areas where there are few or no asylum seekers and the problem is worst where little meaningful interaction takes place (Lewis, 2005). There are, however, some positive stories, which are predominantly reported in the local press. A campaign in rural Dorset against the deportation to Malawi of the Kachepa family won huge local support and positive reporting in local and national media. The campaign won the support of the local Conservative and Labour candidates and the re-election of the Labour candidate in the 2005 general election was widely held to be partly a result of his involvement in the campaign.

The media influences the terms in which the public debate occurs and can provide the stories and material to justify prejudices (Lewis, 2005: 23), but it is politicians and the policy process that set the terms for public discussion of these issues, framing the way in which asylum seekers are spoken about. Jack Straw, then home secretary, was criticised, together with the Conservative opposition, by the UNHCR for using 'inflammatory language' against asylum seekers.[5] Rather than confront the language of racism, politicians who respond in this way give credence to the view that asylum seekers are a threat. This is not a new phenomenon, but has been a theme running through the history of British immigration policy (Paul, 1997). The targets may differ but the language remains remarkably similar.

The nature of the immigration debate

Immigrants have become the focus for insecurities brought about by global and national changes since they are the most visible signifier of these changes, 'while the real causes are invisible, complex and difficult to influence' (Castles, 2000: 128). By drawing on notions of the 'national interest', these complex developments can be presented as stemming from the presence of 'outsiders'. The conception of national interest assumes that different classes within the same territory share the same fundamental interests, despite the disparities in wealth and power.

Immigration policy making has been characterised by the narrowness of the public debate. Brubaker (2004: 903–8) argues that in liberal democratic states there is 'a chronic struggle to define the boundaries of legitimate discussion', and 'both to stigmatize, exclude and marginalize certain themes as illegitimate and to legitimate or "naturalize" previously illegitimate themes'. The debate both reflects and shapes the development of policy making. The consensus on immigration policy in Britain has embraced the necessity of controls for the past century but has shifted in its attitude towards settled migrants. Freeman argues that from the 1970s to the 1990s, when the process of settlement and incorporation of immigrants was developing, liberal democratic states developed an approach to migration in which the boundaries of legitimate discussion excluded 'critiques that reflect the (less "liberal") popular sentiments' (Freeman, 1995: 73). This happened earlier in Britain, when in the 1960s Enoch Powell gave voice to 'sentiments that had been rendered to some degree unspeakable' (Hewitt, 2005: 24). The liberal consensus at this period also excluded views that challenged the legitimacy of controls.

Since 2000, this consensus has shifted towards a greater recognition of the economic benefits of immigration, combined with a more punitive response towards asylum. This was evident in the British government's White Paper, *Secure Borders, Safe Haven* (Home Office, 2002a), which welcomed the social and economic benefits of migration while proposing harsher measures to deter asylum seekers. The subsequent debate around the 2002 Nationality, Immigration and Asylum Bill (Home Office, 2002b) focused almost exclusively on asylum and was highly restrictive. This reflected the priority given to measures to control entry, both in relation to its domestic agenda of attempting to 'outflank' the racist right, and to the wider European Union agenda of harmonisation of controls (Geddes, 2000). It also reflects the nature of policy making on immigration in Britain. Many policy changes are dealt with under

'Immigration Rules' or administrative changes, which are not debated in Parliament. Policy making within the EU is even more remote from public scrutiny, taking place 'behind closed doors' in intergovernmental committees or in bodies such as the Schengen Group, outside the formal European Union process. Freeman argues that there are '[s]erious barriers to the acquisition of information about immigration and ... the highly constrained process by which immigration issues are debated that distorts the information that is available' (Freeman, 1995: 883).

Some analysts argue that this lack of open debate stems from fears of provoking anti-immigration sentiment. Statham suggests that politicians appear to believe in the 'racist public thesis', that there are untapped resources of public grievances against asylum seekers, verging in many cases on racism or outright xenophobia and that their policy proposals must compete for this political territory (Statham, 2003: 167). Saggar argues that the existence (of anti-immigration sentiment) 'and the unspoken boundaries such opinion creates, have come to be assumed as a factor in modern British attitudes. It has led to the "race card" thesis', in which anti-immigration attitudes are 'viewed – and accepted – as a semi-permanent feature of the political landscape' (Saggar, 2003: 178). According to Hewitt (2005: 155) 'a form of strategic illiberalism has been employed by New Labour ... governed by a concern with not being wrong-footed again by the issue of immigration'. Restrictive policy on immigration, however, is not just a response to these real or imagined public views: it also creates and nourishes this type of sentiment. In focusing attention on 'benefit scroungers' and 'illegal entrants' the government legitimises hostility to immigrants and undermines public acceptance of its pro-migration stance in relation to economic migration.

The hostile terms in which immigration is presented also undermine the credibility of politicians in relation to their management of policy. Harsh talking is not seen to work and each attempt to toughen up the language and system has led to a belief that the 'problem' is worse than acknowledged (Lewis, 2005: 21). This fuels the public perception that they are getting limited information about the issues. Respondents to Lewis's survey described themselves as 'powerless bystanders' of a process over which they had no control (Lewis, 2005: 21). This echoes the powerful appeal to the British people made by Enoch Powell in 1968 when he suggested that '[f]or reasons which they could not comprehend and in the pursuance of a decision by default, on which they were never consulted, they found themselves made strangers in their own country' (quoted in Hewitt, 2005: 26). More recently, Charles Clarke was sacked as home secretary in 2006 as a result of a media witch-hunt about foreign prisoners who were released without being deported. In spite of the tough language he adopted on this issue, and his failure to challenge the assumption that these prisoners should be deported, he was seen as not in control, and moreover to have deceived the public by not making public the information earlier.

According to Statham (2003), contrary to the racist public thesis, civil society interventions are mostly pro-immigrant and the state's anti-immigration politics is not a result of mobilised public pressure. Business is broadly pro-immigrant, although it will normally campaign quietly through private channels for changes, for example the successful lobbying for an increase in the speed with which work permits were processed (Duvell and Jordan, 2003). The journal *Human Resources* has led a campaign for asylum seekers to be allowed to enter employment. There is a considerable array of pro-immigrant groups who lobby and campaign for migrant and refugee rights both in general and in relation to specific issues and individual campaigns. In Britain these include the major refugee and immigration voluntary agencies, the Refugee Council, the Joint Council for the Welfare of Immigrants (JCWI), church groups, individual anti-deportation campaigns, many of them affiliated to the National Coalition of Anti-Deportation Campaigns (NCADC). Many of these have international links, and similar groups exist in many European countries, in North America and Australia and other major immigration countries. The JCWI has been a leading player in broadening the debate on immigration, and has recently taken a leading role in the Migration Alliance to campaign for a more open immigration policy. Trade unions, which were often initially hostile to immigration, are now prominent advocates of migrant rights, often supporting individual members against deportation. The largest British trade union, the Transport and General Workers' Union, played a leading role in the campaign to end the voucher system for asylum seekers and in 2006 campaigned for an amnesty for irregular migrant workers. This change has also occurred within the CIO-AFL, the major federation of trade unions in the United States (Castles and Miller, 2003: 98).

There is perhaps no area of policy making in which the government's agenda is so distant from the majority of academic commentary. The study of migration has increased dramatically in recent years and most commentary is broadly 'pro-migrant' and critical of current policy making. Some researchers have attempted to influence government policy. The think tank Ippr has a particularly close relation with policy makers, and its research has been influential in changing the view of the British government on labour migration (see for example Spencer, 1994). The British Home Office commissions some research from academics, but there is considerable wariness from researchers of being seen to be colluding with the Home Office agenda. The main thrust of policy, particularly on asylum, is driven by other factors, in spite of New Labour's emphasis on 'evidence-based' policy. Compulsory dispersal, for example, was brought in despite the experience of problems in previous attempts (Robinson et al, 2003).

A crucial group of participants in the migration debate is migrants themselves but they lack political rights and it is often difficult for them to find a way of intervening within the public arena. Nevertheless, there is a network of refugee and migrant organisations that both provide services to their members and often campaign on their behalf locally and internationally. Refugee children have often been active in these campaigns, mobilising their teachers and fellow pupils on their behalf, often succeeding in preventing their deportation.

The problems of immigration policy making

Immigration policy shares with many policy arenas the difficulties of contending interests and lack of information on which to plan and base decisions. These problems are sharpened by the fact that policy links the international and national levels and has an impact across several domains. Immigration policy is therefore in many ways 'exceptional' (Sciortino, 2000), an issue that will be discussed further in Chapter Five.

A recurring theme in policies towards labour migration has been the attempt to gain the benefits without incurring its costs. Post-war European guestworker systems, for example, aimed to bring in temporary workers who would return to their countries of origin when they were no longer needed (Castles, 2004b). Migration, however, is a social as well as an economic process, and inevitably brings settlement, changing social relations and the development of social networks and institutions. Max Frisch, speaking of the Swiss guestworker system, said 'Wir riefen Arbeitskräfte und es kamen Menschen' (we asked for labour and people came).[6] This contradiction between labour in the abstract and the real people in whom it is embodied is characteristic of capitalist production in general. Human beings resist the power of employers and governments, attempting to gain some control over their own lives and the conditions in which they work. Labour migrants may resist attempts to control their migratory strategies and, for example, refuse to leave when their labour is no longer required.

Immigration policy is fraught with another series of contradictions, which relate to the link between the international system that propels it and the bounded national state. These states gain their legitimacy at the national level, and governments' claims to defend national interests and the rights of their citizens. While the notion of a 'national interest' is ideological, it is a powerful myth, often underpinned by notions of common culture and history. Immigration, by opening up borders, potentially confers rights on others, and challenges notions of national identity.

This raises the 'liberal paradox', which Hollifield (2004: 888) describes as the conflict between the economic logic of liberalism, which is one of openness, and the political and legal logic, which is one of closure. These conflicts are expressed differently in different migration streams. Labour migration raises tensions between 'globalising market forces and continuing closed territorial politics' and the extent to which rights are conferred on non-citizens (Kofman, 2005a). The development of permanent settlement and particularly family reunion sharpens this question, as it potentially changes the cultural and ethnic composition of the national polity and thus questions what constitutes national identity. The conflicts between universal principles and national interest are raised in their sharpest form in the case of refugee flows, where the justification for allowing entry is altruistic rather than for the benefit of the receiving country. In practice, asylum policy has been closely tied to international politics (Joly, 1996; Schuster and Solomos, 1999). Universal principles are embodied in international treaties but it is nation states that implement them. Human rights law is based on the freedom of individuals to move, but no state is compelled to accept specific migrants. There are growing normative clashes between international human rights norms, particularly as they pertain to the 'rights of others' – immigrants, refugees and asylum seekers – and continuing assertions of territorial sovereignty (Benhabib, 2004: 6).

Cole (2000) poses the liberal paradox in another way, arguing that there is a fundamental contradiction between liberal national states, which require closure in order to provide welfare systems, and liberal principles of justice and equality, which are fundamentally universal. He argues that these principles cannot be restricted to the citizens of the state and that therefore there is a conflict between these principles and the development of the citizenship rights that are essential to democratic states.

These conflicts and contradictions feed into the process by which immigration policy is made. It is often assumed that immigration policy operates in the interests of particular classes (Sciortino, 2000: 216), but policy making is a complex social process and does not always achieve its intended outcomes. This was demonstrated in relation to guestworker systems when closing off new migration led to permanent settlement and demands for social and political rights for migrants (Castles, 2004a). Policy making reflects national legal and administrative institutions and their interaction with democratic structures as well as national histories of immigration. With the intense politicisation of immigration, states have a greater stake in immigration policy and responsibility crosses many areas of the state. Hollifield (2004) suggests that we are seeing the emergence of the 'migration state'. Attempts to manage the complex and difficult processes of immigration encompass a range of departments, including police, technology, foreign affairs, labour, welfare services, all of which contain and promote different interests. Contemporary migration policy also involves international institutions, for example the UN, which governs refugee law, and within the European Union national immigration policy is increasingly influenced by Europe-wide policy making.

Conflicting views about migration policy

Different views about the aims of migration policy reflect the different interests and positioning of those involved as well as ideological and moral stances. Thus the attitudes espoused by policy makers, businesses and migrants will to some extent reflect their positions within the system. The views expounded in academic writing, although most are broadly pro-immigrant, also vary from hostility to immigration to the advocacy of completely open borders and equal rights for migrants. Views on immigration also cut across the political spectrum with freedom of movement advocated both from a neoliberal perspective and from the point of view of human rights, anti-racism and social justice.

Much of the debate about immigration policy is about different interpretations of facts, and their implications for the benefits or costs of migration. For example, in relation to welfare, some argue that migrants use up proportionally more national resources, while others say that they contribute more through taxes and as providers of welfare. Other disputes concern the numbers of migrants. The anti-immigration pressure group Migration Watch claims that the number of migrants in Britain has been grossly underestimated by governments, while others argue that migratory flows are less than these 'alarmist' predictions (ICAR, 2004).

Underlying this debate is the question of which facts are seen as important or relevant. For Kearns (2004: 3) the issues at stake, 'who matters and why?', are dependent on fundamental beliefs that are immune to empirical interrogation. Ruhs and Chang (2004) discuss two key issues that distinguish different positions on immigration and therefore the significance accorded to particular facts: first, the importance given to the interests of the receiving nation, compared with those of migrants, or the 'moral standing' of nationals versus migrants (Ruhs and Chang, 2004: 83); and second, the importance of the consequences of policies compared to a concern for rights regardless of their expected outcome. Cohen (2002: 248) argues that the right to free mobility is a fundamental principle and that arguments based on evidence of the benefits or costs of migration are irrelevant, thus in Ruhs and Chang's typology placing the moral standing of immigrants as equal with that of nationals and valuing rights above consequences. He rejects the frequently held view that there is an inherent contradiction between supporting both the free movement of capital and immigration controls. This view, he argues, is logical in that it reflects the interests of capital and is the dominant political view in western states.

There have been increasing challenges to the established common sense that border controls are essential and morally justifiable. The advocacy of a world without borders does, however, raise serious issues concerning the relationship between free movement and the allocations of political and social rights, which have not been adequately explored by the advocates of the abolition of controls. These issues will be explored further in the final chapter.

The scope of the book

This book is divided into two parts. The first, 'Understanding migration', focuses on contemporary migration and refugee flows, and discusses alternative frameworks for understanding these processes. The second, 'Understanding migration and refugee policy', discusses the policies that have accompanied these developments. Part 1 is broader in geographical scope, examining global trends in migratory movements and theory. Part 2 is predominantly British focused, although this is placed within the context of European Union policy.

Chapter Two, 'Contemporary migration flows: continuities and new directions', discusses some key developments in contemporary migration and the extent to which new patterns are emerging. Chapter Three, 'Explaining migration', discusses alternative theories of migration; it argues that a framework for understanding migration must take account of the intersections between different levels in the migration process, the individual, structural and the intermediate layer of networks and institutions that facilitate migration. The last chapter in this section, 'Forced migration', focuses on the debates surrounding the definition of refugees and the blurred boundaries between economic and political movements and discusses the notion of the 'refugee experience'.

Part 2 begins with a general chapter on 'Contemporary immigration policy making', discussing some of the broad issues in relation to immigration policy making that are explored in more detail in relation to Britain in subsequent chapters. It discusses first the specificity of immigration policy and the tools of immigration control, second the link between immigration and citizenship, and third the different levels at which immigration policy is made: national, local, regional and global. Chapter Six, 'The development of British immigration policy', provides an overview of immigration policy from 1905, discussing continuities and changes and drawing out some of the specific characteristics of British policy making. The following chapter, 'Britain's managed migration policy', focuses on the most recent policy developments, particularly the attempt to bring labour migration, controls and citizenship into a common framework reflecting national interests. Chapter Eight, 'Living with immigration policy', shifts the focus to the people who are the objects of immigration policy, examining its impact on the lives of those affected by it. The final chapter, 'The future of immigration policy', draws together some of the key themes from the book in order to discuss possible future immigration policy. It examines in more detail alternative views about migration policy, in particular the case for movement without borders, and the implications this would have for citizenship rights.

The book is based on a range of secondary sources and also draws throughout on research projects carried out during the 1990s and 2000s, some of which are ongoing, mostly in collaboration with other colleagues. This material is referred to through the publications and reports arising from them as well as unpublished interview material. This research has been mainly with the *objects* of immigration policy – migrants and refugees and those working with them – rather than with those who make the policy. The voice of the latter is contained in the policy documents and sets the mainstream agenda but those of the former have been less heard.

Immigration policy is complex and rapidly changing. In the period since 1993, there have been six major pieces of legislation on immigration and asylum, and new rules and policy statements are produced with increasing frequency. The appendix includes a number of sources that provide detailed information and commentary on contemporary developments in legislation as well as a list of sources of relevant statistical data. While the policy and legislation change, and the processes of migration develop, the issues in this book and the questions it raises remain relevant to our understanding of migration and migration policy.

Notes

[1] Prime Minister Tony Blair, speaking to the Commons liaison committee, 4 July 2006.
[2] Reported in the *Guardian*, 9 June 2005.
[3] Speaking on 24 August 2006. Reported in the *Guardian*, 25 August 2006.
[4] Reported on BBC News, 6 August 2006.
[5] Reported in the *Guardian*, 10 April 2000.
[6] Quoted, eg, in UNESCO (2005).

Part 1
Understanding migration

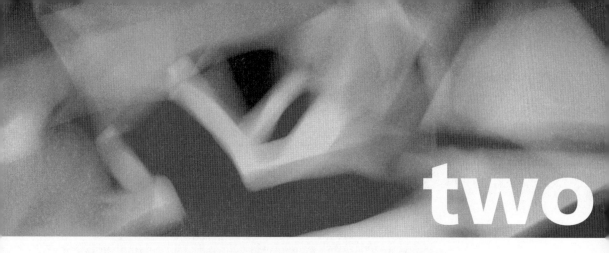

two

Contemporary migration flows: continuities and new directions

Overview

This chapter discusses contemporary migration and explores both continuities with the past and new trends. This has been characterised by a rapid increase in migration, the geographical spread of migration systems to incorporate every part of the world, increasing diversity in the motives and strategies of migrants and in their status in countries of immigration, and an increase in the proportion of female migrants. The chapter is based on both global data and specific examples that illustrate these trends.

Key concepts

Globalisation; acceleration; diversification; feminisation; irregular migration; migration regime

Introduction

Contemporary international migration has been widely described as 'new' both in relation to its scale and to the types of migration that have developed (Koser and Lutz, 1998; Papademetriou, 2003). Every country in the world now participates in international migration, while complex migratory systems have developed at global and regional levels (Castles and Miller, 2003) involving movement in many directions. Established countries of immigration have seen a diversification in their immigration flows in relation to both the countries of origin and the types of migrant involved, while they remained major exporters of labour. Traditional emigration countries in Europe, such as Italy and Ireland, themselves became destinations for immigrants during the 1970s and 1980s. Turkey, which was a major source of labour for post-war European economic reconstruction has become a place of transit for migrants bound further west but now hosts new migrants from the states of the former Soviet Union. While emigrants have poured out of Eastern Europe, particularly following EU accession in 2004, other migrants have entered to fill gaps in their labour markets. Thus the categorisation of states as 'immigration' or 'emigration' countries is becoming harder to sustain.

There is also growing diversity in the motives for migration. People migrate for economic, political and family reasons and to study and pursue new opportunities and personal goals. New types of migratory strategy are developing including temporary and 'commuter' migration (Wallace, 2002), while a growing body of literature is pointing to the continuing attachment of migrants to their country of origin, through the maintenance of transnational connections (Portes, 2004). The insertion of economic migrants into labour markets has also become more uneven. There has been growing competition among developed[1] countries for skilled migrants, who have been able to gain permanent residence, and for overseas students, while unskilled workers have faced restrictions on the length of residence and access to social rights.

Vertovec (2006) uses the term 'super diversity' to describe the combination of the range of migrants' countries of origin and the differentiation in their immigration status. This has brought large groups of people who are marginalised in terms of their status and rights, and who have little previous connection with the country of migration, raising important issues for policy. Vertovec refers specifically to London, but these processes are evident, though at different stages, in other major cities in Europe and elsewhere.

Koser and Lutz (1998) date the onset of 'new' migration in Europe from 1989, when the end of the Cold War and subsequent economic and political crises precipitated mass migration both within and from the former Eastern bloc. The collapse of state structures also led to the redrawing of national borders and new boundaries defining who was included in these new nations. The globalisation of trade, finance and investment had been accelerating since the 1970s, with the internationalisation of production through multinational corporations and the growing influence of international financial institutions on development programmes. The triumph of capitalism over alternative forms of economic organisation intensified this process.

Globalisation has, however, been associated with widening inequalities between both regions and social groups. There has been both consolidation of economic wealth in established centres, with the dominance of three major regional economic centres (NAFTA, the European Union, and Japan and the ASEAN countries)[2] and the development of new growth poles such as the oil-rich countries of the Middle East and the newly industrialising countries of South-East Asia, with China and India competing to become the new global superpower. Other regions, particularly large parts of Africa, have participated on unequal terms. Migration reflects this concentration of power and wealth; the uneven consequences of the spread of markets have deprived some people of the possibility of making a living, forcing them to seek work elsewhere to sustain themselves and their families. Higher levels of education in developing countries have also produced people with new skills who are unable to find appropriate work in their home country. The increasingly globalised media, including the internet and satellite television, makes global differences in income and living standards more visible, while rapid improvements in transport and communications make it easier and cheaper for people to move between countries and to live in new contexts (Castles and Loughna, 2003).

Structural changes in the developed countries, including declining birth rates and sectoral changes in the economy, also encourage migration. The influential global cities paradigm (Sassen, 1991) suggests that the expansion of high-level employment associated with leading global companies feeds demand not only for new skilled and elite workers but for low-status casualised labour in services such as cleaning, hotels and catering and domestic labour. Another sector where migrants have been an important element in the labour force, particularly in Britain, is professional services such as medical, teaching and social work. Thus new forms of brain drain have developed that reinforce global inequalities.

In 1993, in what has become a major text for students of migration, *The age of migration*, Castles and Miller highlighted four key features of contemporary migration: **globalisation**, **acceleration**, **diversification** and **feminisation**. These continue to be relevant, and provide a useful framework for the discussion of the current migratory scene. By 1998, with the second edition of the book, they added a fifth characteristic: **politicisation** (Castles and Miller, 1998: 9), an issue discussed in Chapter One. While recognising what is new in contemporary migration, it is also important to acknowledge continuities with the past. Thus, before turning to these features of contemporary migration, the first section summarises briefly some historical developments in migration.

Migration past and present

Migration has been a feature of all recorded history, although its importance is not always acknowledged in dominant versions of the past. Castles and Miller (2003: 50) argue that the denial of the role of immigrants in nation building has been crucial to the creation of myths of national homogeneity. These myths have drawn on notions of common origins and culture, including language. On the other hand, in settler countries such as the United States and Australia, migration has formed part of the myth of nation building. This included the notion of original 'empty lands', denying the existence of the previous indigenous population. These myths have also been selective, with particular forms of migration welcomed at different times: in the early twentieth century both states adopted policies that selected on racial grounds, while more recently selectivity has been based predominantly on the possession of skills.

Early large-scale migration was related to conquest and the creation of empires. Mass migration also occurred as a result of religious and other forms of persecution, for example the periodic expulsion of Jews from European states (Zolberg et al, 1989). Migration took qualitatively new forms with the development of capitalism and the economic and social upheavals involved in the privatisation of resources and the transformation from subsistence production to production for the market. As the industrial revolution in Britain became established, the concentration of ownership forced people off the land. Some sought work in the cities, while others went abroad to seek work in the developing economies of the United States, Australia and other lands settled by Europeans. Emigration was an integral part of Britain's industrial development, and also included its 'unwanted' population of the poor, orphans and the criminalised, as well as the colonial class of officers and administrators, and entrepreneurs. Immigration, especially from Ireland, also played a major role in the development of industry and infrastructure, including the railways. Hirst and Thompson suggest that recorded voluntary mass migration was at its height in the century after 1815 when the global market in commodities was developing, arguing that, 'the present highly internationalized economy is not unprecedented ... in some respects the current international economy is less open and integrated than the regime that prevailed from 1870 to 1914' (1999: 2).

The world economic order established at this period was unequal, with imperialism and colonialism imposing various forms of unequal exchange. Some settler colonies were able to retain more economic (and later political) independence. The development of the United States and Australia involved mass immigration from Britain and other parts of Europe. A total of 28 million Italians left Italy between 1861 and 1900, mainly for destinations in the 'New World' (IDOS, 2003: 7). Other colonies, notably in Africa and India, primarily experienced the disintegrating effects of involvement in the world market with few of its expansionary effects. Restrictions on trade, the imposition of cash crops and monoculture with the consequent decline in subsistence, and structures of ownership that saw surplus drained in the form of profits, rents and interest, contributed to processes of 'underdevelopment' (Gunder Frank, 1966). Forms of 'involuntary' migration were a continuing feature of this process: the slave trade was part of the 'primitive accumulation' process of capitalism, while indentured labour, such as the movement of people from India and China to work in the plantations in Malaysia, and from Africa to Mauritius, was an integral part of this internationalised economy. These movements created some of the ethnic complexity throughout the world (Cohen, 2006) that has been an element in current refugee-producing conflicts.

The crisis in imperialist relations arising from growing competition between European powers for markets and raw materials culminated in the First World War and curtailed international movement. It was in the aftermath of the Second World War that the transformation of the political and economic structures became most apparent. The United States emerged as the unchallenged superpower, while the expansion of the sphere of influence of the Soviet Union through the Warsaw Pact in Eastern Europe and the revolution in China in 1949 led to the Cold War, which dominated international relations for some 40 years. The long process of decolonisation coincided with renewed mass labour migration, as the demands of post-war reconstruction, especially in Europe, created labour shortages. This migration involved a major shift in relations with citizens of the former colonies as they took up their rights of citizenship in the former colonial centres. These movements brought unintended consequences (Hansen, 2003: 25), with what had been thought of as a temporary expedient to overcome an economic difficulty bringing long-term social and economic change. Although migration from the colonies had taken place in earlier periods, especially Irish migration to Britain, the visible presence of minorities in substantial numbers was new.

A number of 'migration regimes' were established in Europe, reflecting different relations between sending and receiving countries and national traditions of citizenship that had distinct implications for the composition of migrant flows and the rights of migrants (Kofman et al, 2000). Although there has been considerable convergence, national differences remain. **Colonial states** such as Britain, France and the Netherlands permitted migration from former colonies as part of the decolonisation process, and, at least initially, ceded full citizenship rights. The permitting of family reunion, as well as a high proportion of female labour migrants, meant that the gender balance was fairly even. Although it was not expected (either by migrants themselves or by policy makers) that their stay would be permanent, many settled, forming ethnic minority populations. With '**guestworker**' systems, most notably in Germany, labour was recruited directly through bi-lateral contracts, mainly with neighbouring countries in the Mediterranean and North Africa as well as Turkey. Workers were expected to return to their country of origin at the end of their contract, and had minimal rights. Their costs of reproduction were borne in the country of origin, while richer nations gained the benefit of their labour. Migration thus became another means of transferring resources from poor to rich countries. Family reunion was permitted in Germany only following a court ruling after a long campaign by voluntary groups (Hansen, 2003: 27). The less developed countries of Western Europe (Italy, Spain and Portugal and Ireland) remained predominantly **countries of emigration** until the 1970s or 1980s, with a large proportion of their populations emigrating to other parts of Europe or to the United States, Canada and Australia. The majority of Irish migrants went to English-speaking countries, while France was the main destination for Italians.

These regimes were not exclusive; France, for example, had a number of bi-lateral agreements, while Britain developed a form of guestworker arrangement with Polish workers in the early post-war period. Emigration remained important for states that were also experiencing immigration, with Britain a net exporter of people during much of the period (Paul, 1997). Other European states, such as the Scandinavian countries, which did not have empires, became large-scale importers of migrants only in the 1980s, although there was considerable population movement between them, especially between Finland and Sweden, and some immigration, particularly in the early post-war period, from the new states of the Soviet Union. Eastern Europe remained a 'non-departure regime' with emigration officially discouraged. There were continuing small outflows of individuals, and larger outflows linked to specific events, for example the Hungarian uprising that brought refugees to the West in 1956.

The official end of mass labour migration came during the early 1970s in most parts of Europe with the crises in the Fordist mode of accumulation that had underpinned the post-war consensus on Keynesian demand management and welfare policies (Kofman and Sales, 1996). The oil price rise of 1973 was the trigger for a recession, which brought mass unemployment and demands for cuts in migration. In Germany in the period leading up to the imposition of controls, immigrants were forced to make the choice between returning home, and thus being excluded from entering Germany in the future, or making their home in Germany. Instead of a temporary population, controls led to the establishment of permanently resident ethnic minorities (Castles, 2004b). In Britain, controls had been imposed earlier, and following membership of the European Community in 1973, the government attempted to replace migration from former colonies with Europeans.

In spite of official rhetoric of 'zero immigration', migration from outside Europe did not end, but European states promoted greater selectivity in the skills and geographical origin of potential immigrants. New forms of labour migration were introduced that sought to retain 'the economic benefits of migration labour while divesting itself of its social cost' (Fekete, 1997: 1). Skilled migration became increasingly important, but here too a common feature was the casualisation of labour contracts with the removal of permanent rights of residence, and the reduction in social rights (Rudolph, 1996).

This period also saw the migration transition in European states that had previously been predominantly countries of emigration. The exhaustion of traditional labour reserves in agriculture opened up demand for labour within industrial sectors, while the employment of women created new demands for labour to care for children and older people. In the Italian model of immigration in the 1970s, which shared many characteristics with other Mediterranean states (Pugliese, 2000: 797), the incorporation of migrants into the labour force was precarious, and often involved informal labour (Principe, 1998: 17). Immigrants had only severely restricted access to state welfare, making them reliant on the voluntary sector, both religious and secular. The long seacoast made the border difficult to police and the relative ease of entry and lack of control made it an attractive location, either for settlement or as a port of transit. Italy was thus seen as the 'weak link' in the EU's defences, the gateway to Northern Europe, and there was pressure from the EU to seal its borders.

In the United States and Australia, the post-war period saw similar processes of migration, but both operated explicit policies of racial selection. Australia abandoned this policy in 1973, adopting a multicultural policy that became highly institutionalised and comprehensive. In the United States, national quotas were gradually abandoned in favour of a points system based on skills and experience. The United States remains more open to migration than Europe, both in policy terms and in relation to public discourse.

While global linkages embrace every geographic area and every human group (Castles, 2000) the gap between rich and poor nations widened during the period associated with the era of globalisation as a result of the operations of the market system (Freeman and Kagarlitsky, 2004: 9). Trade, investment and intellectual property regimes that favour the industrialised countries maintain underdevelopment in the South (Castles and Loughna, 2003: 5). Long-term underdevelopment has been intensified by debt payments, and this economic insecurity means that natural disasters can become the trigger for major crises. These disasters are often themselves the result of economic and social processes that destroy traditional methods of production, for example the production of cash crops can involve cutting down vegetation, encouraging erosion and flooding.

Inclusion in the world economy intensifies the processes of emigration in the short and medium term (Hollifield, 2004: 902). Rather than acting as a substitute for migration, as many policies based on tackling the 'root causes' of migration assume, the social change that it brings stimulates emigration, at least initially. These new migrants from today's developing countries face a very different situation from those who migrated from Europe to escape the destructive consequences of its industrial development. There are no 'empty lands' to absorb surplus population or to provide opportunities for individual enrichment. Instead the dispossessed of the contemporary underdeveloped world find themselves at the bottom of an established hierarchy. They are forced to move, but the core countries at the top of this hierarchy are unwilling to 'import' the consequences of poverty (Hirst and Thompson, 1999: 75). They are thus either refused entry or find themselves in precarious economic and legal situations.

Another difference concerns the rights of citizenship. In the nineteenth century, there were no rights for migrants to claim in the country of immigration and they had only the possibility of selling their labour power in order to survive. The development of welfare systems and other citizenship rights has created bounded states in which the differential inclusion has been seen as crucial to the maintenance of these regimes.

Contemporary migration

The characteristics that Castles and Miller (2003) suggest define contemporary migration are reflected in a review of trends in migration by the International Organization for Migration (IOM) (IOM, 2005). This covers the period from the 1970s – the era associated with contemporary globalisation and the closure of mass migration – to the early 2000s. These statistics are based mainly on national data that are uneven in quality, since there is a lack of credible statistics in many parts of the world (Koser and Lutz, 1998: 4). In the developing world, migration in African countries is least well documented, but there is good data on Latin America (IOM, 2005). However, even in developed countries, the reliability of some figures is limited. For example, an investigation for the BBC programme *Newsnight* revealed that official figures for Eastern European migrants working in Britain were significantly underestimated (CRONEM, 2006; see also ALP, 2005). Irregular migration is particularly difficult to estimate since by definition it is not counted through normal statistics–gathering processes. Phizacklea (1998) argues that the figures for women migrants, who often work in 'invisible' occupations within the domestic sphere, are particularly likely to be underestimated. Despite these reservations the review provides a comprehensive overview of the contemporary situation. While the individual figures may not be accurate, the trends that they point to are likely to be real, since the inconsistencies in the data will point in a similar way. The next sections drawn heavily on these data, together with other sources that illustrate particular trends.

Acceleration

The most obvious trend revealed by the IOM figures is an increase in the number of international migrants in recent decades. Their numbers increased from 76 million in 1960 to 175 million in 2000, one for every 35 people (IOM, 2005: 379).[3] World population only doubled during this period, and the proportion of migrants increased from 2.5% in 1970 to 2.9% of world population in 2000. Later estimates show an escalation of these trends.[4] In 2005, there were an estimated 191 million migrants in 2005, an increase of some 15 million or approximately 8.5% from 2000, with migrants comprising 3% of the world's population.

Some of this increase in international migration can be attributed to changes in state boundaries. With the disintegration of the Soviet Union, there was a dramatic rise in the number of migrants 'as people previously considered internal migrants among the Soviet republics became international migrants' (IOM, 2005: 380). Changing boundaries also opened up migration within the European Union. Intra-European Union migration was promoted by the Maastricht Treaty of Union, and is a significant element in the migrant population in many member states. In 2001, EU members made up 29% of immigrants in the 15 states that were then members (IDOS, 2004: 36). Immigration from Eastern Europe also increased considerably in the wake of the opening up of borders (Wallace, 2002). In 2003, Polish migrants made up 2.4% of the total foreign population in the 25 members of the European Economic Area and 4.3% in Germany (D'Angelo, 2006: 53). These figures are likely to be grossly underestimated since a very high proportion of these migrants are undocumented. With the accession of eight Eastern European states in May 2004, migration to the West accelerated considerably, particularly to those countries that allowed entry to their labour markets.[5] The UK established a Workers' Registration Scheme that requires employees from these countries to register. Between 1 May 2004 and the end of September 2006, 510,000 workers registered (Home Office, 2006a: 4). A survey of recent Polish migrants, who make up over half of this group, found that only 64% had registered, suggesting that the true figure for those working is much higher (CRONEM, 2006).[6]

The majority of migrants were classified as 'voluntary', including labour and family migrants, with 'forced' migrants – those who migrate as a result of conflict, persecution and natural disasters – a substantial minority. The boundaries between what is considered forced and voluntary migration, however, are not clear-cut and depend on policy change as well as the reasons for migration. In 2000 there were an estimated 17 million refugees or 9.7% of all international migrants. This represented an absolute and proportionate increase from 1990, when they represented only 5.5% of total migrants (IOM, 2005:

381). The definition of refugees is contentious, and excludes many categories of people in need of protection. According to the UNHCR, there were 20.8 million people 'of concern' at the end of 2005, just under half of whom were classified as refugees, and over a third were internally displaced people.[7]

Globalisation

According to the IOM, the most significant recent change in migratory patterns has been the increased concentration of migrants in the developed world, although there were some new 'poles of attraction' for migrants in the Middle East and South-East Asia and other newly industrialising areas. In 2000, 28 countries accounted for 75% of the stock of international immigrants, compared with only 23 in 1970, but there was an increased concentration within this group (IOM, 2005: 382) (see Table 2.1). By the 1990s developed countries were absorbing all the increase in international migrants. Developing countries as a whole have consistently lost population through international migration, but their overall rate of natural increase is still so high that net emigration has had only a small impact on population growth. In sharp contrast, net inflows to more developed regions have been crucial for population growth, or in some cases, to preventing population decline (IOM, 2005: 383).

Some of the fall in the developing world's share of immigrants was due to conflict resolution. Africa has the largest number of refugees per head in the world (Castles and Miller, 2003: 7) with people fleeing to neighbouring countries from armed conflict often linked to the lengthy processes of decolonisation. The number of refugees there fell from 5.4 million in 1990, a third of total migrants, to 3.6 million in 2000, just 22% of migrants (IOM, 2005: 291). This was largely due to the end of conflicts in Southern Africa. The foreign population in Latin America also fell as a result of refugee repatriation following the restoration of democracy in several states. Asia too saw a drop in its share of international migrants, from 35% in 1970 to 25% in 2000, although there were increases in some areas. Pakistan, one of the poorest countries in the region, absorbed substantial proportions of refugees, especially from Afghanistan (Blitz et al, 2005).

The proportion of migrants in the population of major countries such as Australia, Canada, France, Germany and the UK increased, with a particularly sharp rise in the share of the United States, from 12% to 20% between 1970 and 2000. Some newer countries of immigration also experienced rapid increase. Between 1990 and 2000, the stock of non-citizens more than doubled in European countries such as Finland, Ireland, Italy, Portugal and Spain.

As well as the concentration of immigrants in developed countries, there has been a diversification in their countries of origin. Major new flows have developed from the former Warsaw Pact countries, both to other countries in

Table 2.1: Countries hosting the largest number of international migrants, 1970–2000

Country	1970 Migrants (millions)	1970 % of world migrants	Country	2000 Migrants (millions)	2000 % of world migrants
1. United States	9.7	11.9	1. United States	35.0	20.0
2. India	9.1	11.2	2. Russian Fed.	13.3	7.6
3. France	5.2	6.4	3. Germany	7.3	4.2
4. Pakistan	5.1	6.3	4. Ukraine	6.9	4.0
5. Canada	3.3	4.0	5. France	6.3	3.6
6. USSR	3.1	3.8	6. India	6.3	3.6
7. UK	2.9	3.8	7. Canada	5.8	3.3
8. Germany	2.6	3.2	8. Saudi Arabia	5.3	3.0
9. Australia	2.5	2.8	9. Australia	4.7	2.7
10. Argentina	2.3	2.8	10. Pakistan	4.2	2.4
11. Poland	2.1	2.6	11. UK	4.0	2.3
12. China, HK	1.7	2.1	12. Kazakhstan	3.0	1.7
13. Congo DR	1.4	1.7	13. China, HK	2.7	1.5
14. Israel	1.4	1.7	14. Côte d'Ivoire	2.3	1.3
15. Brazil	1.3	1.6	15. Iran	2.3	1.3

Table 2.1: continued

Country	1970 Migrants (millions)	1970 % of world migrants	Country	2000 Migrants (millions)	2000 % of world migrants
16. Indonesia	1.2	1.4	16. Israel	2.3	1.3
17. Côte d'Ivoire	1.1	1.4	17. Poland	2.1	1.2
18. Switzerland	1.1	1.4	18. Jordan	1.9	1.1
19. South Africa	1.0	1.2	19. U.A. Emirates	1.9	1.1
20. Uganda	1.0	1.2	20. Switzerland	1.8	1.0
21. Italy	0.9	1.1	21. Occ. Palestine	1.7	1.0
22. Occ. Palestine	0.9	1.1	22. Italy	1.6	0.9
23. Sri Lanka	0.8	1.0	23. Japan	1.6	0.9
			24. Netherlands	1.6	0.9
			25. Turkey	1.5	0.9
			26. Argentina	1.4	0.8
			27. Malaysia	1.4	0.8
			28. Uzbekistan	1.4	0.8
World	**81.5**	**100**	**World**	**174.9**	**100**

Source: IOM, 2005: 397.

Eastern and Central Europe and to the West. There was a substantial increase in migration from Latin America, particularly from Brazil. Emigration was dominated by flows to the United States, particularly from the states on its borders, and to a lesser extent to Canada (IOM, 2005: 392). There has also been substantial recent migration to Europe from this region, particularly to Spain (Jubany et al, 2004).

Migration from China has become a significant element in contemporary migration flows (IOM, 2005: 386). The economic and political reforms from 1978 brought a new emigration regime (IOM, 1995). China's economic success has been achieved through its ability to enter the global market on its own terms and outside the standard International Monetary Fund (IMF) framework (Freeman and Kargalitsky, 2004: 11). Until the end of the 1980s, most emigrants were sent by the Chinese authorities or educational institutions and some applied for political asylum after the political disturbances in Beijing in 1989. These flows have continued and increased, together with highly skilled migration in technological sectors (Lee et al, 2002; Pieke, 2004). China supplies more overseas students than any other state to universities in the West. At the same time, China's uneven economic expansion means that some areas witnessed a shrinking of local industry, and farmers have lost their land to new developments. From the 1990s, farmers from southern China's Fuzhou and Fuqing coastal areas were forced to migrate to survive and have often travelled to the West clandestinely (IOM, 1995).

As well as the diversification of countries of origin, there remain distinct patterns of concentration of ethnic groups in particular destination countries. These reflect strong historical ties, including colonial links. For example virtually all emigrants from Algeria in 2000 went to France (IOM, 2005: 386).

Castles and Miller's (2003) detailed analysis of migratory systems in different regions of the world reveals that beyond these broad trends were complex flows involving most countries of the world in both emigration and immigration. These reflect both long-standing inequalities and newly emerging hierarchies of economic and political power. Some parts of the Middle East, for example, have developed diverse migratory movements as a result of oil wealth and the resulting new manufacturing and technological power, attracting migrants from neighbouring countries and from outside the region. The latter include the two ends of the migratory spectrum. The poorest, mainly from South-East Asia, have often been forced out by impoverishment at home and work in low-status occupations such as domestic work, often in conditions of semi-slavery. At the other end of the spectrum are significant ex-patriate communities, mainly from the West, in business and professional occupations, whose skills and privileged national status allow them mobility and the ability to command high salaries. There are also substantial refugee populations in the region, largely as a result of the Israel–Palestine conflict. This population increased substantially as a result of the war in Lebanon in 2006.

In the Black Sea region, at the crossroads between Asia and Europe, the ending of the Cold War and the widening and deepening impact of globalisation have brought expanded migratory movements and blurred the boundaries between countries of origin, transit and destination. Turkey, for example, attracts large numbers of migrants from the countries of the Black Sea such as Moldova, including a large number of trafficked women (Aybak, 2004). East Central European states have become attractive to migrants, including those using these states in transit to the West (Castles and Miller, 2003: 87–8; IOM, 2005: 387). These are also becoming regions of settlement, particularly as the exodus of labour to the West opens up shortages and a 'brain drain'. This process follows the earlier pattern of Italy, which is in the process of a second transformation, from a country of transit towards Northern Europe – a 'trampoline' (Petrillo, 1999) – to a country of settled immigration. In 2001, 31.6% of immigrants had lived there for over 10 years (IDOS, 2004: 82).

Most countries have become labour importers as well as labour exporters, part of complex processes of labour circulation at both regional and global levels. Western European states, however, are seen predominantly as labour importers, in spite of continuing large-scale emigration, reflecting the dominant popular perceptions of immigrants as people from developing countries, and the problematisation of certain migratory flows. Since the resolution of the conflicts in Eastern Europe, refugee-producing states have been mainly confined to Africa, Asia and the Middle East, but although most refugees remain in their region of origin, the countries of asylum are now spread across the whole globe.

Diversity

As well as diversification in countries of origin and destination, there is increasing diversity in migrants' motives for migration and their status in the country of immigration. The three major types of migration status – labour migrants, family migrants[8] and refugees – have varied in importance over time and in different states and there has been increasing complexity within each category. With the closure of mass migration during the 1970s, family migration became the main source of migration to developed countries. Family migration usually involves spouses (mainly but not exclusively women) and children, but others, such as parents, may be included. The proportion of refugees also increased during the 1980s, especially in the West. The main source of refugees at this time was from Eastern Europe as a result of the conflicts following the breakdown of state structures and the resurgence of nationalism. Improved communications also made it easier for people to travel from Africa and Asia to seek asylum.

An analysis of eight OECD states (IOM, 2005: 400) showed significant changes in the proportions of migrants with different statuses between 1991 and 2001. The proportions and direction of change varied between states, reflecting differences in migration policy and migratory history. In Australia and the United States, the proportion of labour migrants increased considerably but their shares were quite different, with a rise from 45% to 55% in Australia but from only 10% to 19% in the United States. Labour migrants represented over half of total migrants in Australia, Switzerland and the UK, but only 2% in Sweden. Refugees were the smallest category in all except Sweden where they represented a third, and Switzerland had the lowest proportion, of just 3% in 2001.

These figures need to be viewed with caution. They exclude those working or entering irregularly and for those entering through formal channels, their legal status on entry may not reflect their migratory strategy. This is particularly important in the light of restrictions on labour migration, which may force people to enter under other statuses. Family reunion migrants may enter the labour force and indeed this may be their primary motive for migration (Kofman et al, 2000). Others may claim asylum even if their main motive is economic, since this is one of the few possible routes to entry. In previous periods, on the other hand, people emigrating primarily for political reasons may have been counted as labour migrants as they did not need to go through the process of claiming asylum. Many Turkish migrants to Europe during the 1980s, for example, faced political repression, but since they were able to enter legally for work, they did not register as refugees (Kofman et al, 2002).

These categories have themselves become diversified. Refugees who flee to neighbouring countries are generally automatically deemed de facto refugees and may be accommodated in camps pending return or resettlement. Those who move on elsewhere as 'spontaneous' refugees in third countries have to go through a formal process to become recognised. There has been a proliferation of statuses for this group, with an increase in temporary forms (Morris, 2002: 155). Family reunion migrants to Europe have also experienced a diversification in the conditions under which they are able to enter and reside, but in general the conditions of entry became more stringent (Kofman and Sales, 1998).

The admission of skilled workers increased in the developed world in both absolute terms and as a proportion of total migrants between 1991 and 2002, except in the US where there was a slight fall (IOM, 2005: 389). This reflects state policies aimed at recruiting skilled workers. These policies, for example those based on points, embody gendered notions of skills that tend to favour male migrants (Kofman et al, 2005). Qualified family members entering with skilled migrant workers are counted in the number of skilled migrants in

Australia, Canada and the US, but not in the UK, which had the largest rise, from 7% in 1991 to 32% in 2001 (IOM, 2005: 388). Another element in skilled migration is students. Developed countries have competed to attract fee-paying students from the developed world (Castles and Miller, 2003: 171).

A particular concern in relation to skilled migration has been the consequences of 'brain drain' and 'brain gain' for sending and receiving states (Mahroum, 2000) and its role in exacerbating international inequality. This is particularly important in relation to health; emigration may deprive poor states of basic health care (Cole, 2005; Mesquita and Gordon, 2005). Hospitals in the Philippines have been forced to close down operating theatres because all trained staff had gone to the UK (Castles and Miller, 2003: 170). Emigration from Poland is now leading to similar concerns. The rise of professional registrations of Polish-qualified doctors in Britain, which almost doubled during 2005, from 784 to 1,506,[9] gives an indication of the scope of this problem.

At the same time, there has been increasing demand for unskilled workers, including those carrying out cleaning and caring work to service the economies of global cities. Domestic work in private households became the main area of employment for migrant women in Europe during the 1990s (Anderson, 1997: 37). While the emphasis of policy makers has been on skilled migrants, the majority of migrants are classed as low or unskilled. There have been new openings for particular forms of low-skilled work, through for example Italy's programme of labour migration quotas (IDOS, 2006). In many parts of Europe where migrants are barred from the public sector, informal work provides the main form of employment for migrants.

Temporary migration

With the ease and cheapness of international travel, particularly air transport, the possibilities of temporary migration have increased. Although by no means a new phenomenon, in the past it was largely confined to migration between neighbouring countries, for example Irish seasonal migration to Britain during the nineteenth century. For those migrating further afield, for example to settler colonies such as Australia and New Zealand, migration was not just a one-way process, but often meant that they would not see family members again. Their descendants have now come to see a period of working in Europe as a 'rite of passage' before settling into 'real life' back home (Conradson and Latham, 2005: 298).

The term 'skilled transient' has generally been applied to the, largely male, group of workers who move between different branches of the same company (Appleyard, 1991). Welfare professionals are becoming an increasingly important form of skilled transient, especially in Britain, which is heavily dependent on migrants in health, education and social work. In 2003, the number of social workers qualified abroad who registered to work in Britain was 59% of the number who qualified in Britain.[10]

The migratory experience differs markedly depending on country of origin and personal circumstances. New Zealand professional migrants working temporarily in London are able to find employment in areas 'related closely to both their previous employment and their professional aspirations' (Conradson and Latham, 2005: 293). Those from the New Commonwealth have had more difficulty in finding work appropriate to their qualifications and experience, deskilling even within their profession (Robinson and Carey, 2000; Jubany et al, 2004).

For some temporary migrants, work abroad in unskilled jobs may be part of a strategy aimed at securing their status back home. This has become particularly important in migratory flows from Eastern Europe. With the end of the Cold War, and the fall of the Berlin Wall, Eastern Europeans were not only 'free to leave' but 'free to leave and to come back' (Morokvasic, 2004: 7). Migration thus no longer necessitated permanent exile, but could involve 'short-term and circulatory' movement (Wallace, 2002: 606). Temporary or 'incomplete migration' has become a particular feature of Polish society (Kepinska, 2004). Morokvasic's study of what she calls 'Post Wall' migration suggests these strategies are aimed at improving or maintaining the quality of life at home, with mobility an 'alternative to emigration' (Morokvasic, 2004: 11). Germany's geographical proximity and long-established guestworker systems encouraged temporary movement, but as transport links made migration easier, migrants moved further afield, and migration to Britain was a marked feature of the 1990s.

There is evidence of growing diversity in the migratory strategies of Polish migrants to Britain, especially following EU accession. In contrast to the male domination of previous flows (Kepinska, 2004), nearly half of workers registered with the British Workers' Registration Scheme are women (Home Office, 2006a: 11) and they are more likely than men to be concentrated in permanent employment. Women may have different and more complex motives for migration (Kofman et al, 2000) and are more likely than men to develop personal and household strategies consistent with long-term or permanent settlement abroad (Pessar and Mahler, 2003: 827). Current research with Polish migrants in London[11] has found that family considerations often underpinned migratory decision making, and there is some evidence of family reunification. CRONEM's survey of Polish migrants found that 15.4% wanted to stay permanently and 30% stated that they intend to bring their families to join them in the UK (CRONEM, 2006).

Remittances, money sent by migrants to family or social networks in their home country, have become an increasingly important element in migratory strategies, particularly for temporary migrants who maintain family connections back home. These have important social and economic impacts on the receiving country. Remittances represented 10% of global capital movements at the end of the 1980s (Koslowski, 2004: 11). By 2005, they were estimated at $233 billion worldwide, of which $167 billion went to the developed countries.[12] These figures are likely to be underestimates, since a large proportion of remittances are sent back through informal channels. Migrants may take back savings when they travel home, entrust them to friends and relatives, or send them back through illegal organisations. Furthermore, much of the money is sent back through money orders, which are not counted separately for statistical purposes (IDOS, 2003: 130). Remittances are now recognised as an important source of development finance, and by the 1990s, they exceeded aid flows (Somerville, 2006).

Irregular migration

Irregular migration[13] is a product of policies that deny entry, residence or employment to certain categories of people (see **Box 2.1**). In the context of closure and increased selectivity in immigration policy, with an intensification of the forces that propel people to migrate, irregular migration has become a major component of contemporary migration. This includes both clandestine border-crossers and those who enter legally and overstay their permission to stay or, for example, fail in their application for asylum. The IOM report uses the term 'unwanted migration' for this group (IOM, 2005: 283), thus conflating the notion of 'desirable' with the specific polices that determine people's status. It was estimated that there were 30–40 million unauthorised migrants in 2005, around 15%–20% of the total migrant stock.[14]

Box 2.1: Types of irregular migration

- Entering by avoiding immigration inspection (including with the assistance of smugglers).
- Entering using false documents (wittingly or unwittingly).
- Overstaying visas or otherwise violating visa conditions (for example by working more hours than the visa stipulates).
- Staying after an asylum claim is rejected (failed asylum seeker).
- Being without papers (*sans papiers*) (for example if a passport is destroyed or taken by an employer).
- Having already applied for asylum elsewhere.

Source: Ippr, 2006: 5.

As governments have attempted to control and manage migration, we have also seen the development of a 'migration industry' aimed at facilitating migration. This involves both legal institutions such as recruitment agencies and organised smuggling to bring in workers clandestinely. This 'industry' is becoming more formalised as large institutions replace networks of friends and acquaintances, and organised gangs are increasingly involved in smuggling. Irregular migrants tend to follow the same routes as other migrants (UNHCR, 2006: 56). It is estimated that half of the 4.8 million Mexican-born population in the US in 2000 was irregular (IOM, 2005: 393). Europol estimated that 500,000 enter the EU annually, using smugglers (Koslowski, 2002: 175).

A large proportion of new Chinese migrants in Europe have insecure immigration status, and often use dangerous and difficult routes to enter. This issue received widespread publicity with the discovery of the bodies of 58 Chinese people in the back of a lorry in Dover on the south coast of England in 2000. The deaths of 20 Chinese cockle pickers in Morecambe Bay in 2004, and the subsequent trial of two 'gang masters' who had employed them, drew attention to the extreme forms of exploitation many undergo after arrival. While it is generally assumed that these types of migrants are predominantly male, 'Chinese women are just as willing as their male counterparts to search for better earnings and a more promising future' (Song, 2004: 138). Several of those who died at Morecambe Bay were women.

The trafficking of human beings for the purposes of exploitation has received increasing attention. While smuggling involves consent by the person moving (although it may involve financial exploitation), trafficking involves the transport of people against their will. The relationship of the migrant with the smuggler is assumed to end when they reach their destination, whereas trafficking involves a continuing relationship based on coercion (Morrison, 2000: 62) as the following example describes:

> A contract labor agency in Bangladesh recently advertised work at a garment factory in Jordan. The ad promises a three-year contract, $125 per month, eight hour workdays, six days of work a week, paid overtime, free accommodation, free medical care, free food, and no advance fees. Instead, upon arrival, workers (who were obliged to pay exorbitant advance fees) had passports confiscated, were confined in miserable conditions, and prevented from leaving the factory. Months passed without pay, food was inadequate, and sick workers were tortured. Because most workers had borrowed money, at inflated interest rates, to get the contracts, they were obliged, through debt, to stay.[15]

Human trafficking now involves millions of people across the world. The UN under-secretary general estimated that 200 million people were involved worldwide in some way in the late 1990s (Castles and Miller, 2003: 116). The number of cases that are prosecuted is a tiny proportion of this. The IOM had 9,376 registered cases of victims of trafficking in its database in 2006.[16] Much of this trade involves the sex trade; immigrant women are over-represented in prostitution in Italy, much of which involves coercion and trafficking (Carchedi et al, 2000; Bernardotti et al, 2005). In Britain, a special task force of police and immigration services named 'Operation Pentameter' raided 375 brothels and arrested more than 150 people for trafficking-related offences in the four months following its establishment in February 2006. The traffickers were said to have been paid as much as £8,000 for each woman.[17]

People may move from regular status to irregularity as a result of overstaying their visa or failing in their asylum application. They may also move in the opposite direction. In Italy most migrants who entered during the 1970s experienced some form of irregularity or precarious status, and some were able to take advantage of periodic legalisation programmes from the 1980s. In the United States, regularisation programmes in the 1980s meant that the number of irregulars declined from 4 million in 1986 to 2.5 million in 1989 (IOM, 2005: 388). Polish migrants in Europe have become regularised as a result of shifting boundaries within the EU. They represented a significant proportion of undocumented migrants to Britain in the 1990s (Duvell, 2004: 4) and the lack of internal controls on employment meant that once they had entered the country, generally using tourist visas, they were able to find work without much difficulty (Duvell, 2004: 7).

Feminisation

By 1970 overall female migration had nearly reached parity with male (IOM, 2005: 394). The feminisation of migration, or the increased share of women in migration flows, is thus a long-standing trend. The proportion increased slightly in the next 30 years, from 47.2% to 48.6% in 2000, with a slightly larger share (51.0%) in developed countries, and 44.6% in developing countries. As well as representing an increasing proportion of labour migrants, women make up the majority of family reunion migrants, and significant proportions of the world's refugees, although they are rarely the main applicant in asylum claims. These broad figures hide wide variations in the gendered composition of specific migratory flows. In Italy, for example, among the largest 25 national groups of immigrants in 2001 46.7 % were women, but the proportion varied from 8.6% in migrants from Senegal to 68.4% in the case of Spanish migrants (IDOS, 2003: 43). Among the largest groupings, 31.9% of Moroccans were female and 63.9% of Filipinos. These differences reflect patterns of incorporation in Italy, with Filipinos long established in domestic labour while Moroccans are concentrated in agriculture. They also reflect length of settlement, with more-established groupings developing family reunion.

Feminisation is a product of structural changes in both sending and receiving countries. Women have been disproportionately affected by Structural Adjustment Programmes that, by undermining subsistence production, can deprive them of their livelihoods (Kofman et al, 2000). In the Philippines a culture of emigration has been officially promoted; women, who are often highly educated, are encouraged to migrate and send back remittances to support their families. Shifting demand in immigration countries has also encouraged migration into female-dominated occupations. Increasing inequalities between households have fed demands for paid labour in traditionally female servicing roles. This phenomenon has been particularly important in Italy, where demand for domestic labour has grown as a result of the increase in women's paid employment, the insufficiency of services for children, older people and disabled people, and men's limited participation in domestic work within the home (Tacoli, 1999). This demand has been filled primarily by women from particular countries, mainly the Philippines, Cape Verde and Peru, so that a 'commodified racialised identity plays a key part in the labour market for migrant domestic workers' (Anderson, 2001: 677).

While female migrants have often been identified with unskilled work and particularly with 'invisible' labour in the private sphere, women increasingly migrate as skilled workers. There has been an expansion of professional migrants in female-dominated sectors such as nursing, teaching and social work (Kofman et al, 2005).

Conclusion

The current migratory scene displays increasing numbers of migrants and increased diversity in relation to the areas of origin of migrants and to their motives and strategies for migration. This has resulted from a growing concentration of power and wealth, which has created the conditions for migration while states operate increasing closure and selectivity in relation to migrants. New hierarchies are developing in relation to the ease of international mobility and the ability to take advantage of these global opportunities.

This complexity raises important issues for the way in which migration is understood. It suggests the needs to move beyond some of the binary categories that have tended to dominate thinking about migration, such as notions of forced or voluntary; temporary or permanent; regular and irregular. The redrawing of boundaries, through shifts in national borders or in the groupings that are included in policy, creates new forms of migration and destabilises these categories. These issues will be explored further in the following two chapters.

Notes

[1] According to the UN there is no established definition of 'developed' and 'underdeveloped' country. For convenience this is used here to refer to states with high GDP, including states of Europe, North America, Japan and Australasia. The terms 'developing' and 'underdeveloped' are contentious (see for example the use of the term 'underdeveloped' in Frank, 1966).

[2] The 15 members of the EU before 1 May 2004 were: Austria, Belgium, Denmark, Finland, France, Germany, Greece, Ireland, Italy, Luxembourg, Netherlands, Portugal, Spain, Sweden and the United Kingdom. On 1 May 2004, the following 10 countries joined: Cyprus, the Czech Republic, Estonia, Hungary, Latvia, Lithuania, Malta, Poland, Slovakia and Slovenia. Romania and Bulgaria joined in January 2007. NAFTA comprises the United States, Canada and Mexico. ASEAN countries are Brunei, Darussalam, Cambodia, Indonesia, Laos, Malaysia, Myanmar, the Philippines, Singapore and Thailand.

[3] An international migrant is defined as someone resident in a country other than that in which they were born.

[4] IOM Global estimates and trends, www.iom.int, accessed 20 November 2006.

[5] The United Kingdom, the Republic of Ireland and Sweden were the only EU states to do this immediately.

[6] Five hundred Polish people were interviewed in different parts of Britain.

[7] www.UNHCR.org, accessed 8 August 2006.

[8] Family migrants include those entering through family reunion (spouses and other dependants joining family members) and family formation (partners joining migrants in order to form a new family).

[9] Figures supplied by General Medical Council, UK.

[10] Figures supplied by the General Social Care Council.

[11] 'Polish migrants in London and European enlargement: social networks, transience and settlement', research project funded by the Economic and Social Research Council, 2006–7, carried out by Louise Ryan, Rosemary Sales and Mary Tilki, Middlesex University.

[12] See note 4.

[13] The term includes those entering clandestinely or those overstaying their permission to stay or working without authorisation.

[14] See note 4.

[15] US Department of State report on trafficking, June 2006, www.state.gov, accessed 10 August 2006.

[16] www.iom.int, accessed 11 August 2006

[17] Reported in the *Guardian*, 8 May 2006.

Summary

- Migration is a feature of all recorded history, including voluntary and forced migrations.
- Contemporary migration processes are shaped by global inequalities of wealth and power.
- Contemporary migrants face selective controls on their movement, which privilege those with skills and particular nationalities.
- Contemporary migration is characterised by acceleration, globalisation, diversification and feminisation.

Questions for discussion

- To what extent can contemporary migration be described as 'new'? Is there an 'immigration crisis' in developed countries?
- What trends are likely to emerge in migration in the next 30 years?
- Does interest in the feminisation of migration reflect a new phenomenon or a new way of viewing migration?

Further reading

Castles, S. and Miller, M.J. (2003) *The age of migration* (3rd edn), Basingstoke: Macmillan.

International Organization for Migration (IOM) (2005) *World migration: costs and benefits of international migration*, IOM World Migration Report Series vol 3, Geneva: IOM.

Koser, K. and Lutz, H. (1998) 'The new migration in Europe: contexts, constructions and realities', in K. Koser and H. Lutz (eds) *The new migration in Europe: social constructions and social realities*, Basingstoke: Macmillan.

three

Explaining migration

Overview

This chapter examines the development of theories of migration, focusing on voluntary, or economic, migration. It begins with individualist theories that emphasise individual decision making and 'push' and 'pull' factors. Structuralist theorists criticised these models as ignoring relations of power and inequality within and between nations. A focus on the meso level of analysis, particularly on social networks and migrant institutions, provides a bridge between individual agency and broad structures. Feminist analysis contributes to an understanding of the complexity of migrant decision making and migration strategies. It explores notions of diaspora and transnationalism, which acknowledged that migration is not necessarily a once and for all decision and that migrants maintain connections in more than one country.

Key concepts

Structure and agency; macro, micro and meso level; gender; migratory institutions and networks; transnationalism; diaspora

Introduction

Migration is both an individual decision and a social process. Individuals, families and groups make these decisions within a social, political and economic context that provides opportunities and constrains their movement. The choice is rarely made alone, but involves negotiation with family and friends and wider networks. Migration can be an overwhelmingly important event in people's lives but may also be seen as an 'ordinary' activity (Burrell, 2006: 1) that is part of a well-trodden path taken by friends and family members, as Irish migration to Britain became at certain periods. For some, migration is a positive choice, through which they hope to attain a better life, economically, socially or physically. For others it may be forced by economic and political circumstances that allow limited choice in relation to timing or destination.

The study of migration has increased dramatically from the 1980s as migration and its implications for migrants themselves and for society in sending and receiving states have become of major interest to academics and policy makers as well as the subject of heated political debate. The field has been dominated by sociology, geography and economics, with their different though overlapping concerns but the nature of migration lends itself to interdisciplinary study and major contributions have come from, among others, history, political science, social policy, law and psychology. Migration, with its themes of displacement and loss, of new possibilities and multiple belonging, has long been an important subject of literature, which can throw a particular imaginative light on the migratory experience, and increasingly of film and other cultural media. These approaches both build on each other and retain distinct focuses of interest, while within disciplines there are alternative theoretical and ethical standpoints. The methods used to analyse migration reflect these disciplinary traditions and theoretical approaches as well as the research agendas of different stakeholders, including funders. These methods include quantitative analysis of large data sets, analysis of broad social, economic and political structures, documentary analysis, policy evaluation and qualitative studies of the experience of individuals and groups. As well as being alternative ways of understanding migration, these approaches can complement each other, and most contemporary studies use a combination of several methods. The limitations of quantitative data on migration and the difficulties in ensuring comparability (see for example Barbesino, 1998; Kofman et al, 2000) also suggest the need for multiple methods.

Most early models of migration focused on individual migrants, who were conceived of as rational actors making decisions on the basis of the perceived individual costs and benefits of migration. This individualist thinking was challenged by structural models, which sought to place migration within the context of global processes of power and inequality. More recently, there has been greater emphasis on migrants' own agency, their ability to exercise choice within the constraints of these broader structures and, for example, to resist controls that constrain their movement. This has allowed an understanding of the diversity of migrant experience, which challenges the rather undifferentiated view of migrants that characterise both the individualist model and the structural approaches.

Feminist scholarship and the growing interest in the gendered nature of migration have been crucial in stimulating these developments. By viewing migrants as social beings with specific characteristics (gender, but also class, ethnicity, family situation and so on), it becomes possible to explore diverse experiences and strategies, and the social context in which migrants participate. Migratory strategies are linked to social networks and institutions that facilitate migration and settlement, as well as to migration policy in the home and receiving country.

Migration theory has moved away from some of the binary divisions of the past where migration was seen as a once and for all event in which migrants leave their country of origin and settle into society in the 'receiving' country. Studies of temporary or transient migration and the transnational ties that migrants maintain provide a more nuanced understanding of the diversity of migratory strategies. Migration is a long-drawn-out process that may encompass a whole lifetime and may even extend beyond it as bodies are brought back for burial in the original 'home'.

Migration theorists have tended to treat 'economic' or 'voluntary' migration, as distinct from 'forced migration'. The field of 'refugee studies' has developed to some extent separately from other migration research with its own specialist journals and research centres. The boundaries between the two are not as clear cut as is often claimed in the literature and more particularly in state policy, where the distinction between 'genuine' refugees and 'economic migrants' has been fundamental to current policy and discourse on asylum. The developments that produce refugees are often linked to those that produce economic migration. The networks they use, based on historical ties between states and on established communities in the country of migration, mean that economic and forced migrants often move to the same destinations. Nevertheless, there are some important features of forced migration that deserve specific exploration, and these will be discussed in Chapter Four.

This chapter focuses on explanations for voluntary migration. It broadly follows the chronological development of the various theoretical approaches. It suggests that, in order to explain particular migratory processes, we need to understand individual experience within a wider social and structural context and incorporate the intervening layer of networks and institutions that facilitate migration.

Individualist theories

Modern migration theories have their origin in the political economy of the late eighteenth century, which developed 'general laws' of the workings of the economic system. With the development of private property and production for exchange, individual economic behaviour was seen as predictable, shaped by the market system of supply and demand, or Adam Smith's 'invisible hand' (Smith, 1976). Malthus's famous theory of population linked migration to 'overpopulation'; he argued that population would, if left unchecked, grow geometrically while the potential increase in output that these extra people could produce from the land was limited. This, he suggested, would lead inevitably to a decline in subsistence income per head, and thus to either starvation or emigration for individuals (Rubin, 1979). The nineteenth-century geographer Ravenhill used similar thinking to develop his 'general laws of migration', which he based on what he saw as the tendency of people to move from areas of dense population to more plentiful land where the output per worker would be higher (Kofman et al, 2000).

The Malthusian assumptions of a fixed amount of land and diminishing returns from labour have remained at the root of much contemporary theorising about migration. Although neoclassical theory, which came to dominate mainstream economic thought at the end of the nineteenth century, abandoned many of the tenets of classical political economy, these assumptions have continued to underlie economic theories of migration (see for instance Todaro, 1969, 1976; Borjas, 1989). Neoclassical economics rejected the labour theory of value developed by Adam Smith that underpinned classical political economy and that Marx extended in his theory of exploitation. Labour, capital and land were seen as three 'factors of production' and the relative 'endowment' of different states of these factors provided the basis for migration. Migration would tend to take place from areas of scarce land and capital, low wages and poor employment opportunities towards areas where there was available land, economic opportunity and high demand for labour. Individuals weighed up the costs and benefits to themselves of moving, or the 'push' and 'pull' factors. As well as purely economic factors, Todaro (1969) also saw political freedom as a pull factor, a reflection of the political context of the Cold War. Thus migrants were said to move to destinations that maximised their net personal returns of migration or, as Borjas put it, 'individuals "search" for the country of residence that maximises their well-being' (1989: 461). Conventional international trade theory sees the migration of individuals to high-wage areas as tending to equalise wages on a world scale thus acting as a substitute for international trade (for example, Sodersten, 1978).

This framework embodies implausible assumptions about market perfection, including the perfect substitutability of labour and perfect knowledge. The state is either excluded from consideration or seen as external to the model, imposing 'imperfections' on the market rather than as central to the creation and regulation of migration flows.

The factors identified in these models are clearly important in individuals' decision making, but this model of migration is ahistorical and ignores the structural conditions in which migratory decisions are made and the constraints on these choices. Migration is rarely a simple individual action (Castles and Miller,

2003: 21) but is a result of social and economic change that may open up new possibilities or make it difficult for some people to make a living at home.

More fundamentally, states do not become 'over-' or 'under-' populated, or capital rich and capital poor as a result of historical accident, but as a result of the development of the market system itself and of social and political processes including war, conquest and forcible intervention into social and economic life, through for example colonialism. Thus Malthus's expectation of some form of equilibrium through emigration from Ireland was confounded in the haemorrhage of its people, which continued for over a century after the great famine of 1846, and that saw its population fall from 8 million to 5 million by 1851 (Sales, 1997). The root of this emigration lay not in population density or 'absolute' over-population, but in the social structures within which production took place. Peasants were compelled to produce crops for export in order to pay rents to absentee landlords, thus reducing the availability of land for subsistence while removing the surplus product, which could have been used to improve the land. Emigration, rather than providing the means to increase output per head, helped to perpetuate these structures, removing the most dynamic and productive elements of society and impoverishing agriculture still further.

The causes of migration, and its impact on both sending and receiving country, therefore depend on the social relations within which it takes place. Contrary to the assumptions underlying this approach, migration tends to be from areas of low to higher population density, which are generally the more developed states. Thus Irish migrants moving to the densely populated cities of Britain during the nineteenth century were absorbed into its expanding industrial economy. Furthermore, migrants are not generally those with the lowest income and employment opportunities, but have resources, education, skills and experience that make them employable in the country of immigration.

The model of an individual carefully weighing up the costs and benefits of alternative destinations ignores the structural limitations on access to information. Information is difficult and costly to obtain, and much of the relevant data are uncertain and unknowable. This has proved a problem even for states with huge administrative apparatuses at their disposal. Migrants increasingly depend on social networks for information and support in facilitating migration. The spread of the internet has, however, allowed access to information on a much wider scale, with people able to find out about job opportunities in distant places.

Individualistic theories take for granted the very factors that need to be examined in order to explain migration. They are therefore of limited value in explaining past or contemporary processes of migration and the reasons why particular flows have developed. As well as understanding why individuals may chose to move, migration theory needs to understand the constraints and opportunities open to different social groups and the broader context in which these decisions are made.

Structuralist accounts

From the mid-1970s a new approach developed, drawing on Marxist political economy, as well as dependency theory and world systems theory, which analysed migration in broader social and political terms (see for example Castles and Kosack, 1973; Castells, 1975; Phizacklea and Miles, 1980; Meillassoux, 1981). Central to these accounts were global inequalities in the distribution of economic and political power as a result of colonialism and imperialism and the unequal insertion of different regions into the world market. They also focused on the antagonistic class relations that are central to capitalism. Migration, rather than a means of equalising incomes, was seen as a mechanism for mobilising cheap labour for capital based within the rich states.

This group of theorists focused primarily on the migration of people from former colonies and peripheral areas of Europe to the rich nations of Europe and North America during the post-Second World War period. These migratory flows were generally relatively new and consisted mainly of young, able-bodied migrants who were often skilled in relation both to labour in their home countries and in the country of immigration, although they tended to be incorporated into low-level jobs. They often migrated alone, either as single people or leaving families in their home country. They made few demands on the welfare system in the country of migration, because of their own life stage and restrictions placed on their access to welfare rights. The countries of immigration thus benefited from the resources that had been invested in their education and upbringing in their counties of origin. Castles and Kosack (1973), in a memorable refutation of much of the established 'common sense' on immigration, suggested that labour migration represented a form of aid from the poor countries to the rich.

These theorists argued that it is unrealistic to assume that individuals exercise free choice over migration since long-established structural inequalities drain resources from the poor countries by sustaining underdevelopment. People may be compelled to migrate in order to sustain themselves and their families. Economically dominant states, moreover, control migration to suit their labour supply needs through selective migration policies. These writers were also concerned with the unequal incorporation of migrants into the labour force. They argued that processes of racialisation, based on visible difference or cultural practices and migrants' unequal social status, divided workers and undermined solidarity in the workplace. Racism was viewed as an essential mechanism for the 'over exploitation of the so-called under-developed peoples' and for keeping the latter in a constant state of fear (Meillassoux, 1981: 121), especially where lack of citizenship rights and insecurity of residence undermined working conditions.

Some of these accounts tended to view migrant workers as 'passive agents tossed around in the turbulent seas of international capitalism' (Kofman et al, 2000: 23) rather than as individuals making active choices within the constraints and opportunities open to them. Human agency was reduced to the interests of the collective, the global working class (Kofman et al, 2000). They focused on class almost to the exclusion of other divisions, although Castles and Kosack (1973) and Phizacklea and Miles (1980) did acknowledge the importance of the gendered division of labour. Early structuralist theorists also underestimated the importance of non-economic factors in precipitating emigration. This was particularly important to an understanding of the reasons for women's migration, which may include issues linked to the private sphere such as abuse within marriage and conservative social legislation and practices in relation to sexuality and the family.

Another criticism of the structuralist approach has been its adherence to a 'capital logic' approach, which implies that states operate in the interests of capital (Sciortino, 2000). This embodies a simplistic notion of the 'interests of capital' that ignores conflicting interests between different elements of capital and assumes that the state apparatus has no independence from this class. It also assumes that states have both the information and the means to operate such policies. Immigration policies, on the contrary often produce 'perverse' results, as in the unplanned movement from guestworker systems to settlement in Europe.

In spite of these criticisms, the structuralist approach marked a significant advance on previous theorising, providing the basis for an understanding of migratory flows in the context of broader historical processes. Building on this approach, we can develop the notion of a **migration regime** that encompasses particular types of migratory flows in a specific historical context (Kofman et al, 2000), which was used in Chapter Two to discuss the different types of flows to Europe established in the post-Second World War period, such as the 'guestworker' and 'colonial' regimes. This notion encompasses the economic and political relations between the country of emigration and the country of immigration and the way in which conditions of entry and rights of residence and employment, including the rights of family members, are managed through state policy.

Gendering migration theory

Acknowledgement of the importance of the feminisation of migration grew partly out of changing patterns of migration and the increased importance of flows in which women predominate. It also arose from the increased attention to the phenomenon of female migration as a result mainly of feminist scholarship (Morokvasic, 1984 was one of the earliest gendered analyses of migration). Despite Ravenstein's remark that women are 'greater migrants than men' (cited in Kofman et al, 2000: 22) both individualistic and structuralist accounts have tended to ignore the role of women or, where they are mentioned, treat them as 'followers' rather than as active agents. Bohning's model of the 'stages of migration', cited in Castles and Miller (1998), which was based on the notion that men migrate first and then women join them after a period that has enabled settlement, reflected the generally accepted understanding of women's role within migration streams.

This view of women, which simultaneously ignores them and confines them to the status of dependants, embodies the dualism at the heart of liberal theory and neoclassical economics (Waylen, 1986). It uses the notion of a 'universal' individual economic actor without social characteristics (including gender) but at the same time assumes a traditional gendered division of labour in which domestic labour is carried out by women within the home. This thinking flows from the ways in which the public and private spheres became separated, both in material and ideological terms, in the process of the development of capitalism, which entailed the separation of production from the household. Women were often excluded from the public sphere of work, politics and education and confined to the private sphere. Their labour within the household, though essential to the market system, is deemed unproductive since it receives no monetary reward. The gendered division of labour is taken for granted and women's role within it assumed rather than subject to examination. Mainstream structuralist accounts also focus on productive labour, since their main interest is in class relations within waged work and tend to ignore the gendered power relations that underpin them.

Evans (1997: 122) argues that 'feminism can claim to have developed one of the now great critical traditions within the Western academy, that of suggesting that the universalistic assumptions of knowledge in our society are false, and partial, because they are drawn from the experiences of only one sex'. Feminist research has challenged the dominant tradition in migration theory and, by investigating the hitherto unexplored experience of women migrants, has contributed to a wider understanding of migratory processes. One concern has been to make women's migration visible, showing that they have been significant actors in migration in their own right. Women, for example, have been the main migrants from Ireland for over a century (Rossiter, 1991; Gray, 1996). A gendered analysis, however, goes further than righting the historical balance sheet. By treating migrants as social beings with particular attributes, it raises important questions about the different ways in which migration is experienced and understood, the diversity of motivations for migration and the differential impact of policy.

The conventional approach to the gendered division of labour underpinned early studies of the household and migration decision making (for instance Stark, 1984). In treating the household as the primary unit of analysis, it retained the notion that households are based on altruistic principles as distinct from the rational individualist motives of the market (Barrett and McIntosh, 1980). Portes argued for an understanding of 'how these small social units pool resources to organize a process as complex as international migration' (Portes, 1997: 816). Goss and Lindquist (1995: 327) suggest, however, that the migration literature conflates the interests of household members with those of the male head of household. Households are sites of conflict, including the exploitation of labour as well as cooperation, affection and mutual support. As Grasmuck and Pessar (1991: 202) argue in their study of Dominican migration, the household 'has its own political economy, in which access to power and other valued resources is distributed along gender and generational lines'. Migration decisions reflect these power relations and are a product of conflict and accommodation between the members of the household, rather than a straightforward collective interest. Research with new Polish migrants in London has shown the complexity of these negotiations within the household. These negotiations continue after the initial migration decision has been made, and encompass longer-term migratory strategies and gender roles, particularly in relation to the care of children.[1] Pessar and Mahler (2003: 827) suggest that migrant women are more likely to develop personal and household strategies consistent with long-term or permanent settlement abroad, while men pursue transnational strategies that link them more closely to their homelands and to an eventual permanent return.

The contributors to Phizacklea's (1983) edited collection on migrant women showed how migrants' labour market experience is both racialised and gendered. Specific sectors have become niches for particular groups of migrant women or men. Cypriot women, for example, were concentrated in garment making as 'outworkers' for factories in which they face patriarchal control as well as isolation and exploitation (Anthias, 1983). Much research on women migrants focuses on the lower end of the labour market in which women face extreme exploitation, often within the private sphere. There have been extensive studies of domestic labour (Anderson, 1997: 2001) and homeworking (Phizacklea and Wolkowitz, 1995). These sectors are often not officially considered 'work' because they are hidden within the home. Studies have also shown that they may involve deskilling, with migrant domestic workers often having high levels of educational qualifications (Tacoli, 1999; Andall, 2000).

There are also particular gendered flows such as 'mail order brides' (Kofman et al, 2000: 70), 'sex workers' and women for the 'entertainment industry' (Truong, 1996). However, some have challenged the view that women engaged in these trades are merely victims, and suggested that women operate a degree of choice, albeit a tightly constrained one. They may see such work as a way of supporting themselves and their families, or of escaping difficult situations at home. The degree of choice that it is possible to operate, however, may vary at different stages of the process, so that, for example, women who make a conscious choice to migrate for sex work may find themselves coming under the control of pimps at a later stage in their journey (Carchedi et al, 2000).

Others have criticised the tendency to focus on the most exploited groups of women, which they suggest tends to stereotype women as victims (Kofman, 2006). Recent studies have shown the extensive migration of skilled women, particularly those working in welfare sectors (Raghuram, 2004; Kofman et al, 2005). These have challenged the notion of skill embodied in much of the earlier literature on skilled migration, which identified skill with the male-dominated professions such as accounting, finance and IT rather than caring professions.

Recognising the role of agency is particularly vital for a gendered account of migration because it is often assumed that women simply follow men and that their role in migration is reactive. Morokvasic's research in the mid-1970s showed the extent to which migration represented not simply an enforced response to economic hardship but also a deliberate, calculated move to escape from societies where patriarchy was an institutionalised and repressive force (see for example Morokvasic, 1984). Accounts of Irish women's migration also show the diversity of migratory motives and strategies (Gray, 1996). The ease of entry and access to the labour market in Britain meant that women were able to migrate for a variety of reasons, including to escape violent marriages or to live outside marriage, for example, without having to fit into particular categories in order to satisfy entry requirements.

Other work has shown how the gendered assumptions discussed above are embedded within immigration policy. Women's residence status is conditional on their husband's status in such things as family reunion or asylum applications, making her dependent on him even where she has been an active participant in the labour market. This dependence can make women vulnerable to abuse, for example where they are forced to make a choice between remaining in a violent marriage and facing deportation (SBS, 1997). On the other hand, the assumption of the genderless individual embodied in refugee law does not take account of the specific experience of women, for example, of persecution such as rape in the private sphere (Crawley, 1997).

Analysis of the gendered experience of migration often involves primarily qualitative methods, which provide insight into particular stories of migration. In contrast to the undifferentiated units of individualist theory, migrants are seen as social beings whose migratory experience and strategies are conditioned by gender and also by other social characteristics such as social class, age and life stage, and ethnicity.

Between structure and the individual

Introducing a gendered understanding helps to expose some of the limitations of both the individualist and structuralist approaches and places migrants' humanity at the centre of the analysis. Their migratory strategies need to be understood both within the broader structural context and within the social context in which they live their lives. As Boyd suggests, 'structural factors provide the context within which migration individuals or groups make decisions. However, at this micro level analysis, the decision to migrate is influenced by the existence of and participation in social networks, which connect people across space' (1989: 645).

Interest in this 'meso', or intermediary, level has helped to provide a bridge between explanations at the level of the migratory regime and those that focus on individual experience. This middle layer ranges from informal networks of family, kin, friendship and communities to more formal structures or 'migrant institutions'.

Social networks

The role of social networks became a major focus of migration theory during the 1980s. Networks, comprising households, friends and community ties, link migrants to their place of origin and are crucial in facilitating and sustaining migratory flows (Portes, 2004: 831). Once migration begins, networks come to function as causes of migration in themselves, lowering the costs and risks of migration and increasing its expected returns (Massey et al, 1993). The development of these networks is often linked to long-established historical ties between countries of emigration and immigration, including colonial links. Networks function across a range of countries including countries of origin, destination and transit (Koser and Pinkerton, 2002: 36). Migrant networks tend to be fluid and are maintained as migrants adapt to the new environment (Vertovec, 2004: 977).

The existence of networks may be a major encouragement to migrate and to choose a particular destination. As a social worker from New Zealand explained:

> In London there is this network of loads and loads of shared houses and accommodation that Australians and New Zealanders let out. So it was not difficult at all. (Interview with social worker, May 2005)[2]

Social networks sustain migratory flows by providing information and practical support to migrants in undertaking their migratory journey, negotiating immigration controls and finding their way in the country of immigration through assisting with accommodation and employment, for example. The first two are particularly important where migration is irregular. Before 2004, Polish migrants in Britain were mainly undocumented and did not have formal permission to work. They developed strategies to avoid the suspicion of immigration officers using advice from networks in Poland and Britain:

> She [a friend] also gave us some instructions what to say to the Immigration Officer at the port of entry: that we were students, that we were coming to see some interesting places in England, and that we had about £300 to show at the port of entry, so we were prepared. (Jordan, 2002: 8)

Schaefer et al (cited in Oakley, 1992) distinguish between the different forms of support provided by networks: emotional, informational or instrumental support. Emotional support is generally provided by family and friendship groups and is crucial in preventing social isolation. Information may be provided through friends and more formal channels such as advice centres and community centres. This may include things such as advice on how to look for accommodation and employment and on everyday aspects of living in a new setting, such as registering with a doctor and finding shops and services. Instrumental support may involve wider networks and include support in finding employment, interpretation and help with legal status.

There are no fixed boundaries around these three aspects of support, and networks may provide different types of support at different stages. Current research with Polish migrants demonstrates the fluidity of networks and their international dimensions. With ease of communication, through email and mobile phones, migrants rely heavily on family and friends at home for both emotional and practical support. One group of students in London described how they initially relied on friends already in London for help in finding their way around, knowing 'which tickets to buy', which places to avoid. Once they were more settled maintaining the friendship became more important and they themselves were able to provide support to newer migrants, helping them negotiate life in London (focus group with Polish university students, London, April 2006).

Misunderstanding of the functions of more formal networks can lead to frustration and disappointed expectations. As migrant communities become more settled, community members are increasingly used as 'mediators' between the welfare services and the community. Maintaining professional boundaries in such circumstances is difficult, and many experience 'burn-out' (Hoggart et al, 2000). Lutz (1993), describing the work of Turkish women social workers and teachers in the Netherlands and Germany, also suggests the difficulty of establishing boundaries between professional and community roles. Hynes (2007) found similar issues in relation to members of refugee communities who provided services such as interpretation for dispersed asylum seekers. Some were not familiar with the notion of professional boundaries and looked to interpreters and other service providers for emotional as well as instrumental support. As well as supportive relationships, networks can be exploitative, as in the case of some Polish networks in London (Sales, 2006). In other cases, casual payment is made in return for help. One young man described how his friend found work: 'He bought the job from some bloke. He had to pay £50 for it. There is a trade like this' (focus group with young Polish migrants, 9 October 2004).[3]

The building of broader networks in the country of migration depends on relations with pre-existing communities. Different generations of migratory flows may reflect different social groups with different relations to the homeland. For Poles, the development of networks in London is impeded by the lack of connection between different generations of migrants, with their very different attitudes and attachments to Polish society (Sales and Siara, 2006). The differences may also be reflected in language. Chinese community organisations in London mainly reflect the needs of older generations of migrants who are predominantly from Hong Kong and Cantonese speakers. They are ill-equipped to meet the needs of new migrants, mainly Mandarin speakers from China (Chan et al, 2004: 30).

Migration may involve the separation of families as children or parents and other relatives are left behind temporarily or permanently. Networks become crucial to the ability of families to sustain themselves across international boundaries. Family networks, while providing emotional and practical support for migrants, may also make financial and emotional demands. Different aspects of support are important at different life stages. Grandparents may provide help with childcare, looking after young children during holidays in their home country or through extended visits to the country of migration. As they become older and dependent themselves, however, they may also make demands for caring, often involving frequent travel across national boundaries (Ackers, 1998). Financial obligations to family back home may place heavy burdens on migrants, restricting their living standards in the country of migration. Kofman (2006) found that Latin American women with children in their home country often send back virtually all they earned. When migrants become older themselves, they may find themselves most isolated, as this manager of a Chinese community centre explains:

> We have a lot of old Chinese people, that in their younger days worked in the kitchen in a restaurant and they didn't socialise with anybody outside their own family. Now their children are grown up

and they moved away and they end up on their own. (Manager of
a Chinese community centre, focus group, 8 December 2006)[4]

For temporary migrants, maintaining strong links with home may be more
important than establishing close relationships in the host country and
'social networks and family support are tied to the home base and form an
essential element of the survival strategies of households' (Wallace, 2002: 617).
Technological advance allows them to keep in close touch with networks
at home, including previous migrants, as this young woman explained: 'It is
important, that our network was in Poland and we can contact Polish friends
via email. They have experience, they email us back with important things like:
be careful about this, be careful about that' (focus group with young Polish
migrants, 9 October 2004).[5]

This group relied heavily on these networks to find work, sometimes taking
over jobs from friends as others returned to Poland. In some cases people
are brought over from Poland to 'cover' while the job holder returns home
temporarily, while in the building trade friends or relatives are brought over
when specific skills are needed.

Transient networks of acquaintances reflect and reinforce the transient nature
of their migration. Polish migrants in the period before EU accession made
few links with British society. Their migration involved 'only an instrumental
accommodation to the host society, and few claims upon its social provision or
public infrastructure' (Jordan, 2002: 3). Their temporary stay meant that they
made only a limited investment in British society, for example often learning
only enough English to function in low-level employment. Participants in
a focus group of young Polish migrants just after EU accession stated that
they socialised mainly with other transient groups, including Poles and other
migrants, with little social contact with British people (focus group with young
Polish migrants, 9 October 2004).[6] Although they used services established
by earlier migrants, especially the Polish Church and Polish Centres, they did
not see themselves as embedded in these networks.

Conradson and Latham's study of professional transient migrants from New
Zealand in London suggests that their involvement with networks based in
the home country was a way of maintaining their sense of 'being at home'
despite relatively transient connections to the particular places in which they
were located (2005: 268). For some 'their movement to London was actually
about ensuring that they remained socially embedded' (Conradson and Latham,
2005: 297), since what they saw as their 'real life' was centred in New Zealand
rather than in Britain and thus these were the important connections they
needed to maintain. For other migrants this lack of rootedness may be felt
as a problem. Research with social workers from Australia and New Zealand
working temporarily in London suggested that feelings of transience inhibited

the development of strong local ties, particularly with work colleagues. One explained:

> Even on a friendship level I have experienced people not wanting to get too close as they think that I will leave. People make assumptions about what you do at the weekends, for example that I go to the Walkabout pub. There is an assumption that you are likely to move on ... and [they question] how committed you are to your work as well. (Interview with social worker, 20 July 2004, for 'SMILING' project)[7]

Rejection of close relationships by colleagues reinforced reliance on existing networks. Most lived with people from their home country, sharing accommodation in order to be able to afford London rents and they had little scope for developing a social life outside their existing networks. Their perceived transience reinforced feelings of temporariness and lack of settlement within work. Transience thus becomes self-reinforcing, and 'home' remains firmly linked to their country of origin.

Ties to the home base 'change once larger migrant communities are established abroad' (Wallace, 2002: 617). With more settled migration, they have more incentive to develop local networks. Ryan (2007) stresses the importance of 'propinquity' as help with children in the absence of extended families or affordable childcare is dependent on ties to people living locally. As the strategies of Polish migrants to London have become more complex following EU accession, family migration has developed and with it has been the development of local networks involving friends and neighbours, and often more formal groupings such as schools and mother and toddler groups (focus group with Polish mothers, April 2006).[8] Building these networks involves considerable personal investment and complex relations of reciprocity.

As well as caring for their own families, migrants, especially women, may be engaged in caring for others through paid work. Hochschild (2000: 131) describes 'global care chains' as 'a series of personal links between people across the globe based on the paid or unpaid work of caring'. She argues that global gendered inequalities are transferred along these chains of care, with care provided by Third World women in households in affluent societies, leading to a care deficit at home that is then filled by an internal migrant. Networks thus embody social divisions of class, income, status and ethnicity in which wealthier households in richer countries outsource their care deficits and requirements to poorer households. Morokvasic (2004: 13) describes how transient Polish migrants in Germany share caring roles with other migrants, filling gaps for each other during their absence from home, while taking on caring roles for other families in Germany, thus forming complex care chains across national boundaries. Yeates (2004: 82) suggests broadening the concept of care chains to incorporate market and non-market domains and shows that care work undertaken by migrants involves not just low-paid and 'invisible' care, but professional care undertaken by, for example, nurses and other health workers.

Migratory institutions

The importance of social networks in facilitating migration is well established, but they do not by themselves provide an adequate bridge between broad structures and the individual migrant. Goss and Lindquist (1995: 335) argue that a key component of large-scale international migration is the complex of international and national institutions, transcending the boundaries of states, which link employers in the developed or rapidly developing economies with individuals in the furthest peripheries of the Third World. These 'migrant institutions' articulate between various levels of analysis (Goss and Lindquist, 1995: 317). They suggest that individuals 'act strategically within the institution to further their interests but the capacity for such action is differentially distributed according to knowledge or rules and access to resources' (Goss and Lindquist, 1995: 345). Thus these structures are both constraining and enabling and the ability to use these institutions depends on one's social characteristics. Hondagneu-Sotelo, in an analysis of Mexican migration, suggests that although 'traditionally, gender relations in the networks have facilitated men's and constrained women's migration', gendered power relations may change with migration and 'through migration women and men reinterpret normative standards and creatively manipulate the rules of gender' (1994: 96). Goss and Lindquist's work was developed in a study of migration from the Philippines, where emigration has become institutionalised, with the encouragement of the government in order to provide a flow of remittances. This involves state institutions and a huge ensemble of recruitment agents, overseas employment promoters, manpower suppliers and other intermediaries, both legal and illegal.

Migratory institutions are particularly important for skilled migrants. Research in this field developed significantly in the late 1980s when the movement of migrants was linked to the growth in circulation of goods and initially focused on occupations such as banking workers, IT engineers and technicians, and managers and executives of transnational corporations (for example Beaverstock and Boardwell, 2000). These studies saw the state as playing a limited role in the regulation of migratory movements and the recognition of qualifications, since much of this migration involved transfers of staff within companies with implicit recognition of qualifications. Other studies have shown the importance of intermediaries such as recruitment agents in facilitating migration in the IT sector, particularly in relation to labour flows from India to the United States (Aneesh, 2000).

Recruitment agencies have become crucial in facilitating this flow in health, education and social work, and studies of welfare professionals have shown the importance of the state and other agencies in regulating these flows (Raghuram and Kofman, 2002: 2072), implementing policies that increasingly differentiate between migrants on the basis of their skill and the recognition of professional qualifications (Iredale, 1997). Lower-level posts within social work in Britain are increasingly filled through recruitment agencies, many of which operate overseas and offer advice on the whole process of migration and professional registration as well as placing people in posts (Jubany et al, 2004). These agencies, however, find it easiest to place social workers from the 'traditional' areas of recruitment, primarily the 'Old Commonwealth', while those from the, predominantly black, 'New Commonwealth' are much less able to find work this way (interview with social work recruitment agency manager, 27 July 2004). The proliferation of these agencies 'confirms the fact that globalisation of the highly skilled labour market does not occur without massive network investments' (Meyer, 2001: 102).

The role of institutions changes with developments in the migratory regime. With Poland's accession to the European Union, there was a surge in recruitment from there by British employers. Many British employment agencies opened up offices in Poland. This role is increasingly being taken by Poles who have established themselves in the country of immigration. Previously informal networks are being replaced by more formal networks, including Polish-run employment agencies and magazines (Garapich, 2005: 10–11). Thus a new Polish-run 'immigration industry' (Garapich, 2005: 12) is developing, servicing the needs of this more stable and legal workforce.

The introduction of more stringent entry controls has also provided opportunities for entrepreneurs and organisations that facilitate clandestine transnational population movements (Massey et al, 1993). Their activities include smuggling across borders, faking papers and arranging marriages. In turn, because these practices create a highly vulnerable underclass of migrants, new humanitarian organisations have been set up to provide services such as legal advice, shelter and help with obtaining papers (Massey et al, 1993).

The existence of these institutions helps to reproduce and sustain migratory flows. Portes (2004: 839) suggests that, faced with the combined forces of migrant networks, the migration industry and structural labour demand, receiving states cannot consistently and effectively control their borders. As Massey et al (1993: 451) conclude: 'the international flow of migrants becomes more and more institutionalized and independent of the factors that originally caused it. ... Governments have difficulty controlling migration flows once they have begun because the process of institutionalization is difficult to regulate.'

Transnationalism

The study of migratory networks and institutions has also encouraged interest in the phenomenon of transnationalism, the array of social, economic and political links that migrants retain with their country of origin. These links continue and develop in new ways following migration and migrants may move regularly between and participate in more than one society. They also involve ideologies of connectedness with those left behind (Vertovec, 2004). Levitt and Glick Schiller (2004: 1003) describe this 'simultaneity', or 'living lives that incorporate daily activities, routines and institutions located both in a destination country and transnationally' as a prevailing feature of contemporary migration. The concept of transnationalism is now well established in migration research (Vertovec, 2003; Portes, 2003, 2004; Levitt and Glick Schiller, 2004) but the extent and forms of transnational activism vary with the contexts in which people exit and the reception they receive in the country of migration (Portes, 2003: 878). They may also vary with the life stage. Levitt and Glick Schiller (2004: 1018) suggest that at the 'point of marriage or child rearing, the same individuals who showed little regard for a parental homeland and culture may activate their connections within a transnational field in search of spouses or values to teach to their children'.

Transnational links have a number of dimensions. These include **political**, for example participation in political parties in the country of origin or in solidarity work to change the regime in which many Latin American refugees have been involved; **cultural**, including celebration of traditional cultures and the development of new and hybrid forms such as 'Bangrarap'; and **economic**, ranging from multinational business, through small import businesses, to individual remittances. Portes et al (1999) distinguish between transnationalism from above, conducted by powerful actors such as states and multinational business, and transnationalism from below, which involves grass-roots initiatives from migrants. Portes (2001, cited in Vertovec, 2003: 643) also distinguishes between what he calls 'international' links, to describe activities and programmes of nation states; 'multinational' links to describe activities of large-scale institutions such as corporations or religions that take place in multiple countries; and 'transnational' links to refer to activities 'initiated and sustained by non-institutional actors, be they organized groups or networks of individuals across borders'.

These links do not involve only recent migrants. Indeed, Portes (2004: 835) suggests that participants in networks are 'not generally the most recent or least integrated immigrants but those who had managed to establish a more solid foothold in the receiving country'. Transnational practices may thus increase with the time since immigration. As Levitt et al (2003: 571) suggest, host-country incorporation and transnational practices can occur simultaneously. Tilki (2003), in a qualitative study of the health of Irish migrants to London, found that the most well-settled participants were those who maintained strong links with Ireland, while those who had cut off ties with home tended to be more marginalised in Britain, with fewer close supportive networks.

In a review of theories of transnationalism, Portes (2003) points to a number of convergences. He suggests that it represents a novel perspective rather than a novel phenomenon, although its importance has been boosted by new technologies in transportation and communications, which greatly facilitate rapid communication across national borders and long distances (Portes, 2003: 875). Transnational links have been an enduring (and perhaps inevitable) feature of international mobility, although the scope and strength of these links have been limited due to practical difficulties, including distance and, for example for refugees, political constraints. During the nineteenth century, Irish migration was often temporary and seasonal. Those who migrated permanently maintained close links with home, often going back regularly for holidays. A study of London's Chinatown (Benton, 2005) revealed a long history of Chinese transnationalism with ties based on the initiative of ordinary immigrants and their hometown counterparts as well as states and other formal institutions.

Immigrant transnationalism also has an impact on those left behind. Levitt and Glick Schiller (2004: 1003) suggest that 'migrants are often embedded in multi-layered, multi-sited transnational social fields encompassing those who move and those who stay behind'. Vertovec (2004: 976) discusses the 'bifocality' of many people 'left behind' but whose lives are transformed by transnational activities and ideologies among those who actually move. Transnational links may be maintained by individuals or groups but have macro social consequences in the country of origin. As Portes puts it, although:

> from an individual perspective the act of sending a remittance, buying a house in the migrant's hometown or travelling there on occasion have purely personal consequences, in the aggregate they can modify the fortunes and the cultures of these towns and even of the countries of which they are part. (Portes, 2003: 877–8)

Remittances have been recognised as an increasingly important element in transnational activity. Family remittances are often conflated with 'unproductive' activities but they can involve supporting family members or communities to gain education and health care, which increase productivity and have a broader social impact (Kofman, 2006: 9). They may also support further migration.

Koslowski suggests that development strategies of sending states are changing as they shed fears of a 'brain drain' for the hope of remittances from workers who stay in touch using new technology. These remittances may also become 'migration capital' to pay smugglers (Koslowski, 2004: 12).

Diaspora

Not all immigrants are transnationals and Portes suggests that this 'new theoretical lens in the field of immigration is grounded on the activities of only a minority of the members of the population' (2003: 877). This assumption of common experience is also apparent in another currently fashionable term, 'diaspora'. The notion of a diaspora implies that populations scattered across the globe maintain enduring attachments to the notion of a 'homeland'. Originally associated with the Jewish expulsion from the land of Israel, it has been more recently expanded to define a range of different situations including forced and voluntary migrations (Cohen, 1997). Brubaker (2005) suggests the use of the concept has become inflated and that it tends to assume some sense of collective identity and common responses to the migratory situation. The notion of diaspora embodies three key characteristics: dispersion of a people in space; orientation to a 'homeland'; and maintenance of group boundaries (Brubaker, 2005: 5). Discussion of diaspora can reinforce essentialist notions of these groups and assumptions of a common diasporic consciousness. Brubaker argues that diaspora is not a 'bounded entity' but a 'category of practice' (2005: 12) that acquires practical and symbolic significance in particular circumstances. Rather than this being a part of migrants' lives that is taken for granted, Castles and Miller (2003: 30) suggest that this should be used only where diasporic activity is a 'central part of a person's life'.

Chinese migrants are often viewed as a classic diaspora (Cohen, 1997) but many writers have cautioned against the unchanging notions of 'Chineseness' that this can assume. Ang stresses that Chineseness 'acquires its peculiar forms and contents in dialectical junction with the diverse local conditions in which ethnic Chinese people construct new, hybrid identities and communities' (1998: 7). With the dispersal of Chinese people across many states, myths of return may not easily or straightforwardly hark back to one specific 'homeland' and the trajectory of 'multiple migrations' is becoming more common (Song, 2005: 73). Furthermore the 'breezy and celebratory writings about diaspora and hybridity' (Song, 2005: 64) can downplay the inequalities of market exchange and the international division of labour (Wong, 2003: 12) and the constraints imposed by immigration policy. Diasporic communities are themselves a reflection of the marginalisation of these communities within the societies they inhabit as well as providing a vision of other lives, which makes the present more bearable (Ma Mung, 2002).

Transnationalism raises important issues concerning the relationship between rights, identity and citizenship. Levitt and Glick Schiller (2004: 1003) suggest that central to the project of transnational migration studies 'is a reformulation of the concept of society'. For many migrants with transnational networks and lifestyles, 'the country of origin becomes a source of identity and the country of residence a source of rights' (Kastoryano, cited in Vertovec, 2004: 980). This statement implies, however, too sharp a dichotomy between rights and identity. Rights may be accessed in multiple ways, including through links to the country of origin and through migrant networks in the country of migration. For temporary migrants, such as Polish people in Western Europe, their lack of entitlement to benefits during the transition period of EU accession and difficulties in accessing welfare services encourages people to retain residence at home (Morokvasic, 2004: 12). Furthermore, identity is not fixed, but changes in response to changing relations in both the home country and the country of immigration. Migrants may establish hybrid identities, for example as British-Pakistani, emphasising both their ethnic origin and their claims on rights (Hussain and Bagguley, 2005). Different identities also acquire importance in particular contexts. One may, for example, be at different times a Londoner, a Pole, an EU citizen, a migrant or white, depending on the situation, one's personal view of the world and the identities imposed by others. The separation between citizenship and residence, and the implications for belonging are discussed further in Chapter Five.

Conclusion

The discussion in this chapter suggests the need to incorporate all three levels of analysis, the individual, the macro economic and social structures, and the meso level, into our explanations of migration. An understanding of particular migratory processes must therefore encompass:

- **the migratory regime** that governs the relations between the country of emigration and the country of immigration, including the conditions of entry and rights of residence and citizenship, employment and welfare, and the rights of family members;
- **meso-level institutions and networks**, including formal state structures as well as mediators and facilitators, recruitment agencies and informal networks through which individuals and households negotiate migratory regimes; and
- **individual migrants** whose migratory strategies are conditioned by their own histories, social identities and resources.

In this three-tier conception, migratory institutions mediate between the individual and the broader migratory regime and provide a link between the agency of individual migrants and the structures in which they make their decisions. These structures both constrain and provide opportunities, but structural constraints can also be challenged by individuals and groups. The development of transnationalism and temporary migration also suggests that migration needs to be thought of in more complex terms than the traditional notions of 'once and for all' movement followed by gradual settlement into the country of origin. Migration involves continuing links between countries, which are growing more complex with multiple moves and often multiple destinations.

Notes

[1] 'Polish migrants in London and European enlargement: social networks, transience and settlement', research project funded by the Economic and Social Research Council, 2006–7, carried out by Louise Ryan, Rosemary Sales and Mary Tilki, Middlesex University.

[2] Interviewed for 'Skilled migrants in the labour market' (SMILING) project, funded by European Union Framework VI, 2003–4.

[3] At London-based Zjednoczenie Polskie w Wielkiej Briytani (Federation of Polish Societies in Britain).

[4] 'The changing Chinese community in London: new migration, new needs', project funded by the Big Lottery Fund, with the Chinese in Britain Forum.

[5] See note 3.

[6] See note 3.

[7] See note 2.

[8] See note 1.

Summary

- Early migration theories focused on individual migrants and were ahistorical in approach.
- Structural theorists placed explanations of migration within the context of relations of power and inequality but tended to ignore migrant agency.
- Gender analysis represented a significant advance, drawing attention to the social characteristics of migrants and their specific experiences and strategies.
- Migrant networks and institutions mediate between individuals and structural processes and play an important role in sustaining migration.

- Migrants tend to retain transnational connections and have economic, political and personal links with their country of origin.
- An understanding of specific migratory processes involves understanding the interconnection between different levels of analysis: individual, structure (or migratory regime) and the 'meso' layer of networks and institutions.

Questions for discussion

- How important is gender in understanding migration?
- What are the strengths and limitations of a focus on individuals in understanding migration?
- Is migrant transnationalism a new perspective or a new phenomenon?

Further reading

Boyd, M. (1989) 'Family and personal networks in international migration: recent developments and new agendas', *International Migration Review*, vol 23, pp 638–70.

Brubaker, R. (2005) 'The "diaspora" diaspora', *Ethnic and Racial Studies*, vol 28, pp 1–19.

Goss, J. and Lindquist, B. (1995) 'Conceptualizing international labor migration: a structuration perspective', *International Migration Review*, vol 29, no 2, pp 317–51.

Kofman, E., Phizacklea, A., Raghuram, P. and Sales, R. (2000) *Gender and migration in Europe*, London: Routledge.

Portes, A. (2004) 'A cross-Atlantic dialogue: the progress of research and theory in the study of international migration', *International Migration Review*, vol 38, no 3, pp 823–51.

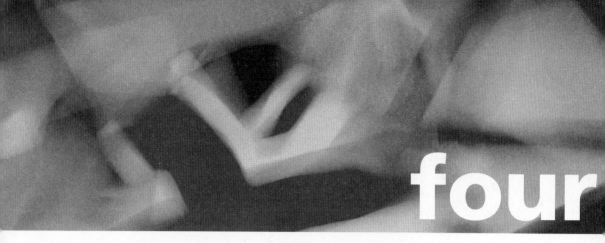

four

Forced migration

Overview

This chapter explores forced migration, in particular the definition of refugees and the notion of a refugee experience. The political and economic causes of forced migration are closely connected. The 1951 Geneva Convention is the basis for refugee law and policy. Its definition of a refugee emphasises individual persecution and involves both subjective and objective elements. The notion of a 'refugee experience' is highly contested. Some reject it due to the diversity of individuals' experiences while others point to commonalities arising from the lack of choice in moving and the emotional and physical loss it entails.

Key concepts

Forced and voluntary migration; asylum; asylum–immigration nexus; Geneva Convention definition of refugees; refugee experience

Introduction

The movement of refugees has been the most visible and controversial aspect of international migration since the 1980s. Unlike the migratory movements discussed in the previous chapter, the migration of refugees is seen as involuntary, or forced, and a result of non-economic motives. The number of forced migrants has expanded due to the escalation of conflicts and the collapse of state structures. The closing-off of other routes to migration has also increased asylum claims. The Third World generated huge refugee flows before 1960 but the overwhelming majority settled in their region of origin (Zolberg et al, 1989: 228) and were therefore of limited concern to the West.

The end of Cold War, rather than leading to a more peaceful world, has brought renewed, and in many cases more entrenched, conflicts. Civilians are increasingly the targets of human rights abuses and account for 90% of deaths in contemporary conflicts (Castles, 2003: 50). While the majority continue to remain in their country of origin, a minority move across continents to seek asylum in developed countries.

Not all of those forced to leave their homes are counted as refugees in international law, and are able to claim its protection. The basis of international refugee law is the Geneva Convention on Refugees and its Bellagio Protocol, which had been signed by 146 of the 191 member states of the UN in 2005. The rights embodied in the Convention include the right of individuals to apply for asylum and an impartial refugee determination process (UNHCR, 2006), non-refoulement (protection against being sent back to face danger or persecution) and minimum standards of living in the country of asylum for those granted refugee status. The 'classic' refugee, for whom the Geneva Convention was developed, is an individual who has suffered persecution in his (sic) country of origin. Today's forced migrants increasingly do not fit that model and are often deemed to be 'caught up in conflict' rather than refugees within the meaning of the Convention. The process of refugee determination is based on the assumption that it is possible to make a clear-cut distinction between refugees and 'economic migrants', and between forced and voluntary movement, distinctions that in reality are increasingly blurred (Bloch, 1999).

Policies concerning the acceptance and settlement of refugees are based on humanitarian principles, whereas it is the interests of the receiving country that govern policies on economic migration. In spite of its humanitarian basis, refugee policy has often been an arm of foreign policy, and political and strategic considerations inform individual countries' decisions about whom to admit (Joly, 1996). Refugee-receiving states are unwilling to accept refugees from their allies since by granting this status to those who have fled they imply that the regime has breached human rights. The United States has been the most political in its decision making (Zolberg et al, 1989: 27). It shifted to a more generous stance on admissions at the start of the Cold War as those 'fleeing communism' were seen as votes for liberal democracy (Harrell-Bond, 1999: 144). During the 1970s and 1980s, when much of Latin America was governed by authoritarian right-wing regimes, it did not accept asylum applicants from these states because of its alliances with their governments. Similarly, the British Conservative government refused to accept refugees from General Pinochet's coup in Chile in 1973 and it was only with the return of a Labour government in 1974 that some were admitted. More recently this position has been formalised with the development of a 'white list' of states deemed to be 'safe' and from which asylum applications are deemed to be unfounded.

There is an increasing contradiction between a more widespread adherence by states to core common humanitarian values as expressed through international instruments, and the increasing inequality and insecurity that produce refugees who are then confronted with closure on the part of the rich countries. Most EU and other western states now operate strict policies towards the entry of refugees, who have to resort to clandestine means of entry. Refugees are increasingly associated with poor countries. There have, however, been a small number from western states, for example some US soldiers have claimed political asylum in Canada after refusing to serve in the war in Iraq.[1]

This chapter focuses on the extent to which it is possible to make a distinction between forced and voluntary migration. After briefly outlining the background to contemporary forced migration flows, it discusses this in relation to two main issues: first, the definition of a refugee in international law, and second, the notion of the 'refugee experience'.

Why forced migration?

The scope of refugee flows

There were 20.8 million people 'of concern' to the United Nations High Commission for Refugees (UNHCR) at the end of 2005, of which 40% (around 8 million) were classified as refugees (UNHCR, 2006: 2). This represented a rise of more than a million during that year. A minority of these had gone through a formal asylum process: most are recognised as de facto refugees when they are given assistance by the UNHCR after crossing international borders in situations where they are fleeing conflict. There were 668,000 initial asylum applications and appeals submitted to governments in 2005, the majority registered in Europe (UNHCR, 2006: 7). Internally displaced persons (IDPs) represented 32% of the people 'of concern' to the UNHCR in 2005 and 11% were stateless. Pakistan and Iran remained host to the largest refugee populations, with around 21% of the global refugee population each, followed by Germany, Tanzania and the United States, while Afghanistan was the largest refugee-producing country. The majority of the world's refugees continued to be based in poor countries with just under 2 million in Europe at the end of 2005. These included 293,459 refugees and 13,400 asylum seekers in the United Kingdom. Other people 'of concern' are even more concentrated in developing countries: Colombia hosted over 2 million people, almost entirely IDPs, followed by Iraq (1.6 million), Pakistan (1.1 million) and Afghanistan (912,000).

Global refugee numbers reached a peak of 18.2 million in 1993 after the end of Cold War. Asylum applications in European Union states quadrupled between 1985 and 1992, rising from 159,176 to 674,056 (Levy, 1999: 16).

The decline in refugee numbers since then is mainly a result of repatriation; the UNHCR declared the 1990s the 'decade of return'. Nine million people returned to their country of origin between 1991 and 1996 (UNHCR, 2006: 130). Return programmes were the result of changing international policy towards return as well as the resolution of some protracted conflict situations. Repatriations included 3.4 million to Afghanistan and over a million to Bosnia-Herzegovina. The number of IDPs, however, has increased due to the closure of state borders preventing refugee flight and the changed nature of intra-state conflict as well as growing recognition of IDPs as a group in need of protection (UNHCR, 2006: 18). Natural disasters create forced migration and directly affect an average of 21 million people per year (UNHCR, 2006: 27) with displaced populations disproportionately vulnerable. Even greater levels of displacement are caused by development projects, but although people forced to move by natural or 'man-made' disasters are entitled to protection and assistance from the UNHCR, those displaced through development policies and projects are not. It has been estimated that in India 33 million people have been forced to move in this way (UNHCR, 2006: 28).

Figures for forced migrants are notoriously unreliable, particularly for stateless persons (UNHCR, 2006: 9). Refugees and IDPs who do not – or are unable to – register with the UNHCR are not counted and are denied access to material assistance and family tracing and reunion, and their children become effectively stateless (UNHCR, 2006: 44). The figures are often not broken down by gender and estimates are based on the assumption of a male 'head of household'. Official figures for adult asylum applications do not include dependants and no reliable figures exist for the numbers of refugee children (Dennis, 2002: 4). Unaccompanied minors are counted separately in many countries and constituted an average of 5% of asylum claims in 21 European countries for which data was available during 2001–3 (UNHCR, 2006: 4).

While particular refugee situations have become highly visible, more than 60% of refugees are trapped in situations far from the international spotlight (UNHCR, 2006: 105). In 2004 there were 33 situations of 'protracted refugee exile', defined as situations involving at least 25,000 people over a period of five years (UNHCR, 2006: 106). This excludes the chronic Palestinian refugee situation, which is dealt with by a separate authority.

The causes of forced migration

Refugee flows are often perceived as 'unruly' since they result from events such as civil strife, abrupt changes of regime, arbitrary governmental decisions, or international war, all of which are generally considered singular and unpredictable occurrences (Zolberg et al, 1989: v). Although specific events that propel refugee flows may appear to be sudden, refugee-producing situations are not random events but part of global power structures that reflect inequality between people and regions and are thus subject to analysis (Zolberg et al, 1989). The causes of refugee flows are strongly linked to those that precipitate economic migration, with both movements arising from the unequal incorporation of states into an international system of economic and political power. Conflict and forced migration are an integral part of the North–South division (Castles and Loughna, 2003: 5).

Forced migration has accompanied war and conquest throughout history but it took new forms with the development of the nation state and the political and economic changes associated with capitalism. The formation of nation states implied that only nationals could be citizens, and national belonging was often associated with religious or ethnic identity, so that minorities became 'misfits' (Zolberg et al, 1989: 12) and suffered discrimination and expulsion. During this period refugees were often sheltered by co-religionists in neighbouring states, such as the Huguenots, who went to Britain and also formed a sizeable group in Protestant areas of Belfast. Jews were frequently excluded from the countries in which they had settled and this took particularly virulent forms in the pogroms of the late nineteenth century in Russia and Eastern Europe. They often met with hostility from states where they sought refuge and their entry was deemed 'exceptional' rather than taken for granted (Zolberg et al, 1989: 25). Struggles with the old order and with the nascent capitalist class also led to the development of new political ideologies and political refugees who were deemed undesirable or dangerous because of their political opinions.

The twentieth century produced refugees on an unprecedented scale. Totalitarian regimes practised persecution on political, religious and ethnic grounds. The Second World War led to massive forced and voluntary movement, with 30 million people internationally displaced at the end of the conflict (Zolberg et al, 1989: 21). The Cold War brought new refugee movements, mainly small groups of individuals, although following the 1956 Hungarian uprising 200,000 refugees fled to Western Europe. Colonial struggles and post-colonial state formation brought civil conflicts across much of Africa and Asia in the 1970s and 1980s. Unequal social and economic relationships outlasted formal independence and the failure to build independent economic and social development in much of the South was accompanied by weak states, predatory ruling cliques and human rights abuse (Zolberg et al, 1989: 17). The arbitrary state boundaries bequeathed by colonialism often produced the conditions for ethnic conflict within the newly independent states. The independent Nigerian state, for example, incorporated three major ethnic groupings and political parties were constructed on ethnic lines with each competing for state resources. This competition led to a civil war in 1970 with the secession of Biafra from the federal state and large refugee flows.

With the end of the Cold War, 'globalization and the dominance of a single superpower have increased conflict and forced migration' (Castles, 2003: 5). Attempts to build nation states based on ethnic identity and exclusive notions of nationality have led to the 'denationalisation' of groups not seen as belonging, with forced displacement increasingly used as an instrument of war (Crisp, 2003: 76). Castles argues that ethnic cleansing is not the emergence of 'age-old hatreds' but a 'systematic element of a thoroughly modern new form of warfare' (Castles, 2003: 18). In Rwanda, for example, Hutu and Tutsi identities 'were created and reproduced as separate and conflicting racialised identities under colonialism' (Baines, 2004: 132). During the civil conflict in 1994, one in eight Rwandans fled and 80,000 people, mainly Tutsi, perished in four months of brutal mass killing (Baines, 2004: 164). The collapse of the Eastern bloc states brought a refugee crisis to Europe's door, with the former Yugoslavia the major refugee-producing country in this period as it split into new states based on ethnic identity. Gender was an essential element in the constructions of nationhood, and rape and impregnation of women from the 'other side' became a specific weapon in these conflicts (Baines, 2004).

The post-11 September global 'war on terror' introduced a new dynamic to conflicts as the pursuit of terrorists was used by western powers (led by the United States and Britain) to justify military offensives against other states, including Afghanistan and Iraq. These actions have created thousands of refugees as bombings of civilian areas have left people homeless and escalating civil wars have forced people to flee in search of safety.

The reception of today's refugees has been very different from that given to those fleeing during the Cold War period. During the 1960s and 1970s refugees from independence struggles were often welcomed by neighbours and allowed into their territory. They were supported by western donors through the UNHCR as part of Cold War stabilisation. This strategic interest collapsed with the Cold War. The increase in refugee numbers has thus been accompanied by measures to block them from entering western states, while there has also been a decline in the support they are able to obtain in neighbouring states. In 2001, those fleeing bombing in Afghanistan found borders closed, although Pakistan had hosted refugees from there for decades. Border closure and refoulement is generally associated with developing countries but in developed countries, where refugees arrive in smaller numbers, a broader array of measures is deployed to deter entry (UNHCR, 2006: 34). With the stabilisation of Eastern European states and their incorporation into the European Union as members and associates, these states have been transformed from the refugee producers at the doors of Western Europe to partners in preventing arrivals from further afield.

The role of the 'international community' (which essentially means the powerful northern states and the intergovernmental agencies) in preventing forced migration is ambiguous (Castles, 2003: 18) and contradictory. Underdevelopment is increasingly seen as a threat to security in the rich countries, hence the current concern with investment and trade in Africa of the major economic powers. In bringing these countries into the world market, however, traditional social relations are disrupted, creating the conditions for emigration. In underpinning these unequal relationships, the governments of the developed world do more to cause forced migration than to prevent it.

The asylum–immigration nexus

The causes of conflict and violence that propel refugee flight are linked to those that cause poverty and economic dislocation and that propel people to move in search of better material opportunities. As conflicts are increasingly related to the breakdown of state structures, the economic and political causes of movement are difficult to disentangle. The notion of an 'asylum–immigration nexus' (UNHCR, 2006: 56) encapsulates this connection. Migrants seeking better economic opportunities and refugees fleeing conflict and human rights abuses are increasingly using the same routes and intermediaries, including smugglers. These routes may bring them to the same destinations, chosen because of the existing relations between them.

Another connecting link between forced and economic migration is the secondary migration of refugees after they have reached an initial place of safety. Many move on to seek better economic opportunities as part of individual or household coping strategies. Remittances sent from relatives who have moved in this way are crucial to the survival of those left behind (UNHCR, 2006: 24). These remittances are an increasingly important form of transnational link (see Chapter Three) and refugees play a similar role to economic migrants in the transfer of economic resources. Longer-term strategies may involve age-selective asylum migration, in which a young person is selected to move on in the expectation that they will be able to take advantage of opportunities in rich countries and help support the family back home. A Somali boy, aged 14, described being sent to London alone from a refugee camp in Kenya after relatives had pooled money to pay for the fare and the documents he needed:

> My brother took me to the airport. I was chosen by my family to go. I was the middle one; I was old enough to be sent, but not too old to get an education. They thought I would have a better life in England. I would be able to help. (Interview with unaccompanied Somali refugee, London school, 18 July 1996)

Defining refugees

The term 'refugee' has both an everyday meaning – those fleeing for their lives from violence and persecution – and an exact meaning in law. As Zolberg et al (1989: 3) put it, the definition is 'no mere academic exercise but has a bearing on matters of life and death' and its significance as a legal, social and administrative category has been vastly enhanced in contemporary policy and discourse. The need for precise definitions did not arise under conditions of unrestricted immigration. The Statue of Liberty, which overlooks New York Harbour and the entrance to the city, was erected there in 1886 to proclaim America's openness to newcomers and the opportunities embodied in the American Dream. Its base bears the poem by Lazarus that includes the lines (quoted in Zolberg et al, 1989: 3):

> Give me your tired, your poor,
> Your huddled masses yearning to breathe free
> The wretched refuse of your teeming shore.

These 'huddled masses' are precisely the people whom western states are now trying to turn away. Escaping poverty is not a passport to entry for those 'wretched' people fleeing the 'teeming shores' of the contemporary developing world. The reality was always different from this image, since people were turned back at the Ellis Island processing centre if they were deemed too sick to be productive or failed basic intelligence tests. Now even the able bodied are rejected unless they have skills that are in demand or they can prove that they fit the narrow categories outlined in the Geneva Convention. Western states are interpreting this definition increasingly strictly, attempting to make a firm distinction between genuine refugees who are granted refugee status and those deemed to be economic migrants. The term 'asylum seeker', a person in the process of applying for recognition as a refugee, has developed negative connotations and is often coupled with the term 'bogus' or even 'illegal'.

The word 'refugee' was first used in France in 1573 and in Britain it was used in the late seventeenth century in relation to Huguenots (Zolberg et al, 1989: 5). Most states, however, did not differentiate in law between refugees and other migrants until recently. Britain's 1905 Aliens Act, its first immigration control measure, made special exemptions for refugees. The United States did not distinguish between refugees and migrants until after the First World War (Zolberg et al, 1989: 17).

The formal definition that is now the basis for international refugee law was established with the Geneva Convention in 1951. The foundations of the international institutions for refugee protection were developed by the League of Nations, established after the First World War. It set up High Commissions for Refugees from Russia in 1921 and from Germany in 1933. These embodied a crucial step forward in refugee protection as they involved the international community in taking collective responsibility for the victims of persecution and granting them specific rights (Zolberg et al, 1989: 20).

In the aftermath of the Second World War, the millions of internationally displaced people added urgency to the need to tackle the refugee issue. The Geneva Convention was ratified in 1951 and the definition of refugee that it included remained substantially the same as that developed during the 1930s (Zolberg et al, 1989: 20). People recognised as refugees under this definition ('Convention status') are entitled to protection from return, to family reunion and social rights in the country of asylum, in practice obtaining most formal rights of citizenship except voting. The Convention was at first limited in both time and space, applying only to those forced out of European countries before 1951. This reflected the post-war situation and the expectation that the refugee problem would disappear over time. It was extended to all countries without time limit in the 1967 Bellagio Protocol. Not all states are party to the Convention but the principle of non-refoulement is now recognised as an essential component of customary international law and therefore binding on all states, including non-signatories to the Convention (UNHCR, 2006: 33).

The UNHCR was established as the body with international responsibility for protecting refugee interests. Its work, however, has been beset by tensions embedded in the concept of a refugee. Granting refugee status involves recognition by the international community that one of its members is engaging in persecution. Powerful states have been unwilling to offend their allies, and humanitarian motives have sometimes been secondary to strategic and economic interests in dealing with applications for asylum. The UNHCR has a duty to respond impartially to human rights abuses but is dependent for funding on the major powers, which are the largest donors; this tension has increased as the UNHCR has taken on a wider humanitarian role in conflict situations. Another major area of controversy concerns the definition of refugee and what the UNHCR claims to be the operation by the major powers of 'narrow and restrictive definitions of what amounts to persecution, who qualify as agents of persecution and what constitutes effective state protection' (UNHCR, 2006: 43).

The Geneva Convention definition

> Any person who is outside the country of his nationality ... because
> he has or had well-founded fear of persecution by reason of his

race, religion, nationality, political opinion or membership of a particular social group and is unable or, because of such fear, is unwilling to avail himself of the protection of the country of his nationality ... (Geneva Convention (UNHCR, 1951))

This definition of a refugee, although phrased in universalistic terms, is based on specifically European history with its focus on individual experience (Zolberg et al, 1989: 21). The definition is quite stringent: claimants must prove individual and specific persecution, which involves being able to demonstrate objective (factually 'well-founded') and subjective ('fear') grounds for the claim. They must also show that this relates to them individually on the basis of one of these categories. The definition has been criticised from a range of perspectives, including from those who see it as too narrow as well as those who seek to limit the individual right to claim asylum. These criticisms focus mainly on the concerns discussed below.

The individual character of persecution

The Convention definition requires individuals to show they are individually persecuted or threatened with persecution, rather than merely facing danger. A claim, for example, that the applicant's village has been attacked because of links to opposition fighters will not suffice. This makes claiming refugee status exceptional, rather than permitting a collective response to conflict and persecution and it limits the number of successful claims. Tuitt (1999) suggests that forcing people to fit a particular group of persecuted people focuses attention on the individual reason for their persecution rather than their need. Baines (2004: 65) argues that this focus on persecution compels refugees to appear vulnerable in order to be recognised as 'authentic'.

Zolberg et al (1989) distinguish three categories of refugee: activists who have been engaged in political opposition movements; targets at risk through their membership of particular groups (for example, ethnic) and victims caught up in conflict. Only the first two would be considered refugees under the Convention, although 'victims' may often face serious danger if returned. Zolberg et al (1989: 270) argue that these three categories are morally equivalent. In practice, 'victims' are often recognised by measures such as temporary protection on a collective or individual basis, but these offer fewer rights than refugee status, and protection tends to be conditional and limited in time.

Others, particularly governments in refugee-receiving states, have argued that the individual right to asylum is inappropriate for contemporary conflict situations and they have sought to limit the asylum applications on their territory. The British government has been a leading proponent of this view within Europe. Following an unsuccessful attempt to negotiate these changes through the European Union in 2003, it reiterated its commitment to the Geneva Convention (Home Office, 2005a).

The gendered nature of the definition

The Convention definition is ostensibly gender neutral but the definition of persecution and the processes for determining refugee status derive from a male-dominated institutional and political power structure that reflects male experience and embodies specific assumptions about gendered roles. These affect both women's ability to gain recognition as political refugees in their own right and what is deemed to be persecution.

The criteria for refugee status are drawn from the public sphere (Callamard, 1999: 207) but women's activity, particularly in states where social norms restrict their movements, is often in informal social movements, which are not always recognised as political (Kofman et al, 2000: 73). Women tend to be represented as victims of circumstances outside their own control, rather than as active agents in their own right. Mariam, a science graduate from Somalia, was involved in a women's group in Mogadishu that helped women displaced through civil war to find shelter, food and clothing. She explained why she was forced to flee:

> The warlords hated me because I wouldn't support them. They claimed I was diverting my energies and those of the other helpers away from the war effort. Because we worked with everybody, regardless of which clan they belonged to, they said we were undermining support for the war. I had a lot of enemies. They used to threaten my life. (Quoted in Sales and Gregory, 1998, p 17)

Mariam was initially refused refugee status in Britain on the grounds that she was just 'caught up in conflict'. She was determined to have her political activity acknowledged, and won her case on appeal. On the other hand, the specifically gendered forms of persecution that women endure are not included in the Convention categories. In some conflicts, for example, rape is used as a strategy for winning allegiance. Women may be forced to bear children with men of the opposing ethnic group (Baines, 2004). As Indra (1987: 3) argues, 'an individual risking death at the hands of the majority group institutions for maintaining a minority religion ... fits the definition whereas a woman ... facing death by the same institutions for stepping out of her "appropriate role" or for deviating from misogynous sexual norms does not'.

The refugee-determination process embodies gendered assumptions that do not allow women's specific experiences to be dealt with appropriately (Crawley,

1997). Typically they are expected to discuss their experiences of persecution in front of strangers where their stories are minutely scrutinised for potential inconsistencies. Traumatised people, 'especially victims of torture or rape, may be unwilling or reluctant to discuss their experiences' (Refugee Council, 2005b: 4), particularly in the hugely stressful situation of an immigration interview. They may feel shame as a result of the sexual violence and blame themselves or fear they will be blamed by family and community.

The issue of gender persecution is increasingly acknowledged. The European Parliament recognised in 1984 that women are sometimes persecuted for breaking the social or cultural norms assigned to their gender (Baines, 2004: 29). The UNHCR produced 'Guidelines on working with refugees' in 1989 and gender has been 'mainstreamed' within its work (Baines, 2004: 31). The category 'social group', which was added during the Convention itself in 1951 to cover possible gaps in coverage (Zolberg et al, 1989: 25), has allowed new groups, including those claiming forms of gender persecution, some possibility of successful application. There have been some successful claims, for example on the grounds of fear of female genital mutilation, but these remain exceptional.

Like women, children are not generally seen as political actors, but they are especially vulnerable to certain forms of exploitation, for example forcible recruitment into armed forces, while in some conflicts child civilians become targets for murder and torture (Ayotte, 2000: 9). Unaccompanied minors have to claim asylum in an adult system that does not address their particular needs and situations. A group of children's charities criticised the way children are treated within the British system, suggesting that the procedures 'offer insufficient protection' (Barnardo's et al, undated: 7). Home Office decision making often does not take into account the child-specific forms of persecution that occur in some source countries, leading to a 'protection deficit' (Bhabha and Finch, 2006).

The focus on the sovereign state

Refugee law is founded on the notion that the world is divided into a finite number of sovereign states with mutually exclusive jurisdictions (Zolberg et al, 1989: v). Refugees are seen as victims of persecution by state forces within individual states. The UNHCR faces contradictory pressures in attempting to protect refugees while not undermining state sovereignty. This has intensified as the mandate has been extended to deal with the cause of refugee flows, which involves intervention within states, including in relation to 'protection zones' and responsibility for IDPs. This preventative approach compromises its non-political stance and challenges the notion of state sovereignty (UNHCR, 2006: 6). This insistence of state sovereignty ignores the international dimension of conflict that is recognised in the broader definition of the Organisation of African Unity (OAU):

> The term 'refugee' shall also apply to every person who, owning to external aggression, occupation, foreign domination or events seriously disturbing public order, in either part or the whole of his country ... is compelled to leave his place of habitual residence in order to seek refuge. (OAU, 1969: 2)

This definition reflects the African experience, particularly of white rule in Southern Africa and poverty, which makes individual assessment of status impractical (Zolberg et al, 1989: 29). Zolberg and his co-authors argue that this definition is also 'self serving' as it enabled African states to acknowledge people as refugees without imputing persecution to its members.

The focus on persecution by state agents ignores other forms of persecution that may be as serious and where the state may be unwilling or unable to protect its victims. This applies particularly to women where persecution might take forms (sexual violence; insistence on particular dress codes) that are considered part of the private sphere. The EU has, however, reaffirmed the importance of state actors in this. The focus on state persecution also makes a distinction between receiving and producing states. Baines (2004), writing from a Canadian perspective, suggests that this creates a separation between 'self' (Canada as refugee-receiving and rights respecting) and 'other' (the Third World as refugee-producing and rights abusing).

The focus on non-economic causes

In contemporary refugee flows, conflict and human rights violations overlap with economic marginalisation, poverty, environmental degradation, population pressure and poor governance (UNHCR, 2006: 24). Some recent Chinese migrants to Europe, for example, have been forced to emigrate as a result of political decisions about the nature of development programmes that have undermined their ability to survive at home. Although famines may be triggered by natural events, their underlying causes lie in political and economic structures that create unequal access to resources and their impact is always experienced unevenly as a result of these inequalities (Sen, 1980). Zolberg et al (1989) argue that the important distinguishing mark of refugees is violence or the fear of violence. They argue for what they call an 'ethically grounded' concept of 'life-threatening violence' that recognises these connections, and encompasses: 'both clear and immediate physical violence, and coercive circumstances that have similar threatening effects. Life includes both biological existence and social existence and the basic material and organizational conditions necessary to maintain them' (Zolberg et al, 1989: 269).

The 'refugee experience'

The term 'refugee experience' has been widely used to describe 'the human consequences – personal, social, economic, cultural and political – of forced migration' (Ager, 1999a: 2). O'Neill and Spybey describe some of the tensions embodied in this concept:

> [T]he 'refugee' label is powerful ... both in its use to define human experience and a category of people, but also in terms of the identity and subjectivity of those who bear the label. At one and the same time one can be proud of being a 'refugee' and having survived unspeakable horrors; but it also marks a lack of homeland and of previous social status and identity and self worth, a lack reinforced by racist abuse in all its guises. (O'Neill and Spybey, 2003: 8)

Being defined as a refugee has deeply ambivalent meanings for refugees and their sense of self. This label is increasingly used by others in negative and hostile terms, as asylum seekers are portrayed as 'bogus' and 'a burden'. Refugee policy in the receiving states also forces refugees to prove themselves as vulnerable and 'victims'. Hynes (2007) argues that an active construction of the 'refugee experience' by asylum seekers in the UK was based not on a common sense of solidarity but on the necessity to invoke a particular identity in order to access services. This is particularly important for asylum seekers who are attempting to assert their right to refugee status and thus to protection and rights.

Joly (1996) distinguishes between 'project' refugees and 'non-project' refugees. The former are those who have been active participants in political activity in some form or the 'classic refugee' (Zolberg et al, 1989). The latter are either targets for example due to their ethnic group, or have been caught up in conflict. Project refugees may take pride in their status and engage in political activity in exile related to their country of origin. For non-project refugees, being a refugee does not provide the basis for mutual support in exile; indeed the ethnic and other divisions that formed the basis for conflict may be reproduced in exile, undermining group solidarity. Refugee movements are increasingly made up of people caught up in conflict rather than political exiles. Hostility towards refugees in the countries of exile also means that 'rather than viewing themselves as heroes who have stood up to and escaped from repressive regimes, today many refugees are reluctant to admit their status' (Harrell-Bond, 1999: 143).

Castles argues that the notion of a sociology of 'exile, displacement or belonging' places too much emphasis on the subjective and cultural aspects of forced migration, neglecting its structural dimension (2003: 21). The focus on loss in exile may also be used to suggest that refugees are not able to settle outside their original home and thus the only permanent end to the 'refugee cycle' must be return, a policy increasingly emphasised by the UNHCR and its major donor states. This reifies the notion of 'home', ignoring the structural divisions that may make people feel displaced even before flight (Zarzosa, 1998) and the fact that conflict may so transform the original homeland that returning 'home' becomes unrealisable.

It is frequently reiterated that refugees are 'ordinary people experiencing extraordinary events' (Ahearn et al, 1999: 231). This phrase emphasises that the issues they face in coming to terms with trauma are not due to their own individual psyche, or 'madness'. It can, however, suggest a lack of agency on the part of refugees, who may have been active participants in these events.

The term 'refugee' is a formal status, a social category and part of an individual's 'lived experience'. The last two may outlast the formal status. Refugees who acquire citizenship in their new home may continue to see themselves as exiles, and retain a desire for return even if this is not realistic in practical terms. The refugee label is both chosen and imposed. For some it may represent a stage in life from which they wish to move on while for others it remains central to their identity. Contemporary policy is promoting returns in the expectation that on returning home they will cease to be refugees. Not all refugees are able settle into their original 'home' and the refugee experience will continue to shape their lives.

Turton (2003: 6) argues that there is no 'refugee experience', only the experiences and voices of individual refugees. In spite of the diversity, however, there are some commonalities in experience. Refugees' movement is not based on a positive choice and the scope for planning is often strictly constrained. They experience loss of home, dislocation in their lives and relationships and often the death of relatives and friends before or during flight. Trauma is often repeated in exile, as they face insecurity and social exclusion in the receiving country. These issues are discussed in more detail below. Ager (1999a) suggests that there are some key phases in this experience (see ***Box 4.1***). Not all refugees go through all these phases, and their experiences are shaped by individual characteristics and histories as well as the structural causes that force movement. Just as the distinction between forced and voluntary movement is one of degree rather than an absolute distinction, so elements of the refugee experience are shared by other migrants.

> **Box 4.1:** The phases of the refugee experience
>
> - Pre-flight: Refugees may face economic hardship and social disruption, physical violence and political oppression.
> - Flight: Refugees face dangers in flight and separation from family and home.
> - Reception: This may be in a refugee camp where those crossing borders are recognised as de facto refugees; or in a country of asylum where 'spontaneous' refugees make an individual application for asylum. In both cases this period involves an extended period of dependence and limbo.
> - Settlement: Many refugees settle themselves (self-settle) within a neighbouring country without registering with authorities. They thus do not receive support but may be able to take advantage of opportunities for income generation.
> - Re-settlement: A minority of refugees are resettled in developed countries through collective programmes for those with accepted refugee status. Issues arising in this period may include difficulties with finding employment, health problems, language difficulties and problems in accessing services.
>
> Based on the typology in Ager (1999a).

Lack of choice in moving

> One day they came to my house and they were knocking on the door. There were three of them with guns. ... They took my uncle upstairs, and then my dad came out and they made my uncle run, and they started shooting and there were bullets in him. He had no chance and my father just stood by because he was just scared. (Somali boy, quoted in Hek et al, 2001: 11)

> The place we live ... it's a Kurdish village, but it's ruled by the Turkish government ... there were three people killed there because they were like soldiers, but they weren't Turkish [they were Kurdish] ... Someone reported them to the Turkish army and they shot them dead first and they put them on a donkey ... and they carried them through the village, and everyone could see the dead bodies and there was blood everywhere. They made everyone come out to see, even us very small children. (Kurdish boy, quoted in Hek et al, 2001: 4)

Some conflict situations make immediate flight imperative, while in others there is some degree of choice about when, where and with whom to flee.

Kunz (1973) distinguishes between 'immediate' and 'anticipatory' flight. In the first example, from the Somali boy, the lives of the family were in immediate danger, making flight imperative. For the second, flight was the result of a long build-up of violence and insecurity. Economic deprivation may be the first form of persecution. Before the mass murder of Jews under the Nazis, they were systematically deprived of the means to make a living.

Whatever the level of anticipation, refugee movement is involuntary and generally allows little possibility of planning. It may involve dangerous journeys, often of multiple stages over a long period, and may bring separation from family. Most refugees entering Europe rely on agents, and Koser and Pinkerton (2002) found that smugglers' networks rather than refugees' choices may be decisive in determining their destination. Kurdish refugees interviewed in Rome had had no knowledge of their destination before leaving and most did not want to remain in Italy.[2] This lack of ability to plan means people often have limited prior knowledge of the country in which they settle or of the local language. A Kurdish refugee in London said of his experience of being unable to communicate on first arrival: 'I felt like a newborn baby' (interview with Kurdish refugee, June 2000). The lack of choice also has more intangible implications for the ability to settle. Learning a language may represent for refugees an acknowledgement that they are unable to return, at least for the foreseeable future and therefore be seen as a kind of defeat (Sales, 2002a). Milica, who fled from Bosnia to Rome, described how it only gradually began to seem necessary to become more involved in Italian society:

> It was not easy at the beginning, because psychologically I was not prepared for leaving my country, and it really felt like a total abandonment. Not knowing the language, not knowing the customs, not knowing what I should do here, how long I was going to stay, when the war would finish. I wanted to return. But gradually we began to understand that we needed to settle here because the war was not ending. We could not just sit and wait. We began to study the language and to start doing things for ourselves. (Interview with Bosnian woman, Rome, October, 2000)

Loss

The loss experienced by refugees has many dimensions, both emotional and material. Refugees are torn, often violently, from their past life and thrust into a new environment where they do not understand the rules of social life and where they may be treated with suspicion. They may experience 'cultural bereavement' (Ahearn et al, 1999: 228). Many have faced trauma and violence either directly or indirectly, which can involve a breakdown of trust in individuals and institutions (Hynes, 2003). Ager (1999: 4) argues that betrayal by neighbours adds a specific dimension to the disruption of normal life, undermining security and a sense of reality. In the former Yugoslavia where communities had lived together and inter-married for many generations, people were forced to adopt a new 'ethnic' identity in opposition to other groups (Baines, 2004).

Refugees may have lost family members before or during their flight. One young boy now living in London explained: 'The war happened and I got lost from my family. I don't know where they are. Some people found me on my own and they just brought me here, they left me and then I went in a children's home' (quoted in Hek et al, 2001: 12). Some parents send their children abroad to safety, often leaving them to be cared for by strangers.

Refugees lose control over important elements in their lives and their subsequent experiences often intensify their dependence on others and the sense of living in limbo. Many spend time in refugee camps, often in protracted exile, unable either to return or to make a new life in exile (UNHCR, 2006: 105). Respect for human dignity is often the first casualty (Harrell-Bond, 1999a: 141) and they experience profound loss of individuality, self-esteem and independence (Callamard, 1999: 203). The way in which aid is distributed may undermine individuals' personal coping resources (Harrell-Bond, 1999: 136). This 'warehousing' of refugees means life is lived in waiting and 'idleness, despair and in a few cases, even violence prevails' (UNHCR, 2006: 115). People fleeing to refugee camps are deemed de facto refugees but those who move to a third country, directly or indirectly, must claim asylum. This presents a further extended period of limbo while a decision is made on their application, in which their rights may be severely curtailed and their ability to build a new life is put on hold.

Refugees often experience a profound loss of status. For people who have left high-status occupations, the loss of self-esteem can be particularly hard. Fatima, who had been a nurse in Somalia, said: 'My work was very important in my life. Now when we go to hospital here they think we are nothing, we don't know anything' (Sales and Gregory, 1998, p 19).

The lack of trust engendered by the refugee experience, combined with unfamiliarity with services may make it difficult to access appropriate services. Taylor (2007) found that Congolese refugees in London were unfamiliar with the gatekeeper role of general practitioners and experienced what they perceived to be discrimination and racism. They were profoundly mistrustful of the treatment they received within the National Health Service, believing that they received a poorer service specifically designed for refugees.

There is considerable evidence to suggest that refugee women often find it easier than men to adapt to changed status (Kay, 1989; Buijs, 1993; Summerfield,

1993; Refugee Council, 1996; Kofman et al, 2000). Men may lose status in the home, as they are unable to fulfil their traditional 'breadwinner' role, and they also lose a public political role. In contrast, many women experience new opportunities, for example acquiring for the first time independent income through benefits or employment, and taking on new roles, paid and unpaid. Somali women interviewed in London had taken on the main responsibility for keeping the family together, dealing with landlords, teachers, social security, doctors and lawyers (Sales and Gregory, 1998). Ferhat's husband had had a highly paid government job in Somalia but was not employed in London: 'He feels depressed and isolated. He sits at home and reads newspapers. He hardly ever goes out. He has a problem with his hearing which has got worse, but he won't get it looked at' (Sales and Gregory, 1998, p 18).

Summerfield (1993: 83) found that Somali men suffered from depression more frequently than women and appeared to be less in control of their lives. Divorce is high among Somalis in Britain as women have found more independence and do not need to depend on a husband (Ali, 1997). Exile can, however, bring attempts to reassert patriarchal roles. Zarzosa (1998), in discussing her own exile from Chile, describes how women refugees may feel themselves marginalised in the exile community, with men seen as the main political activists, even if the women had themselves been politically involved.

It is generally easier for younger people to settle and those with qualifications and some form of 'social capital' on which to draw may find it easier to pick up the threads of their life, even if this means developing a new career (Kofman et al, 2002). Children are generally most adaptable and quick to learn a new language. This can bring a reversal in family roles, which may place children in the role of managing and mediating the new culture for their parents (Ahearn et al, 1999: 230). It can rob parents of their traditional authority, making them feel infantilised, while children take on too much responsibility. Parents' dependence for interpretation may lead children to become involved in issues that increase their anxiety, such as parents' medical problems or immigration issues (interviews with Kurdish refugees, London, June 2000).[3] This was an issue for Zamzam from Somalia, who said: 'My older daughter interprets for me at the doctor's but sometimes I don't want to let her know what I am feeling. I get so worried and I don't want her to know how bad things are' (Sales and Gregory, 1998: 20).

Mental health

Refugees have a high rate of mental health problems. They may experience depression and anxiety as a result of witnessing traumatic events (BMA, 2004: 1). A study for the British Home Office (Carey-Wood et al, 1995) found that two-thirds of the 263 refugees interviewed experienced stress, anxiety and depression, which often continued for many years. Traumatic symptoms can include flashbacks, memory disturbance, panic, sleeplessness (Ager, 1999a: 6). They may also feel anxious about people left behind and guilty at their own safety. One boy who left Turkey following threats because of his political activity said:

> I feel I ran away from my friends in Turkey. I was an opportunist, I shouldn't have left my friends – we were five boys, we were always together. Three of them were imprisoned and one died there. I feel guilty. Now I want to study so that I can help. (Interview with Kurdish asylum seeker in London school, 5 June 1996)[4]

Most refugees deal with practical problems first and psychological issues come later, often when they are more securely settled (Sales, 2002b). As Kohli and Mather (2003:208) put it in relation to unaccompanied refugees, 'young people want to face the present first, the future next and the past last'. Mental health problems can be exacerbated by insecurity and exclusion in the country of exile. Leila's husband had been an engineer in Somalia but was unable to work in London: 'When he sees buildings like the ones he used to build, he just stops and stares at them. He would love to be able to do that kind of work. His asthma [a stress-related disease] has become chronic since we came here' (Sales and Gregory, 1998, p 18).

Melzac (1999) suggests that children and young people who become most vulnerable to later difficulties are those who are unable to discuss their situations and where the problems remain hidden. A teacher in a London school described how a project on refugees he initiated helped some pupils to talk about their experiences:

> There were several refugee children in the class, and I wanted them all to be happy about it so I asked each individually. They all said that we should go ahead, but 'don't talk about me'. So I invited someone in to talk about his experience as a refugee. As he was talking, one girl started crying and I felt I had made a terrible mistake. But when I apologised to her she said: 'No, he was telling my story. Now I want to talk about it myself.' (Interview with teacher in London school, 5 June 1996)

The refugee pupils went on to take the lead in developing a video and a play about the refugee experience, and the class developed a 'Charter' of refugee rights. Some professionals working with refugees argue that western psychiatric categories have been used in ways that ignore the social, political and economic factors that are crucial to refugees' experience (Watters, 2001). Psychotherapists Kos and Derviskadic-Jovanovic (1998: 6) report that, when offered psychological help, illiterate peasants politely explained: 'we are not crazy. What we feel is not abnormal – the situation is crazy and abnormal. Our reactions are human and normal.' Refugees who manage to survive dangerous situations and to negotiate the difficult journey and the immigration process have often displayed enormous resilience. Thus rather than portraying them as 'passive victims' suffering mental health problems, Watters (2001) argues that attention should be given to the resistance of refugees and the ways in which they interpret and respond to experiences.

Returning 'home'?

> Afghanistan is a poor dusty country but for me it is heaven. It has a lot of sun, we have good food, good people, kind people. Every one loves their country and I like my own dusty country... my mountains. My dream is to return there. My country is gold. (Interview, Manchester, 22 September 2002)

> This is my home. I don't even want to think about Afghanistan any more. This is my new life! My future is here. To me it is like my life starts now. All I had before was fighting and war. (Interview, Manchester, 22 September 2002)

These two quotations from a study of the views of Afghan refugees (Sales et al, 2003) suggest the variety of feelings about 'home'. A nostalgic notion of home may be maintained as a survival strategy in exile, particularly during the initial period when refugees may reject the host society (Zarzosa, 1998: 193). As for the first person quoted above, this may be an idealised view and the speaker had no concrete plans to return. For the second man quoted, starting a new life in the country of exile was a priority and he wanted to cut himself off from his previous 'home'. The first had secure status as a recognised refugee, while the other was an asylum seeker and fearful of being sent back home.

Desire to return depends on broad political and economic considerations connected with the conflict that precipitated flight, especially the extent to which the country is perceived as safe. It also varies with personal characteristics such as age and education. As people put down roots in exile, the meaning of home becomes transformed and they may feel at home in more than one place. For some refugees, their children represent a future that they feel they have lost for themselves, and as the children progress in the country of exile, return may become less realistic. Milica from Bosnia was single when she arrived in Italy but started a family there and decided to settle permanently. Her parents, however, were unable to make a life in Italy:

> My parents dream of returning. They have never really integrated here. They speak some Italian, they have good Italian friends, they get on well here. But they have their own house in Bosnia, and they want to return to it. ... They don't lack material things here, they have a house, food, clothes but that is not all that matters. For the small amount of life they have left, they want to be there. (Interview with Kurdish refugee, London, June 2000)[5]

Chimni (2004: 59) rejects the assumption that exiles long for return to a particular place. Most refugees who 'return' never actually go back to their previous home. In most post-conflict situations the experiences of war and exile have intensified divisions between ethnic groups. In Bosnia, for example, national boundaries have been redrawn, cutting many off from their original home. Returnees are confronted with a host of difficult problems relating to property claims, employment and education (Blitz, 2003: 63). In Afghanistan, returnees have faced localised violence, persistent drought and lack of employment, basic services and housing. Many have thus left their original homes and headed for Kabul and other urban centres for security and employment (UNHCR, 2006: 20).

Strategies for promoting reconstruction may leave untouched relations of power and fail to address the issues that promoted conflict. Baines (2004) describes this process in Rwanda, where official policy involved creating a modern, non-ethnic nation in which the terms 'Hutu' and 'Tutsi' became irrelevant. As part of the attempt at national reconciliation, women were required to confront people who had been involved in the genocide against their families. As one woman asked, 'how can we welcome back the people who killed our husbands and children?' (Baines, 2004: 146).

The UNHCR and the major donor states are increasingly promoting return as the most viable long-term solution to the refugee crisis. The voluntariness of these programmes, however, is sometimes questionable (Baines, 2004; Blitz et al, 2005). A concern raised by Chimni (2004: 61) is that return is based on a supposedly 'objective' test of the security carried out by the host country, not on the subjective desire of the refugee. He suggests that 'objectivism disenfranchises the refugee through eliminating his or her voice in the process leading to the decision to deny or terminate protection' (Chimni, 2004: 62). The silencing of the refugee voice thus becomes an element in the whole refugee cycle, from flight to return.

Conclusion

This chapter has emphasised the significance of the definition of a 'refugee'. The ability of refugees to meet the criteria of the Geneva Convention determines their rights in exile and may even determine their right to life if they are returned as 'failed asylum seekers'. The definition can be seen, however, as morally arbitrary in that it distinguishes between the causes of violence rather than the danger people face. Zolberg et al (1989) argue for a restructuring of the refugee determination process based on prioritising the immediacy of need rather than the categories of the Convention. The blurred boundaries between economic and political migrants, however, suggest the need for a more radical rethinking of the nature of immigration controls and the case for exclusion of migrants whatever their motivation. This issue will be discussed further in Chapter Nine.

The chapter also discussed the controversial notion of the 'refugee experience'. An understanding of these experiences may help in identifying refugees' specific needs that require support, for example in relation to language learning and mental health. This approach needs to be balanced with 'an appreciation of the common resilience of refugee communities and the resources within them for responding to the challenges of forced migration' (Ager, 1999a: 13). The notion can also risk the danger of unduly pathologising the experience of refugees (Ager, 1999b), creating an image of the refugee as a 'generic and essentialized figure' (Callamard, 1999: 197). Refugee experience is as diverse as the number of individual refugees themselves and the situations from which they have fled.

Two polarised views of refugees have been promoted in contemporary debate. Official and popular discourse portrays refugees and asylum seekers as 'scroungers' who place a burden on an overstretched welfare state. Those concerned with refugee rights have been keen to combat these negative media images and focused on their resilience, their skills and potential contribution to the economy and broader society.[6] While this may have a positive impact on popular attitudes, it also contains dangers. Some individuals are unable to make this kind of contribution. Many are too sick or old to work, and will continue to be dependent. Not all are either 'heroes' or innocent victims. Some have been perpetrators of violence as well as victims and in some conflict situations the boundaries between legitimate and illegitimate violence and between voluntary and coerced activity is difficult to disentangle. The continuing claim for refugee protection cannot rest on the moral or economic value of individual refugees but must be based on more general political and ethical principles.

Notes

[1] A report in the *Guardian* (28 March 2006) said that hundreds went into Canada and are now seeking political refugee status there, arguing that violations of the rules of war in Iraq by the US entitle them to asylum.

[2] All interviews in this paragraph are from a series of interviews with refugees from Turkey and former Yugoslavia, in Rome, 2000, for the 'Civic stratification, social exclusion and migrant trajectories in three European cities' project funded by ESRC, with E. Kofman and C. Lloyd, 1999–2001.

[3] From the series of interviews described in note 2 above.

[4] See note 3 above.

[5] See note 3 above.

[6] See, for example, the promotion of 'Refugee Week' by the Refugee Council.

Summary

- Western concern about forced migration increased as the end of the Cold War changed the nature and response to conflict and brought asylum seekers to the developed countries.
- Forced and voluntary migration are connected in terms of their causes and the direction of migration flows (the asylum–immigration nexus).
- Forced and voluntary migration are matters of degree rather than an absolute distinction.
- Establishing claims to refugee status is crucial to the security and rights granted to refugees.
- The Geneva Convention definition of a refugee is based on individual persecution on particular grounds.
- Many forced migrants do not fit the categories of the Convention but need protection.
- There are commonalities as well as diversity in the refugee experience, including lack of control over their lives, insecurity and loss, but also resilience and survival.
- Not all refugees wish to return home after the end of conflict.

Questions for discussion

- Is the Geneva Convention definition of refugees appropriate for contemporary refugee movements?

- Are the tensions between humanitarian principles and state sovereignty irreconcilable?
- Is the term 'refugee experience' useful?

Further reading

Ager, A. (ed) (1999b) *Refugees: Perspectives on the experience of forced migration*, London: Continuum.

Bloch, A. and Levy, C. (eds) (1999) *Refugees, citizenship and social policy in Europe*, Basingstoke: Macmillan.

Castles, S. and Loughna, S. (2003) 'Globalization, migration and asylum', in V. George and R. Page (eds) *Global social problems and global social policy*, Cambridge: Polity.

UNHCR (2006) *The state of the world refugees: Human displacement in the new millennium*, Geneva: UNHCR.

Zolberg, A., Suhrke, A. and Aguayo, S. (1989) *Escape from violence: Conflict and the refugee crisis in the developing world*, New York: Oxford University Press.

Part 2
Understanding migration and refugee policy

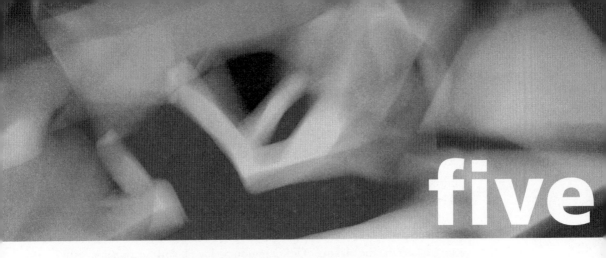

five

Contemporary immigration policy making

Overview

This chapter examines some key features of immigration policy making that will be explored in greater depth in subsequent chapters dealing with Britain. It explores three main issues: first, the specific characteristics of immigration policy making and the complex and conflicting interests involved, which mean that immigration policy may produce unintended results; second, it looks at the impact of migration on different national models of citizenship and the extent to which national citizenship remains important; and third at the different levels at which immigration policy is made. The nation state remains the major actor in immigration policy but national sovereignty is challenged from above by international and regional policies and governance and from below by local institutions.

Key concepts

Policy-making process; immigration exceptionalism; models of citizenship; post-national citizenship; civic stratification; multiculturalism

Introduction

In this part of the book the focus shifts to immigration policy. It examines the development of immigration policy, current policy making and debates about the future. Immigration policy is relatively new and the scope and pace of policy making has expanded rapidly in recent years. The complexity of contemporary immigration processes and the erosion of the distinction between countries of immigration and countries of emigration, together with global and regional governance, have meant that most states now operate some form of immigration policy. Global and regional developments have brought some convergence in policy making but nation states remain the key decision makers in relation to immigration policy.

The following chapters concentrate mainly on Britain and explore in more detail some of the questions raised in this chapter, which discusses some general issues concerning the making of immigration policy. The first section concerns the specific nature of immigration policy or 'immigration exceptionalism' (Sciortino, 2000) and the difficulties in implementing it. It discusses the tools of immigration policy and the strategies open to migrants and their supporters in resisting these controls. The following section discusses the link between migration and citizenship. Migration separates citizenship from residence, raising the issue of which rights non-citizens should be able to access and the process by which migrants are able to become citizens. It discusses different national models of citizenship and the impact of contemporary developments on these traditions. On the one hand there have been moves to acknowledge the importance of transnational mobility by granting more rights to non-citizens and on the other, the perception of a 'migration crisis' and a terrorist threat have led to the promotion of more national forms of citizenship based on notions of national culture and core values.

The final section discusses the different spatial levels at which immigration policy is made. Although control over the national borders and the route to citizenship remain central to national sovereignty and national identity, this power is constrained by the difficulties inherent in policy making discussed in section one, as well as by formal and informal obligations arising from other policy-making arenas. This includes international obligations and procedures, and regional obligations such as those emanating from the EU as well as local responsibilities and initiatives.

The nature of immigration policy making

Immigration policy is concerned with who is able to enter the national territory and on what terms, the rights of non-citizens resident within the state and the conditions by which citizenship is acquired. States claim to make immigration policy in the 'national interest', which presupposes the moral superiority of the national over the rights and interests of outsiders. Claims of a common interest are always illusory since different groups and classes have different interests that are reflected in different attitudes to immigration policy.

Attempting to manage national migration policy is inherently problematic since it involves external flows that are by definition unpredictable and outside the state's control. The difficulties are exacerbated by the relative absence of global governance with regard to international migration (Castles, 2004a: 870). Bhagwati suggests that paradoxically, the ability to control migration has shrunk as the desire to do so has increased (quoted in Castles, 2004a: 852).

Castles (2004a) illustrates the unintended consequences of immigration policies, which have sometimes led to spectacular reversals of policy. One such was the closure of the German guestworker system in the 1970s, which, instead of the expected ending of immigration, led to migration becoming self-sustaining, bringing with it a settled ethnic minority population and the opening up of routes to the acquisition of citizenship. Another was the failure of assimilation in Australia, which led to the adoption of state-sponsored multiculturalism in 1973 (Castles, 2004a: 852). Castles suggests that immigration policy is driven by the bureaucratic belief that rules determine behaviour and that migration can be switched on and off like a tap when no longer useful to the country of immigration (2004a: 858). This belief ignores the fact that migration is a social process. It becomes self-perpetuating over time, fed by structural dependence on migration in both emigration states (who depend on remittances and the relief of social tensions) and in immigration states (to feed labour demand in particular sectors). It is also sustained through chain migration and the development of networks and migrant institutions. Migrants are human beings rather than the 'units of labour' that the proponents of managed migration policy would prefer. They resist attempts to control them, pursuing their own migratory strategies, which may involve extended settlement and evading or challenging the restrictions placed upon them.

Sciortino, describing what he calls 'immigration exceptionalism' (2000: 223), raises another series of dimensions to the specificity of immigration policy. First, it cannot be shaped by interaction with those subjected to its regulation since migrants are by definition outside the polity, either physically beyond its borders or without the right to participate in the political process. There is thus no shared 'vision' (Sciortino, 2000: 224) or the possibility of 'user involvement' in the development of policy. On the contrary, there is often sharp conflict in which migrants are largely powerless in the face of decisions made about their fate on the basis of criteria that do not correspond to their needs or interests. Second, there is uncertainty about the numbers of potential immigrants since immigration is the result of external events. Debates about immigration policy frequently revolve around different estimates of numbers, and the lack of credible data may bring exaggerated estimates from those hostile to migration.

Third, policy-making actors do not have to fear sanctions from those who are the objects of policy and so migration rhetoric becomes an 'empty symbol', which can be deployed to gain votes (Sciortino, 2000). Saggar (2003: 180–1) suggests that the race card can only be effective under certain conditions.

It requires not only that a significant majority are opposed to immigration but that they rank this highly in their agenda of concerns. It also requires an alignment on this issue between party and voter preference. As communities settle and become voters, immigration policy may develop a very real resonance in some localities. For example, the ability to bring in family members is an area of immigration law that directly affects some voters. Political parties have often striven to maintain some form of consensus on the boundaries within which debate on immigration policy takes place, since a high profile can lead to mainstream parties losing control over the issue to far right parties, as has happened in Britain, France and the Netherlands during the current century. The 'race card' is also unpredictable. John Howard won an unexpected victory in the Australian election of 2004 through acting 'tough' on asylum. He was forced, however, to back down on plans for a new law that included indefinite detention of refugees in response to opposition from politicians and voluntary agencies.[1]

Fourth, immigration policy cross-cuts the main cleavages in society, especially class loyalties. Trade unions, for example, may sometimes call for closure to protect what they claim are their members' interests, which can place them on the same side as conservative nationalists. Free-market capitalists and internationalist socialists support freedom from controls for very different reasons. These differing interests are complex with, for example, employers in sectors where migrants predominate favouring more open immigration, while others may reject it. These divisions are not fixed: trade unions for example have been prominent in calling for progressive policies in relation to migration as more settled migrant populations have themselves become recruited to membership.

The policy process

These contradictions feed into the process by which immigration policy is made. This process is shaped by the histories of immigration in individual states as well as the development of their political, legal and administrative structures. National policy is also influenced by international and regional institutions such as the United Nations and the European Union and by local actors.

Most theorists within the political economy tradition assume that migration policy reflects the economic interest of privileged class (Sciortino, 2000: 216). Early work within the structuralist tradition, for example, suggested that immigration policy was aimed at meeting the needs of European capital for cheap labour, while migration also divided workers, thus undermining resistance. The complexity of immigration policy making means, however, that it cannot be a simple response to 'the needs of capital'. States lack reliable information both about the immediate situation and the future implications of migratory processes. They also face contradictory imperatives. Liberal democratic states face the fundamental contradiction between the formal political equality of citizens and gross inequalities in wealth and income. Maintaining legitimacy requires the state to embody a notion of the 'national interest' (Habermas, 1975) that is not just rhetorical but that brings tangible benefits, such as the promotion of domestic employment and social rights (Gough, 1979). Responding to demands for immigration controls in the name of protecting jobs may be a means to maintain social peace. The German state, for example, conceded to demands for control of immigration from trade unions during the economic downturn in 1973 in spite of the negative impact on profits. The capitalist class itself includes conflicting and competitive interests, with those who benefit directly from employing migrant labour most interested in ensuring openness to migration.

National states embody an assemblage of conflicting economic and political pressures that may be reflected in differences between different government departments. In post-war Britain, for example, the minister of labour favoured controls on immigration to protect domestic employment, while the colonial secretary, whose brief involved the maintenance of relations with the colonies and emerging independent nations, opposed them since controls could have jeopardised these relations (Hansen, 2003: 28). State policy is also a site for conflict and struggle in which the interests of the rich and powerful compete with those of others. These struggles may also cut across class divisions as they have in relation to both pro- and anti-immigrant campaigns.

Freeman, using a corporatist model of the state, argues that immigration politics are, 'contrary to what most scholars seem to believe, largely expansionist and inclusive' (1995: 882). He suggests that immigration tends to produce concentrated benefits and diffuse costs and thus 'those who benefit from immigration in direct and concrete ways are better placed to organize than are those who bear immigration's costs' (Freeman, 1995: 885). Immigration regulation and control is thus 'a public good that lacks a concrete and organized constituency to produce it' (Freeman, 1995). He suggests that politicians sometimes give lip service to an anti-immigration rhetoric while actually pursuing policies that lead to more immigration. Castles (2004a: 867) also suggests that there are frequent 'hidden agendas' in immigration policy making. Anti-immigration rhetoric, however, by creating a hostile environment towards immigration, can undermine public acceptance of the immigration that the state deems to be in the national interest. This failure to address economic migration within public debate is partly a result of the political process; migration processes are long term but the policy cycle is essentially short term and related to elections (Castles, 2004a: 871). Politicians thus tend to focus on what they perceive as popular in the immediate term, rather than on the more difficult issues that may arise through examining longer-term developments.

Sciortino (2000: 221) argues that policy making is a 'social process in its own right'. State agencies have their own interests and cultures that are semi-autonomous of political and economic power. The British Home Office, for example, developed a conservative culture (Pellew, 1989) that has tended to favour restricting immigration, particularly from certain regions. During the 1980s, 'virginity tests' were introduced for Asian women applying to enter for marriage. These represented racist and patriarchal stereotypes, were highly intrusive and could not be said to serve any direct 'interest'.

The tools of immigration control

Recent efforts by states to regulate the movement of people have seen the reinforcing of borders and the erection of ever-more technologically sophisticated and militarised barriers (Rosewarne, 2001: 1). These are aimed partly at demonstrating that the state is in control of migration. The British home secretary, John Reid, took office in 2006 following a 'crisis' in the Home Office, which was shown to be unaware of the numbers of foreign prisoners. He immediately announced a plan for a uniformed immigration service, designed to show that he was 'doing something' about the perceived problem. The visible display of controls can, however, be counter-productive since 'in promising more than they can deliver, they only exacerbate the sense of crisis, so that these extraordinary measures seem normal and justifiable' (Bloch and Schuster, 2005: 509).

Immigration control encompasses measures to restrict or select the entry of aliens, and to control the conditions of their residence. These controls have expanded in geographical scope, extending beyond national boundaries and involving more people, including non-state actors, in the checking of immigration status. Hollifield (2004) argues that the intense politicisation of immigration and its growing significance in relation to state policy has led to the emergence of the 'migration state'. The attempt to manage immigration is not confined to immigration departments, but encompasses police, foreign affairs, labour and welfare services. These have different interests and cultures and provide different possibilities for resistance.

Controls on entry

Controls on entry are the most visible and important mechanism for protecting borders. The financial costs of border controls for the 25 richest countries are estimated as between $25 billion and $30 billion per year (Pecoud and de Guchteneire, 2005: 4). Although relatively recent in historical terms, passport checks at border ports have become routine and accepted by travellers. These border checks are now 'enhanced by biometric data (finger printing, digital photographs and iris recognition)' (Cohen, 2006:109). Special techniques have been devised in an attempt to stop people using well-known migrant routes. The US–Mexico border, for example, is policed by high-intensity lighting, high steel fencing, body-heat and motion-detecting sensors, and video surveillance and border patrols follow migrants into US territory (Pecoud and de Guchteneire, 2005: 2).

Halfmann (1998: 520) suggests that some areas have seen the transformation of 'frontiers (peripheral zones of states where authority can not be exerted as strongly as in the centre) into boundaries (highly surveillanced demarcation lines between states)'. Italy's long coastlines made entry easy during the 1980s and it has developed a system of sea patrols to intercept migrants. Some metropolitan states also project their authority outwards, pressuring neighbouring countries to strengthen their border controls; Australia now places immigration officials with airlines at overseas airports (Rosewarne, 2001: 3). Controls also operate before entry, with visa requirements involving pre-entry clearance in the country of origin. States rely increasingly on 'carrier sanctions' (fines and other punishment on transport operators for carrying passengers without correct documentation). They have become increasingly reliant on non-state actors and non-nationals to check immigration status. The British Five Year Strategy for Asylum and Immigration included the commitment to 'fingerprint everyone when they apply for a visa … Airlines will not have authority to carry people until this check has been made' (Home Office, 2005a: 8). Preventing travel by stopping those without proper documentation can have serious implications for refugees, who may not have access to this documentation, and can limit their right to enter the asylum process and reduce protection against *refoulement* (Morris, 2002: 150).

There has been increased reliance on technologically driven techniques that allow more sophisticated checks using computers, fingerprints and biometric data. President George W. Bush announced the 'Smart Border of the Future' in response to 11 September (Koslowski, 2004: 3) and allocated $380 million for a new entry–exit information system in 2003 (Koslowski, 2004: 18). Koslowski argues that the relationship between information technology and immigration control is contradictory. Developments in IT are driving the globalisation processes that undermine state sovereignty and challenge efforts to control immigration, but states also rely on it to control migration. Tracking the movement of cargo and people for security purposes also conflicts with economic goals. Computer checks take several minutes, slowing down traffic. Screening has been focused on the less well off, but the bias dictated by economic imperatives does not necessarily improve 'homeland security' since the 'rich can be dangerous' (Koslowski, 2004: 6). Ironically, migrants recruited into the US IT industry have been crucial to the development of these security tools (Koslowski, 2004: 31).

Detention

Detention of immigrants is increasing in western countries and is generally the prelude to deportation. In Australia, detention of all asylum seekers on arrival has become standard practice and there has been an increase in the use of detention and deportation against asylum seekers across Europe (Bloch and Schuster, 2005). In Italy, the development of mass immigration in the 1980s led to the establishment of 11 detention centres, mainly in the south, to hold those arriving irregularly. Over 500 people were imprisoned for infringement of immigration law in 2001 (IDOS, 2003). The British government promised in 2005 that it would detain more people and use 'other means of contact like tagging to prevent people absconding when they are ready to be removed' (Home Office, 2005a).

Most European states impose a limit to the length of time someone may be detained for immigration purposes. In Britain the period of detention remains indefinite. It has opted out of European Union directives that would have forced the government to abide by common limits (Nienhuis, 2006).

Internal controls

Internal controls involve measures to monitor migrants in the country of migration. They involve reliance on a range of agencies, including non-state actors to prevent access to employment or services and to alert the authorities to illegal presences. Employer sanctions, which allow for fines on employers who employ those not entitled to work, were developed in the 1970s in the US and Western Europe (Castles and Miller, 2003: 95) and were introduced in the UK in 1996. Germany has imposed particularly intense monitoring on employment (Duvell, 2004: 7). Employers tend to resent these controls since implementing controls is costly and disrupts relations with the workforce (Duvell and Jordan, 2003), and employing undocumented workers is often cheaper. In the US some employers have sufficient clout to prevent implementation (Castles and Miller, 2003: 96).

Controls on access to welfare have been a major element in immigration policy. Conditions placed on those entering for family reunion across Europe involve, in the British phrase, 'no recourse to public funds' and the availability of suitable accommodation (Kofman and Sales, 1998). Asylum seekers have also seen their rights to welfare reduced across Europe (Bloch and Schuster, 2002). As benefit agencies and service providers are required to scrutinise immigration status, this may run counter to professional codes, for example in the case of social workers or health workers (Hayes and Humphries, 2004).

Opposing immigration control

As immigration controls become wider in scope they create new forms of resistance. Stricter controls force migrants to use more ingenuity to get around them. Smugglers use the latest technology to switch routes and avoid detection (Koslowski, 2004: 13) and the declining cost of communicating allows individuals and networks to plan strategies and to keep in touch with the homeland. Migrants take risks, often endangering their health or even their lives in entering clandestinely and resisting controls.

'Illegal' entry

As border controls become more sophisticated and legal entry routes are closed off, migrants have found new ways of entering states. This takes a huge toll: it is estimated that one migrant dies every day attempting to cross the US–Mexico border (Pecoud and de Guchteneire, 2005: 3), but many thousands still attempt the crossing. Migrants often receive assistance in crossing borders; recent research by the British Refugee Council revealed that 69.4% of those surveyed had relied on agents (Refugee Council, 2004: 4). Some offer this help out of personal moral or religious conviction as did some German and Polish people who helped Jews to escape during the Nazi period or more recently the 'coyotes' who guide Mexican workers across the Rio Grande (Cohen, 2003: 114). Political refugees may rely on fellow political activists. Italy's 1998 Immigration Law, which introduced a 14-year sentence for facilitating illegal entry, recognised the variety of situations by allowing a defence based on humanitarian motives, a distinction that does not exist in British legislation.

Resistance to controls

Campaigns against immigration controls involve activities ranging from direct action to prevent a deportation to more conventional campaigns such as letter writing and picketing government offices. Campaigns may be mobilised to support a single person or family facing deportation, or may be more long standing, for example attempts to change particular laws, such as the campaign by Southall Black Sisters in Britain against the discriminatory 'primary purpose rule'. Campaigns may be based on friends, colleagues, fellow students and neighbours. Sometimes they involve people whose lives migrants happen to cross at a particular moment. Activists have, for example, been able to prevent deportations by asking passengers to refuse to sit down until the person is removed.[2] Trade unions are increasingly involved in collective action to reject elements of migration control. The main trade union umbrella body in the United States, the AFL-CIO, campaigns against employer enforcement that affects its members (Castles and Miller, 2003: 98). In France the main union federation, the CFDT, has demanded that Air France management should not use planes and staff for removals (Cohen, 2003: 17).

Migrants themselves are central to these campaigns and some take desperate action to publicise their situation. Refugees in Australia sewed up their mouths during a hunger strike to protest against their detention in 2004. They may go 'underground' in the face of the threat of deportation, or resistance may be more mundane, involving the failure to comply with bureaucratic demands. In Britain, asylum seekers who are due to be compulsorily dispersed outside London often remain in temporary accommodation rather than allow themselves to be moved (Hynes, 2007). Central to all these activities is a challenge to the idea that the state should decide where and how people move.

Migration and citizenship

The notion of a nation state is based on the supposed fit between geographical territory and the nation. Nation states are a combination of a political unit that controls a bounded territory (the state) and a national community (the nation or people) that has the power to impose its political will within those boundaries. Citizenship implies belonging to the 'imagined community' of the nation, which is 'both inherently limited and sovereign' (Anderson, 1983: 15). An aspect of states' struggle for legitimacy is the claim that they represent the aspirations of their people (citizens) based on cultural consensus allowing agreement on values and interests (Castles and Miller, 2003: 40). In reality the construction of nation states has involved the spatial extension of state power and the incorporation of hitherto distinct ethnic groups. Luhmann suggests that 'state formation can be understood in terms of the territorialisation of political dominance' (quoted in Jessop, 1990: 350). This process may involve the exclusion, assimilation or even genocide of minority groups.

Migration challenges this notion of national homogeneity (Castles and Davidson, 2000: 12) and raises the 'liberal paradox'. Democratic states are based on universal principles, involving equal access to some level of rights, but also on national particularity (Castles and Davidson, 2000: 12). The notion of citizenship itself implies some form of universalism above cultural difference yet it exists only in the context of a nation state that is based on cultural specificity (Castles, 2000: 188). Democratic decision making and the provision of social welfare presuppose clearly defined boundaries of membership (Jordan and Duvell, 2003: 17). Liberal theory, however, espouses the moral equality of persons and implies that all are equally eligible for membership (Cole, 2000). Moreover, the wealthy immigration-receiving nations also subscribe to human rights legislation, which applies to all those within their borders, not just to citizens (Portes, 2004: 833) and constrains the way in which states may treat unwelcome migrants.

Migration thus poses questions about how non-citizens are to be incorporated. These relate to individual access to the rights – civic, political and social – traditionally associated with citizenship (Marshall, 1950) and the way in which citizenship can be acquired. They also relate to the incorporation of groups (Soysal, 1994): whether, for example, they are able to acquire some group rights and the extent to which the society of immigration tolerates some form of difference.

Traditions of citizenship

There have been three main ways of acquiring citizenship that reflect traditions of immigration and emigration. Under *ius soli* (the law of the soil) people automatically become citizens by birth in a state; under *ius sanguinis* (blood law), citizenship is passed down through kinship; under *ius domicili* (law of residence) it is acquired through settlement. Most European states were until recently countries of emigration and citizenship based on *ius sanguinis*, which allowed ties with emigrants to be retained. The *Aussiedler*, people of German origin living outside Germany, had rights of return, while citizenship was difficult to acquire for foreigners. Israel operates an extreme version of *ius sanguinis*, offering citizenship to all who are 'challarchically' Jewish,[3] even those with no previous connection with the state. Citizenship in the immigration countries of the New World (the US as well as Canada and Australia) was based on *ius soli*, making it easy to incorporate immigrant children into the nation (Koslowski, 2002: 173). They encouraged family reunion and permanent settlement, treating immigrants as future citizens who acquired citizenship through *ius domicili*. In Britain, *ius soli* was linked to its imperial role.

These differences remain but have become less marked as a result of new migratory patterns: Germany now allows migrants to acquire citizenship, though under strict conditions, while Britain has moved towards a more ethnic basis for citizenship with the introduction of 'patriality' (see Chapter Six). Migration has also meant that citizenship is increasingly acquired through residence. The term used for this process, 'naturalisation', implies that membership of a certain nation state is laid down by 'natural laws' (Castles and Davidson, 2000: 15). Those aspiring to citizenship therefore have to prove themselves worthy, and no state grants citizenship as a right; each imposes conditions based primarily on length of residence. Most also demand 'good character' and the means to support oneself. Some exclude people with criminal convictions. The US has stringent rules, barring people with any form of criminal record, drunks, people who have taken drugs and past and present members of the Communist Party (Castles and Davidson, 2000: 86). Germany requires that granting citizenship to an individual is positively in the 'public interest' (Castles and Davidson, 2000: 87). Many states require new citizens to swear loyalty to their new country. The UK added a citizenship pledge in 2002 to the oath of allegiance to the monarchy, which all new citizens are required to swear, and introduced American-style 'citizenship ceremonies'.

These differences are linked to broader national traditions of citizenship. Castles and Miller (2003: 44) distinguish four models that have different implications for the rights of individuals and groups. These are 'ideal types' and actual states may contain elements of several, for example treating different types of migrant differently. They nevertheless provide a useful framework for understanding different approaches.

The imperial model

In this model, belonging derives from being subject to the same ruler, as in the British, Soviet or Austro-Hungarian empires. Castles and Miller (2003: 44) point out that this concept is always ideological, since it veils dominance by one ethnic or national group over subject peoples, as for example the break-up of the Soviet Union has demonstrated. In Britain, until post-war immigration differentiated between different categories of British citizen, all citizens of the colonies and Commonwealth were equally entitled to enter Britain and to full citizenship rights. This contrasted with 'aliens', who faced growing restrictions in the twentieth century. The construction of 'Britishness', however, has been on the basis of the dominant Christian and, until recently, a Protestant identity (Sales, 2005). Although citizens of the colonies and the Commonwealth had formal access to rights, actual rights were limited through racism and discrimination. Post-war immigration policy has differentiated between different categories of British citizen, whereas former aliens from Europe now have the right to enter as EU citizens. Britain has also moved from policies of assimilation of settled migrants towards forms of multiculturalism operated mainly at local level.

The 'folk' or ethnic model

Citizenship is based on ethnicity and notions of common descent and language. Ethnic minorities, even those born in the state, are excluded from citizenship. Germany comes closest to this model. *Aussiedler* were permitted free entry and citizenship rights after German unification. Japan remains one of the most exclusionary states in relation to citizenship, which cannot be obtained even by long residence and marriage to a Japanese citizen.

Guestworker models in Germany and other European states were based on the notion that they were not countries of immigration and that migrants were workers not settlers (Castles and Davidson, 2000: 61). They were accepted only with strict functional and temporal limits and excluded from many basic rights. In countries of recent immigration, such as Italy, migrants were initially excluded from mainstream welfare. Subsequent legislation has opened up more rights for legally resident migrants (Sales, 2002b) but citizenship remains difficult to acquire.

The republican model

The republican model defines the nation as a political community based on a constitution, law and common citizenship. Newcomers can become members provided they adopt the national culture and language. The classic examples are France (with its 'civic republican' model) and the US, which also emerged from a revolution to overthrow rule by a monarchy. France's colonial citizens were also perceived as members of this community.[4] Castles (2000: 138) argues that the republican model 'appears to be purely political, yet it brings culture in through the back door'. The notion of a 'national community' hides the dominance of particular languages and cultures. The spread of French culture 'rested on ensuring that crushed minorities forgot the history of their oppression' (Castles and Davidson, 2000: 46). France's policy of secularism in the public sphere, which has seen the banning of the wearing of headscarves by Muslim pupils, has tolerated the display of Catholic symbols such as crucifixes. The United States was built on the linguistic and cultural dominance of English. Abandoning their mother tongues was part of the process of 'Americanisation' of its new citizens throughout most of the twentieth century.

Although both are assimilationist in their method of incorporation of immigrants, these states have very different relations to their histories of migration. The image of the French nation conceals its history of immigration and conquest. In spite of the importance of language to current French national identity, most citizens of France did not speak French until the end of the nineteenth century (Castles and Davidson, 2000: 45). The US, in contrast, celebrates its tradition of immigration. The 'melting pot', the melding of different languages and cultures into a common allegiance to the United States, is crucial to its myth of nationhood. This melting pot, however, excluded 'people of colour' for most of the twentieth century.

These assimilationist models have come under pressure from the settlement of minorities who have refused to abandon their culture. Since the 1960s the United States has been 'reconceptualised as a multicultural society' (Castles and Davidson, 2000: 160). In France, the failure of the republican model to include minorities is evident in the segregation evident in the *banlieux*, the deprived peripheral regions of major cities, and has led to the development of flexible 'integration policies' (Castles and Miller, 2003: 249) operated mainly at local level (Kofman et al, 2000).

The multicultural model

Multiculturalism is a more recent development. It is also based on the definition of the nation as a political community but newcomers are not only permitted to acquire citizenship but also to retain cultural difference and form ethnic communities within the framework of adherence to common laws. This model became dominant in Australia, Canada and Sweden during the 1970s, states with very different histories of immigration. Multiculturalism was promoted mainly through public policy, with Australia adopting the most systematic policy in 1973 with the National Agenda for Integration (Castles and Davidson, 2000: 165). In the United States, multiculturalism has mainly taken the form of attempts to question previously dominant understandings of history (Castles and Davidson, 2000: 164), with the achievement of the 'American dream' in material terms left largely to market forces.

The first three models shared an important common principle, namely that immigration should not bring about significant change to the culture and society of the receiving nation. Multiculturalism involves some accommodation to immigration, although the extent of cultural autonomy allowed has been contested. Critics of multicultural policies have suggested that they are often based on static and essentialised views of immigrant communities and family structures. These may homogenise minority cultures and for example legitimise conservative practices that restrict women's roles (Kofman et al, 2000). Reluctance to criticise what is claimed to be 'traditional culture' can lead to a failure by service providers to intervene to prevent human rights abuses (Meetoo and Mirza, 2007).

These models are based on the notion that one can belong to only one country and that immigration is a once and for all process. The principle of singular citizenship has been eroded by mixed marriages (Castles and Miller, 2003: 244) and by transnational practices. Some states, including the UK, France, Australia and the US, permit dual citizenship. Others, such as Austria, Denmark, Japan and Germany, require renunciation of former citizenship on naturalisation (Castles and Miller, 2003: 245).

New countries of immigration, such as Italy and Spain, have only recently developed policies towards immigration and models of incorporation. They are two of the very few European countries that are signatories to key international conventions on migrant rights, but the large numbers of undocumented migrants remain unprotected. Both have strongly developed policies towards territorial minorities, such as the Basques and Catalans in Spain, but the development of multicultural policies in respect of migrant minorities has been slower.

Towards post-national citizenship?

Processes of migration have brought considerable convergence in the practices of states in relation to citizenship. This has been intensified by international and regional pressures, for example European Union integration. Germany has opened up citizenship to migrants, and policies for the integration of migrants have been widely developed across Europe. At the same time, powerful states are operating increased closure in relation to 'unwanted' migration, reducing the social rights available to temporary residents. These contradictory trends have led to competing discourses about the continuing importance of national citizenship. Some argue that a new 'transnational' citizenship is developing, rendering formal citizenship status less relevant. Others argue that citizenship continues to be crucial in determining rights and security.

Soysal (1994:1) argues that a 'new and more universal concept of citizenship has unfolded in the post-war era, one whose organising and legitimating principles are based on universal personhood rather than national belonging'. She suggests that, with settled residence, non-citizens gain significant social rights in the country of migration, or a post-national citizenship with quasi-citizenship rights and status. These rights are underpinned by an international regime of rights embodied in treaties and other international agreements (Soysal, 1994: 10). Critics have suggested that Soysal overstates the importance of 'world-level pressures' in securing rights for migrants (Castles and Davidson, 2000: 18). Morris (2002: 145) argues that the effects of international conventions are limited in a number of ways: they grant protection only to those party to the convention; they address the needs of specific groups; deal only with specific areas of rights; and are limited to migrants lawfully in the territory. The 1990 UN Convention on the Rights of Migrant Workers and Members of their Families, for example, has been signed by only a handful of emigration countries, for whom the obligations implied are limited (Castles and Davidson, 2000: 19). In general these instruments do not challenge the right of a state to govern the entry and conditions for the stay of aliens (Morris, 2002: 145). According to Kofman et al (2000), the acquisition of migrants' rights owes more to political and economic developments in the countries of migration than to international human rights instruments. The right to family reunion in Germany was won through legal action taken by migrants and their supporters (Hollifield, 2004: 895).

The optimistic scenario outlined by Soysal reflects the experience of secure residents. Other privileged migrants, for example skilled transients, are able to develop notions of 'transnationalism' that do not involve engagement with society (Jordan and Duvell, 2003: 61). For the less privileged, rights in the country of residence are crucial to their long-term future. Restrictions on access to benefits and residence, which increasingly apply to labour and family migrants, underline the continuing importance of formal citizenship status. Citizenship status remains crucial to the acquisition of political rights and the process by which it is acquired remains largely the domain of national governments. The development of 'supranational' EU citizenship has remained limited, and tied mainly to the movement of labour (Ackers, 1998). This development has, paradoxically, increased the importance of national belonging, since membership derives from citizenship of a member state.

Those with more precarious status have been increasingly excluded from rights. Recent legislation has created a growing disparity between the rights of labour migrants with settled status and those with temporary or insecure status (Morris, 1997, 2002). A common feature has been the casualisation of labour contracts and the removal of permanent rights of residence (Rudolph, 1996). Insecure workers are unwilling or unable to assert their employment rights, for example in relation to health and safety (interview with TUC official, June 2006).[5] This process has been particularly important in relation to asylum policy, where the trend across Europe and elsewhere has been to separate asylum seekers from refugees in relation to welfare and security of residence (Bloch and Schuster, 2002).

Morris (2002) uses the notion of 'civic stratification' to analyse the processes of increasingly differential rights of migrants. She suggests that the 'rights and protections afforded by the state to different "entry" categories constitute a system of stratified rights' (Morris, 2002: 19). Building on the work of Lockwood, Morris distinguishes between three dimensions that impact on rights:

- **inclusion and exclusion**: formal rights attached to particular statuses;
- **gains and deficits**: informal processes through which rights are gained or lost;
- **expansion and contraction**: the general terrain of rights at national level.

She argues that formal rights have become more differentiated in most countries of immigration, intensifying exclusion for some. Gender functions as an informal status that has an impact on rights. It creates deficits through 'the ascription of features which dictate the distribution of private obligations of caring' and 'the associated allocation of esteem, which devalues the private sphere' (Morris, 2002: 123). In some regimes, such as Germany, there has been a general expansion in the terrain of rights, whereas this has contracted in Britain. Comparative research in London, Paris and Rome (Kofman et al, 2002) found that both formal and informal processes were important in securing access to rights. It also suggested that, although long-term third-country residents may eventually acquire rights almost on a par with European citizens, the growth in undocumented migration is creating a population that is 'tolerated' but barred from participating fully in society. The processes of social exclusion that they experience have long-term implications for them, their families and for the society in which they now live (Sales, 2002b; see also Vertovec, 2006).

The renewal of citizenship?

Widespread fears that migration threatens national cultures and societies have led to renewed efforts by states to construct and sustain a sense of common national citizenship (Kymlicka, 2003: 195). This runs counter to attempts to develop more open approaches to citizenship. The politicisation of migration and ethnic conflict, for example in France and Britain, and the 'feeling of uncertainty and loss from the swamping of distinctive cultural practices and forms by a commodified international culture' (Castles, 2000: 182) has been a common theme in the discourse of politicians and in popular media. National states are making increasingly vociferous demands for undivided loyalty and affiliation to national cultures and polities (Kofman, 2005a: 464). This has been exacerbated by the success of anti-immigrant parties in mobilising support and votes.

European nation states have retreated from the supposed 'excesses' of multiculturalism and revived 'neo-assimilationist agendas' (Kofman, 2005a: 454). In the Netherlands, the popularity of Pim Fortuyn and his party Lijst Pim Fortuyn (LPF), dedicated to combating multiculturalism and further immigration, threatened mainstream parties in the election campaign of 2002. Fortuyn's murder by a young Muslim man just before the election and the internal disagreements within the party that followed have led to the disappearance of the party as a political force. Ironically, the Somali-born Dutch MP Ayaan Hirsi Ali, whose life has been threatened by Islamic extremists because of her support for secularism, was stripped of her citizenship on the grounds that she had made a false declaration in her asylum claim. The Dutch system was unable to accommodate the situation of a young and vulnerable person fleeing the very real threat of religious persecution in her home country. In France, a law introduced in 2005 banned religious forms of dress in public places. This action in defence of the secularism embedded in the French Constitution has, however, been perceived as being explicitly targeted at Muslims. It re-ignited the divisions of the 'headscarf affair' of the 1990s that divided the left, feminists, the anti-racist movement and the Muslim population itself (Kofman et al, 2000: 170). The latest law was passed in the context of growing intolerance towards immigrants and in the wake of battles in the *banlieux* of large cities between police and groups of French-born young men of North African origin who had become excluded socially and spatially from mainstream society.

Fear of immigrants' 'divided loyalties' has become prevalent in the wake of the terrorist attack of 11 September. In the United States, the notion of 'homeland security' seeks to naturalise the difference between 'us' and 'them' (Cohen, 2006: 198). Muslims have become the new 'other' and belonging to the *Ummah*, or Muslim world nation, is seen as conflicting with national loyalty and national laws (Kofman, 2005b: 92). The British government has denounced those who suggest that there is a connection between its foreign policy and the existence of home-grown Muslim terrorists.[6] Less seriously, Norman Tebbit's 'cricket test'[7] was resurrected with demands by government ministers that Scottish politicians support the English soccer team in the 2006 World Cup. These concerns hark back to earlier periods when foreigners were seen as potential enemies. In the United States, Japanese-born citizens were rounded up after the attacks on Pearl Harbor in 1941, while in Britain, 'enemy aliens' were interned and deported during both world wars. Britain's Jewish community has long been sensitive to this issue and regularly demonstrates its allegiance. Both the British and Israeli national anthems are played at weddings and *bar mitzvahs*, one of the rare times outside state occasions where the British one is heard.

States have invoked notions of national belonging and presented the national state as 'protector of national identity and social cohesion' (Kofman, 2005a: 455) with a more active national citizenship. This has not generally involved the strengthening of the particularist aspects of citizenship (Halfmann, 1998: 527) but the reassertion of liberal principles that they claim to embody and that are presented as central to the national identity of European states (Kofman, 2005: 461). The meaning of 'Britishness', for example, was located in the 1998 Human Rights Act, passed to bring European legislation into British law. The government claimed that this 'can be viewed as a key source of values that British citizens should share' (Home Office, 2002a: 30). Thus the identity of the dominant group, or 'us', is formulated around its tolerance and adherence to human rights compared to the intolerant other (Kofman, 2005a: 462). The notion that migrants disrupt a 'pre-existing national consensus and culture' (Kofman, 2005b: 91) was given voice in the introduction by Prime Minister Tony Blair to his government's Five Year Strategy for Asylum and Immigration in 2005 (Home Office, 2005a: 6):

> But this tradition [of] tolerance is under threat. It is under threat from those who come here illegally by breaking our rules and abusing our hospitality. And, unless we act to tackle abuses, it could be increasingly exploited by extremists to promote their perverted view of race.

This notion of 'hospitality' suggests that foreigners invade the nation's domestic space. They are presented as uninvited guests living off 'our' good will rather than as workers making an economic contribution. Although this threat to national tolerance is claimed to lie in the 'abuse' of rules, the statement implies that there are too many foreigners. In France, notions of a 'tipping point' (Kofman, 2005a: 459) or a 'threshold of tolerance' were invoked to suggest a 'quantifiable level of tolerance' so that people are 'able to reject the foreigner in the name of science' (Kofman, 2005a: 460).

There has been a shift towards a contractual model of citizenship, in which rights are balanced by obligations and responsibilities. In Britain this has taken the form of language and citizenship tests. As Kymlicka notes, similar requirements are made in Canada, where they have been uncontroversial. Unlike Canada with its trajectory towards greater openness (Kymlicka, 2003: 197), the direction in Britain is towards closure, or to use Morris's terminology, there has been a contraction in the terrain of rights. Citizenship policies, Kymlicka suggests, cannot be seen in isolation from the broader trends regarding the acceptance of newcomers.

Levels of immigration policy making

The national state is the central focus of immigration management and control and, despite some convergence, the rules of citizenship and associated rights remain predominantly national. Individual states' management of migration remains rooted in their migration histories. As national power is eroded through the globalisation of markets and the development of international and regional political institutions, migration policy remains an area for the assertion of national sovereignty with enormous ideological and political importance. Indeed Hirst and Thompson (1999) argue that migration has increased the power of the national state.

National independence in immigration policy is, however, challenged from above, by regional and international obligations and institutions, and from below, by local state bodies to which states may devolve responsibility for immigration control as well as by resistance from individuals and groups. Immigration policy illustrates the precarious balance between the power of global and regional regimes and nation states (Jordan and Duvell, 2003: 17). The entry of labour migrants is primarily determined at national level, but managing migration involves extensive engagement with sending states, including police and immigration officers (Jordan and Duvell, 2003: 18). International bodies also place obligations on nation states in relation to humanitarian principles. Asylum challenges state sovereignty in determining the number and composition of those who enter the nation state (Kofman, 2005a: 459). International regimes may dictate human rights law, but the immediate guarantor of transnational rights is the nation state and the mechanism for its delivery operates at national level (Morris, 2002: 15–16).

Jordan and Duvell (2003: 18) suggest that national sovereignty in relation to border controls has been shored up by supranational bodies like the EU. Free movement for EU citizens, however, reduces the ability of individual states to control entry. The expansion of EU membership has shifted the boundaries of inclusion, with nationals of new member states gaining rights of entry. In those European states where large-scale immigration first developed in the context of European integration, national policies have been strongly influenced by EU policy that may conflict with national interests. Italy, for example, introduced immigration controls largely in response to EU pressure. Newer countries of the EU and its periphery, such as Lithuania, have introduced controls that are primarily aimed at stopping them becoming a stepping-stone to the richer parts of the European Union (Cohen, 2003).

The next two chapters, which deal with Britain's immigration policy, will focus mainly on the national level. The following sections discuss other levels of policy making that influence and interact with the national.

The international level

International regulation of immigration takes place through formal and informal agreements between international institutions and governments. Freedom of movement for business, study and tourism are established through international agreements (Jordan and Duvell, 2003: 17). Contemporary globalisation demands new channels for the movement of financial, managerial and technical elites, and a range of highly skilled workers, or what Jordan and Duvell (2003: 60) call 'global nomads'. Their mobility is often negotiated for them through international companies.

More vulnerable migrants receive some protection from international conventions such as the International Labour Organization's (ILO) 1975 Convention on Migrant Workers, the Council of Europe's 1977 European Convention on the Legal Status of Migrant Workers, and the UN 1990 Convention on the Protection of the Rights of all Migrant Workers and their Families. As suggested above, these have had limited impact, mainly due to the lack of ratification by the most important states. The UN Convention of 1990, for example, has not been signed by any EU member (Morris, 2002: 15).

The 1951 UN Convention on Refugees (the Geneva Convention) is the most widely ratified and implemented international convention and has a significant impact on national states. As the body charged with refugee protection, the UNHCR has struggled to maintain its independence from the major powers. This problem escalated with the end of the Cold War, which produced major changes to international refugee policy.

The international refugee regime

The development of an international 'refugee regime' was tied to the Cold War, and the UNHCR's priorities, particularly in relation to refugee return, have reflected this. The Convention initially applied only to Europe and to people displaced during the war and those fleeing the new Warsaw Pact states. The option of voluntary repatriation was effectively obsolete (Chimni, 2004: 61) since Cold War politics demanded the rejection of this solution. Settlement therefore was seen as the main 'durable solution'. The absence of pressure for return meant that the importance of the voluntary nature of return was not stressed in the Convention, which only required 'safe' return (Chimni, 2004: 55).

The first major challenge to the UNHCR was the Hungarian uprising of 1956, but the focus shifted from Europe during the 1960s and 1970s with decolonisation and civil conflicts in Africa and Asia. The UNHCR took on a wider role in humanitarian relief in the 1980s (Baines, 2004: 105). With increasing refugee numbers, particularly those attempting to settle in the West, western powers attempted to close their borders and there was a shift towards attempting to address 'root causes of displacement' (Baines, 2004: 258). This policy potentially challenges the sovereignty of nation states and the fragile balance that the UNHCR walks 'between protection of refugees and sovereign prerogatives of states' (Baines, 2004: 5). This dilemma was evident in the evacuation of Bosnians faced with 'ethnic cleansing' in Serbia. Evacuation could be seen as colluding with genocide, but leaving people in place would have left them at grave risk (Baines, 2004: 109). A thorough challenge to the root causes of refugee flows would also involve examining the relations between refugee-producing and -receiving states. These create refugee movements indirectly through the unequal relations they sustain and more directly in supplying weapons to those carrying out persecution, for example.

With the end of the Cold War, the strategic interest of the West in protecting refugees declined. The rich states saw no reason to share the burden of the poor through providing asylum or resources (Chimni, 2004: 73). Australia, for example, has taken brutal steps to prevent entry and detains all asylum seekers on arrival in remote camps (Jordan and Duvell, 2003: 24), a policy that contravenes its human rights obligations (Gradstein, 2006).

A hierarchy of 'durable solutions' to the refugee cycle was established, with 'voluntary return' deemed more desirable than the other two solutions of integration into the country of asylum or resettlement to a third country (Crisp, 2004). Refugee returns were initially promoted as a response to the end of conflict and millions were repatriated during the 1980s and 1990s (Koser, 2000). As the imperative to return has increased, repatriation is being pursued at the expense of the safety of refugees. The idea of 'safe return', embodied in the Convention, was re-introduced in an attempt to occupy the middle ground in the 'continuum between voluntary and involuntary repatriation' (Chimni, 2004: 55). Returns policies have increasingly moved towards the involuntary end of this continuum, or 'non-voluntary' return.

Research on returns to Afghanistan following the war in 2001 identified three discourses of return (Blitz et al, 2005): **justice-based** arguments consider return as a means of post-conflict stabilisation and furthering reconciliation (Toft, 2000); return represents the 'end of the refugee cycle' (Black and Koser, 1999). The **human capital** argument is based on the notion that the skills of returnees can be invested in the reconstruction of their home countries. This is the basis for the promotion of return programmes by non-governmental organisations. The **burden-relieving** discourse, by contrast, sees refugees as causing social and political problems in the country of exile, and returns are promoted in the interests of the rich states.

This last motive appears to dominate current return programmes. The UNHCR reported in 1997 that 'it is clear that a large proportion of the world's recent returnees have repatriated under some form of duress' (Chimni, 2004: 65). Castles et al (2003: 48–9), while seeing 'orderly return' as the priority following the end of conflict, point to the increasingly compulsory nature of returns. As Stein noted, political interests 'particularly in the country of asylum, increasingly are trying to influence refugee decision-making and limit its voluntary character through pressure, harassment and direct violence' (1997: 2). Returns to Afghanistan have become increasingly non-voluntary (Turton and Marsden, 2002; Blitz et al, 2005). In June 2002 the UNHCR warned that the 'flood of refugees' into Afghanistan was exceeding the ability of development agencies to cope (Harris, T., 2002). Forcible deportations from Britain began in April 2003 despite warnings from the Foreign Office that the country remained unsafe.[8] At the same time, refugees were arriving in large numbers, fleeing persecution and continuing conflict. They paid several thousand pounds to travel while at the same time some government-backed schemes were offering them £600 to return. As one refugee interviewed at Dover said: 'It is an insult, it is as if our lives are being bought for £600' (Sales et al, 2003: 61).

Another dimension to this regime change has been attempts to contain fighting through the development of 'safe zones' on the edge of conflict regions. This has involved the securitisation of displacement to promote regional and international interests of the West (Baines, 2004: 42). The UNHCR has become more implicated in containment policy, which further undermines its independence from the major donor powers. International refugee policy is increasingly implemented at 'arm's length' through partnerships with the voluntary sector. NGOs are drawn into involvement in programmes developed by the major powers (Duffield and Waddell, 2004), undermining the neutrality of humanitarian assistance (Donini, 2004). Castles suggests that the 'humanitarian sector ceased to be marginal and became part of the bureaucratic mainstream of national and international governance' (2003: 7). This development has been exacerbated following the war in Iraq (Donini, 2004), with aid agencies unable to work independently in the country.

The regional dimension: the European Union

Three major trading blocs have become the focus of regional political and economic power: NAFTA, Japan and the ASEAN countries, and the European Union (EU). This section focuses on the EU, which is by far the most advanced in the development of immigration policy (Morris, 2002: 10) and has the most comprehensive legal enactment of a transnational status for migrants (Soysal, 1994: 147). EU policy involves a complex and contradictory relation to the nation state. The enforcement of EU initiatives depends on national governments, but EU policies may also force states to comply with policies that operate against what they perceive to be their own national interest. EU policy making is highly complex, involving both binding and non-binding regulations on member states. The United Kingdom has tended to opt out of non-binding decisions concerning economic migration, while opting into restrictive legislation on asylum (Nienhuis, 2006: 14). Together with Ireland, it has a 'privileged' position in being able to opt out of proposals on immigration and asylum.

EU immigration policy has two aspects that have been developed in parallel: freedom of movement for EU citizens and the regulation and control of entry of non-EU citizens. The former has given enhanced meaning to EU citizenship and its associated rights. The development of EU citizenship also involved for the first time the construction of a 'European identity' in endogenous terms and not simply in opposition to its colonial presence (Balibar, 1991). This took place during a period of increasingly assertive racism and xenophobia both from the extreme right and within mainstream discourse and practice (Kofman and Sales, 1998) and more recently the panic over Islam linked to the 'war on terror'. There have also been shifting boundaries around who is included within the definition of 'European'. Leibfried, writing in 1993, argued that 'European citizenship has already become a major issue in defining the "outsiders" of eastern and southern Europe' (1993: 12). The former 'outsiders' from Eastern Europe are in the process of becoming 'insiders' as EU enlargement extends its borders eastwards, although they retain an ambivalent status within the established states of the EU as social exclusion, barriers to employment and lack of full social rights mean that they have yet to become full EU citizens. They are expected to replace much of the labour demand within the older EU, particularly for unskilled labour, a policy made explicit in Britain when it opened its labour market to workers from the new member states (the

A8 countries) before most other EU states (Home Office, 2005a). These new boundaries will thus exclude more firmly those from outside Europe. Turkey's attempts to negotiate membership of the EU have so far failed due to opposition both at home and within the EU.

The current European Union has extended in size and scope from the initial European Economic Community (EEC) of six members founded in 1957 with the Treaty of Rome. The EEC aimed to produce a gradual reduction in barriers to the free movement of workers, capital, goods and services between member countries. This process was intensified with an amendment to the Treaty, the 1986 Single European Act, aimed at creating a single internal market in goods, services and free movement of people within the Union by 1992 through harmonisation of the relevant laws of member countries. The Maastricht Treaty, which came into force in 1993, provided the basis for the European Union and involved significantly greater social and economic integration. The areas of justice and home affairs, which were responsible for immigration policy, initially came under the 'third pillar' of the EU, implying that any decisions required unanimous agreement from member states. This was amended with the Amsterdam Treaty of 1997, which transferred this to the 'EC pillar', under which qualified majority rather than unanimous agreement is required (JCWI, 2006: 504). Free movement was extended to the European Economic Area (EEA) in 1994, which included EU countries with some members of the European Free Trade Association, a grouping of European states which are non-members of the EEC.

Freedom of movement regulations allow considerable rights to EU citizens. They are able to move freely across the EU and to take up employment, to seek work, to study or to retire in another member state (JCWI, 2006). The movement of skilled workers is being facilitated by the harmonisation of recognition of professional qualifications across the EU, allowing those qualifying in one EU state to work in other member states. Those taking advantage of EU freedom of movement are entitled to bring in family members, spouses and dependent children and parents. This has led to the anomaly that EU citizens living in another EU state are able to bring in a spouse from outside the EU, while nationals do not have this automatic right. EU citizenship also provides for social rights within other EU states, although these are limited by the fact that freedom of movement is primarily linked to the labour market.

The EU's institutional structure is complex, with several different types of decision-making structure having an input into EU policy on migration and asylum (see *Box 5.1*). EU immigration policy has been driven by inter-governmental bodies rather than the European Parliament and Commission; the former have tended to pursue restrictive policies while the latter have attempted a more positive role but their recommendations are not binding on individual states.

Box 5.1: European Union institutions

European Parliament: Based in Strasbourg. Members (MEPs) are directly elected by each EU country. Debates proposals for changes to European legislation and resolutions on specific areas. Limited powers to initiate new legislation or propose amendments to policies recommended by the European Commission, and does not have the final say on legislation. It can receive complaints from individuals about EU policies and laws and make reference to the European Court of Justice.

European Commission: Based in Brussels. Members are appointed and represent all EU countries. Prepares legislation for the EU (regulations and directives). Has own bureaucracy representing all EU countries. Can receive and investigate individual complaints, for example the application of EU law by member states.

European Council: Also called the 'Council of Ministers'. Consists of ministers from EU member states and takes the final decisions on most legislation, having taken account of the view of the European Parliament.

European Court of Justice (ECJ): Based in Luxembourg. Decides on legal cases brought under EU law. Its interpretation of EU law must be followed by individual countries. National courts and tribunals can refer cases to the ECJ and member states may seek rulings.

European Ombudsman: Established in 1995, receives complaints concerning maladministration by European institutions from anyone living in a member state. Limited to investigating European, not national or local, administrations even in matters concerning European law.

Source: JCWI, 2006: 508–9.

EU migration policy focused initially on controls on entry, particularly of asylum seekers. Race relations and the incorporation and integration of immigrants have remained largely within the domain of 'subsidiarity' the remit of individual member states, although an EU Directive in 2003 set minimum standards for the reception of asylum seekers.

The development of the Single European Market, in which capital, commodities and people were able to move freely, involved the abolition of internal borders. This required both a strengthening of the EU's external border and increased internal surveillance of migration status. The term 'Fortress Europe' has commonly been used to describe the battery of physical and legal controls that have been used to police entry. The 'fortress' has not been impregnable, as people have continued to enter clandestinely while legal entry has been increasingly selective in relation to skills and nationality. The Schengen Group has been responsible for initiating many of the policy developments; this group of ministers of the major EU countries (excluding Britain) meets outside the sphere of democratic scrutiny (Geddes, 2000) and its proposals are then ratified by EU bodies and individual governments. These measures have focused particularly on asylum, and include 'carriers' liability' (fines on transport companies that bring in migrants without the correct documents) and the 'one chance rule', which prevents people from applying for asylum in more than one EU country.

This measure was ratified in the 1990 Dublin Convention, under which many people have been deported to the 'first safe country' in which they landed. The agreement was replaced with 'Dublin II' from 2003. Under this agreement adults may be returned to another country on the basis that they have passed through that state. Unaccompanied children may only be returned if they have previously made an asylum application in that state. The Refugee Council (2006) argues that this poses dangers to children since there is considerable variation between states in their assessments of whether particular children are in need of international protection, and whether particular states are considered 'safe'.

With the 1997 Amsterdam Treaty, the Schengen Convention became part of the EU legal framework. The transfer of responsibility for migration policy to the 'third pillar' of the EU[9] placed it under the EU's institutions rather than inter-governmental structures, although the responsibilities remained ambiguous (Geddes, 2000: 110). This opened up areas for broader harmonisation for example on the rights of migrants. The 1999 Tampere Conference developed the detailed implementation of the Amsterdam Treaty, including proposals to tackle the 'root causes' of migration. The European Commission's Green Paper, 2005, addressed economic migration for the first time, a belated acknowledgement of Europe's dependence on imported labour. It included proposals for regularisation and a green-card system for highly skilled workers. The discussion of the 'root causes' of migration suggested measures to promote 'brain circulation', which would allow migrants to return home periodically to transfer skills, and recognised the role of remittances in promoting economic development (Nienhuis, 2006: 14).

Agreement and implementation of a common EU immigration policy share the problems and contradictions of national policy but these are magnified by the size of the EU and the complexity of its decision-making process. Geddes (2000: 24) gives a comprehensive list of these problems, summarised below:

1. The extent of borders makes the costs of policing for some states enormous.

2. Too much is expected too soon from new countries, which may have an underdeveloped bureaucracy.
3. Effective policy implementation requires resources.
4. Policy needs to be based on a valid theory of cause and effect but migration policy may produce perverse results.
5. The longer the chain between policy decision and implementation, the less likely is policy to be effective.
6. The EU depends on national agencies for implementation.
7. Countries may have differing labour market, and therefore immigration, needs.
8. Tasks and roles need to be specified clearly.
9. The complexity of EU structures tends to bring lack of coordination and communication.
10. EU authority depends on national interpretation and implementation of directives.

Some of these problems (1, 3, 4, 8 and 9) are similar to those experienced by national states, but the scale of the EU gives them qualitatively greater significance. Others (2 and 7) arise from conflicts of interest between member states, some of which may wish to follow more restrictive policies than others. The specific structures of the EU create problems (5, 6, 10) in negotiating between different sets of laws with different priorities. For example, one of the main aims of the EU is the minimisation of the barriers to free movement, while for states such as the UK, the main aim has been to control immigration strictly (JCWI, 2006: 504). This difference led to the negotiation of the opt-out clause from the Maastricht Treaty. These difficulties have meant that the main focus of policy has been on controls that have proved easier to harmonise and that have been promoted by the more powerful countries within the EU.

Geddes (2000:106) describes the various degrees of 'insider' status in relation to the EU as a series of concentric circles, with 'Schengenland' plus UK and Ireland at its core, and 'the excluded' of the underdeveloped world on the outside. The political priorities of the core are, he suggests, the elaboration of restrictive policies and the incorporation of neighbouring states into a regime of controls (Geddes, 2000: 107). The second tier of 'aspirants' in Central, Eastern and Southern Europe (some of which joined in 2004, and others in 2007) have been compelled to adopt restrictive immigration frameworks linked to Accession and Association agreements with the EU. Pre-entry checks on immigration status (for example by British immigration officers on Roma from the Czech Republic) prevented whole groups of people from travelling to the EU. The third layer consists of transit countries, staging posts into the EU, including Turkey and the Balkans. These operate checks on passengers and take action against undocumented migrants and are incorporated through 'temporary protection' systems for refugees. The outermost layer consists of the excluded, the people of underdeveloped states, who are the 'targets' of the control regime.

These developments have also brought a growing diversity in the employment, residence and social rights of non-citizens within the EU. The logic of European integration is sharpening divisions between EU citizens and non-citizens, giving renewed importance to formal citizenship status.

The local level

Most decision making on the conditions of entry and the broad issue of citizenship rights is done at national level but implementation may be at local level. Local institutions can have a significant influence on the way in which decisions on individual cases are made and more generally on the experience of migrants. Devolutionary policies have led to some local control over broader migration policy. The Scottish Executive launched its Fresh Talent Initiative in February 2004 'aiming to attract talented and entrepreneurial migrants to Scotland'. This included 'measures to be agreed with the UK government actively to promote Scotland as a destination for people seeking to use the work permit route to come into the UK'. [10] The establishment of some regional autonomy for the Catalan region of Spain in June 2006 also included regulation of regional migration. [11]

Some states devolve decision making on individual applications. In France, local prefectures (police stations) carry out the initial scrutiny of asylum applications. In 2001, they deployed delaying tactics, leaving new asylum seekers completely destitute and increasing the numbers attempting to enter Britain from France via the Channel Tunnel (Kofman et al, 2002). Local policies may be at odds with national policies. George W. Bush supported expanded admissions of Mexican temporary workers when he was governor of Texas (Castles and Miller, 2003: 11), in opposition to national policy. Internal scrutiny of the status of immigrants has been largely a responsibility of local services (Owers, 1994; Cohen et al, 2002).

Multicultural policies have mainly been implemented at the local level in many states, often at variance with official national policies. In Germany and Belgium local advisory councils on 'ethnic minority issues' are consulted by local elected bodies, although their influence is limited. In France, although Republican orthodoxy refuses any formal recognition of ethnic differentiation (Poinsot, 1993) at local level, multicultural initiatives have been developed since the 1970s, including provision of specific services and the involvement of community groups in a consultative capacity (Hargreaves and Wihtol de Wenden, 1993). At the same time, openly exclusionist policies were carried out in other local areas and these practices were increasingly forced into the arena of national politics.

The French concept of *seuil de tolerance* (threshold of tolerance) was aimed at preventing the development of ethnic communities through quotas for public housing, but some local managers have evaded restrictions to create ghettos (Castles and Miller, 2003: 232) often isolated from French society, as the riots in the *banlieux* in 2006 demonstrated. In Italy, while the national government pursued anti-immigrant policies under the Berlusconi regime, local and regional bodies were established to promote access for immigrants to health care and other services (IDOS, 2003). The major legislation in Italy on immigration and integration, the 1998 Legge Turco Napolitano, placed the responsibility for the implementation of social and cultural policies in the hands of local authorities. In Britain, local initiatives, for example interpretation services and health advocacy, have been incorporated into local health services although they are generally subject to funding problems (Hoggart et al, 2000). Schools have been the main area for implementing multicultural policies, in the absence of national policies (Hewitt, 2005: 116), although their independence has been restricted by the development of a national curriculum.

Conclusion

Immigration policy involves a multiplicity of interests that may conflict with each other so that policies may have unexpected consequences that do not reflect the intentions of policy makers. The globalisation and regionalisation of decision making has added further layers of complexity. In spite of the growing recognition among major economic powers of their dependence on immigration, recent policy making has tended to be dominated by controls. States and regional groupings have developed a growing arsenal of tools to control migration that have also brought new forms of resistance from migrants and their supporters.

Notes

[1] Reported in the *Guardian*, 16 August 2006.

[2] http://www.deportation-class.com/alliance/news.html.

[3] All who can show Jewish descent on the mother's side.

[4] Colonial citizens of other European states, such as the Netherlands and Belgium, also had rights of entry to the colonial state.

[5] Interview for 'Polish migrants in London and European enlargement: social networks, transience and settlement' project funded by the Economic and Social Research Council, 2006–7, carried out by Louise Ryan, Rosemary Sales and Mary Tilki.

[6] Reported in the *Guardian*, 16 August 2006.

[7] Tebbit stated that British citizens from ethnic minorities should prove their integration by supporting the English cricket team.

[8] Foreign and Commonwealth Office, Travel and Country Advice, 27 May 2003 (www.fco.gov).

[9] This change increased the power of the European Commission, Parliament and Court of Justice in relation to policy initiatives, but acceptance of any new guidelines remains with individual member state governments.

[10] Scottish Executive website, www.scotland.gov.uk, accessed August 2006.

[11] Reported in the *Guardian*, 21 June 2006.

Summary

- Immigration policy is 'exceptional' in that it embodies conflicting interests within and between nation states and the supply of migrants is not subject to domestic control.
- Immigration policy frequently produces 'perverse' results.
- The tools of immigration control have become more sophisticated and have brought more sophisticated resistance.
- The granting of citizenship remains a prerogative of national governments.
- Distinct national traditions of citizenship remain, reflecting different histories of migration.
- States claim universal values while national citizenship privileges particular groups.
- The rights attached to different migratory statuses have become more stratified.
- Immigration policy making is dominated by the national state but higher and lower levels are increasingly important.
- International policy has mainly concerned refugees and humanitarian motives are increasingly in conflict with the interest of powerful states.
- Regional immigration policy is most advanced in the European Union and has impacted on member states, particularly in relation to harmonising controls.
- Local institutions have some input into the implementation of policy.

Questions for discussion

- Do the specific features of immigration policy making make it 'exceptional' in relation to other areas of policy? What problems arise in attempting to implement immigration policy?
- How far have international, regional and local institutions undermined the power of the nation state in relation to managing immigration policy?

- Is national citizenship status becoming irrelevant in the face of mass migration?

Further reading

Castles, S. (2004a) 'The factors that make and unmake migration policies', *International Migration Review*, vol 38, no 3, pp 852–84.

Castles, S. and Davidson, A. (2000) *Citizenship and migration: Globalization and the politics of belonging*, Basingstoke: Macmillan.

Geddes, A. (2000) *Immigration and European integration: Towards fortress Europe?*, Manchester: Manchester University Press.

Morris, L. (2002) *Managing migration: Civic stratification and migrants' rights*, London: Routledge.

Sciortino, G. (2000) 'Towards a political sociology of entry policies: conceptual problems and theoretical proposals', *Journal of Ethnic and Migration Studies*, vol 26, no 2, pp 213–28.

Soysal, Y. (1994) *Limits of citizenship: Migrants and postnational membership in Europe*, Chicago, IL: University of Chicago Press.

six

The development of British immigration policy

Overview

This chapter explores the development of immigration policy in Britain. It argues that there have been four major phases in this policy: first, the control of 'aliens' from Europe, mainly Jews, from the early twentieth century up to the Second World War; second, controls that distinguished between the Old and New Commonwealth in the post-war period; third, controls on the entry and rights of asylum seekers from the late 1980s, and fourth, the era of 'managed migration' from 2000. These phases, particularly the last three, have also overlapped and some continuities underlie the whole process, including bi-partisanship agreement on the necessity for controls, the importance of rules and discretion in policy implementation, and the assumption that good race relations depend on controls.

Key concepts

British nationality; British citizenship; Commonwealth citizen; patrial; racialisation; burden sharing; bi-partisan policy; rules/discretion

Introduction

Immigration and emigration have been significant elements in Britain's history. Throughout the nineteenth and for much of the twentieth century, Britain was predominantly an exporter of labour, mainly to its empire. This emigration included the officer class and the settlers who took over land in the empire as well as Britain's 'unwanted' population, who helped provide a labour force in the so-called 'empty' lands. Immigration also has a long history, as a result of conquest by others (for example the Romans, Normans and Danes) and of Britain's own imperialist ventures. Britain has also accepted refugees, including the Huguenots – Protestants fleeing Catholic France – and revolutionaries from Europe. Marx and Lenin both spent time in exile in London and Marx was buried in London's Highgate Cemetery. The first mass immigration was from Ireland, particularly in the wake of the famine of 1846, and Irish people continue to be Britain's largest ethnic minority (Hickman and Walter, 1997).

Britain has an uneasy relationship with its immigration history. Holmes (1988) suggested that official accounts of Britain have been unwilling to admit the extent of immigration since it interfered with myths of nationhood based on a common culture. More recently, diversity has been claimed in the name of a particular form of Britishness. The White Paper *Secure Borders, Safe Haven* suggested that, 'British nationality has never been associated with membership of a particular ethnic group. For centuries we have been a multi-ethnic nation. We do not exclude people from citizenship on the basis of their race or ethnicity' (Home Office, 2002a: 10).

Governments have, however, attempted to control this diversity in relation to the numbers of new entrants and the claimed limits to the 'tolerance' of the British people. Immigration control, although it has become normalised as part of the 'common sense' in which discussion about migration is framed, is only a hundred years old. The first Act barring entry to Britain was the 1905 Aliens Act. This created the presumption 'that an alien had no claim to be received, or to remain, but could enter only as the interest of the state – as defined by the state authorities – dictated' (Dummett and Nicol, 1990: 112) and marked a major change from the free movement that had prevailed up to then. The state had periodically expelled groups or individuals, but had not placed controls on entry. Jews, the main targets of the Act, had been periodically welcomed and deported since they first entered Britain with the Norman invasion in 1066 and there were expulsions of black people, citizens of the empire, from Elizabethan England.

Acceptance of controls within mainstream politics followed swiftly after the passage of the Aliens Act. Various groups have been the primary targets of control, although there have been continuities in the language in which 'undesirables' are discussed. This often embodies notions of threat to the nation's health, welfare and the 'British way of life'. As well as selecting by national origin, controls have had a class and gender dimension. The Aliens Act applied only to the poorest would-be immigrants who travelled 'steerage' class. Current policy continues to differentiate on the basis of wealth, income and skills, while being based on conservative assumptions about gender roles within the family.

The labour and trade union movements have sometimes been accorded a significant role in agitating for immigration controls in some accounts (for example, Cohen, 2002; JCWI, 2006). The tension between the desire to exclude outsiders in the name of their members' perceived interests and the principle of international solidarity has divided them on the issue. Moreover, these movements were formed in the period of empire when scientific racism was at its height and the 'labour aristocracy' that dominated these movements at this time was also imbued with notions of 'respectability' and the need to exclude the 'undeserving' (Hobsbawm, 1964). The importance of the labour movement has, however, been exaggerated in narratives that portray the state as passively responding to popular pressure, rather than as initiating and developing the agenda of controls. The experience of empire ensured that notions of racial hierarchy were rooted in the state itself and profoundly affected the development of immigration policy.

There have been four main phases of immigration controls in Britain (see *Box 6.1*). First, the control of 'aliens' from Europe, mainly Jews, from the beginning of the twentieth century up to and during the Second World War; second, there were selective controls on (black) immigration from the New Commonwealth in the post-war period as British citizenship was reconstructed to exclude this group; third, from the late 1980s, were controls on the entry and rights of asylum seekers, which created a parallel system of welfare support; and fourth, the era of 'managed migration', with the opening up of routes for skilled migration accompanied by tighter controls on asylum and irregular migration. This chapter outlines the key developments in these periods, focusing on the first three. The final section discusses some of the key features of British immigration policy that are common to all these phases. The current policy of 'managed migration' developed under New Labour is discussed in more detail in Chapter Seven.

Box 6.1: Phases of immigration control in Britain

1. Control of mainly Jewish immigration (1905 up to and after Second World War).
2. Controls on New (black) Commonwealth immigration (1960s onwards).
3. Controls on asylum seekers (late 1980s onwards).
4. Managed migration: greater selectivity in labour migration: stricter controls on asylum (2000 onwards).

Phase 1: the beginning of controls

Immigration controls were introduced with the 1905 Aliens Act, following a long campaign that brought together a number of disparate elements including trade unions and reactionary MPs (Cohen, 2002). The immediate trigger was the inflow of Jews from Russia and Eastern Europe fleeing persecution and economic marginalisation.

Jews were not the first sizeable group of unwelcome migrants. Irish people had moved to Britain in large numbers during the nineteenth century, particularly following the famine of 1846. Stereotypes of supposed biological inferiority were prevalent, reflecting colonial relationships between Britain and Ireland (Curtis, 1984). The surgeon general, addressing the Poor Law Inquiry for Ireland, described the Irish as 'the pests of society. They generate contagion' (cited in Jones, 1977: 49). They were also seen as taking advantage of welfare in Britain. The Rev Jonas of Liverpool, in a phrase that echoes demands for immigration control throughout the following century, told the Inquiry, 'It is well known that many of the Irish come over here for the express purpose of availing themselves of that assistance which they are unable to procure at home' (quoted in Jones, 1977: 56). Although they could be deported under the Poor Law, there was no move to restrict entry. Indeed under the 1801 Act of Union Ireland became part of the United Kingdom.[1]

The demand for controls at the end of the century reflected the changing balance of class interests in Britain as well as external factors. The growth of the labour movement and the achievement of universal adult male suffrage in 1884[2] had created new notions of citizenship and the need for politicians to respond to wider claims than those of the elite. Belonging to the nation thus meant more in material and symbolic terms. As welfare provision started to develop, it was easier for the state to argue that a genuine social contract was being forged between capital and labour (Mynott, 2002: 22). This, however, required boundaries around those eligible to benefit and the exclusion of the 'undeserving' was seen as a priority. The subsequent 1908 Old Age Pensions Act and the 1911 National Insurance Act, which paved the way for the welfare state, both included conditions on residence and citizenship (Hayes, 2002: 38). The downturn in the British economy at the end of the nineteenth century, partly due to the competition from new industrialising states of Europe and the United States, brought unemployment and threatened this social contract. The contradictory accusations that immigrants were taking jobs and paupers taking advantage of charities (Jones, 1977: 78) have been a continuing element of anti-immigration rhetoric.

Debates in the East End centred on competition for jobs, housing and amenities (Solomos, 2003: 41) based on the view that the resources of society were fixed and unable to withstand additional pressures (Holmes, 1988: 301). In reality the proportion of aliens claiming pauper's allowance was considerably lower than the rest of the population (Jones, 1977: 89) but it was 'easier to claim that Jewish immigrants were responsible for the economic and social problems of the area than it was to unearth the complex pressures that were at work in the East End in the late nineteenth and early twentieth centuries'

(Holmes, 1988: 301). Jews were geographically concentrated in a small part of London's East End and were thus more visible than the Irish, who had settled in towns across Britain. Jones quotes an East End midwife who, speaking at the end of the nineteenth century, incorporates the Irish into her notion of 'decent people' in contrast to these new outsiders:

> Samuel Street ... used to be a street occupied by poor English and Irish people. In the afternoons you would see the steps inside cleaned and the women with their clean white aprons sit in summer time inside the doors, perhaps at needlework with their little children about. Now it is a seething mass of refuse and filth ... and the stench from the refuse and filth is disgraceful. (Jones, 1977: 75)

When agitation for controls began in the 1880s, opinion was sharply divided both within and outside Parliament. The ruling Liberal Party opposed controls, while right-wing MPs joined elements in the labour movement to form the Immigration Control Association (Saggar, 1992: 72). The TUC raised concerns about the impact on employment at its congresses in 1892, 1894 and 1895 (Holmes, 1988: 68), and immigrants were accused of being blacklegs (May, 1978: 82). On the other hand there was considerable support among Liberals and socialists for Jewish immigrants (Holmes, 1988: 66).

Box 6.2 British immigration legislation – key points

1905 Aliens Act: Excluded 'undesirable' aliens – those who could not support '[themself] and [their] dependants' or with 'disease or infirmity' making them liable to be 'a charge on the rates or otherwise a detriment to the public'.

1919 Aliens Restriction Act: Consolidated powers of home secretary to deport aliens already in UK; made it criminal offence for an alien to 'promote industrial unrest'.

1962 Commonwealth Immigrants Act: Introduced 'entry vouchers' for Commonwealth citizens, issued on the basis of skills and qualifications.

1968 Commonwealth Immigrants Act: Distinguished between UK passport holders with right of abode (patrials – those born or naturalised in UK or with a UK-born grandparent) and those without.

1971 Immigration Act: Set out structure of immigration control, gave power to home secretary to make immigration rules. All those without right of abode required to seek work permit. End of primary migration from Commonwealth (though continued in shortage areas).

1981 British Nationality Act: Those qualifying for right of abode given British citizenship. Children born in Britain of non-British citizens losing automatic right to citizenship.

1987 Carriers' Liability Act: Fines on airlines carrying passengers without correct documents.

1988 Immigration Act: Made deportation easier, withdrew right of family reunion from Commonwealth men, established 'primary purpose' marriage rule.

1993 Asylum and Immigration Appeals Act: Incorporated Geneva Convention into immigration rules, creating processes for dealing with asylum applications. Withdrew rights of appeal for visitors and students.

1996 Asylum and Immigration Act: Withdrew non-contributory benefits for asylum seekers and other groups subject to immigration control, for example work permit holders.

1999 Asylum and Immigration Act: Created NASS system for asylum-seeker support; created single appeal stage; imposed duty on marriage registrars to report suspicious marriages; strengthened powers of immigration officers in enforcing controls; extended carrier sanctions; imposed regulation of immigration advice.

2002 Nationality, Immigration and Asylum Act: Introduced new controls on entry, new citizenship pledge; limited powers of Immigration Appeals Tribunals to hear appeals on human rights grounds.

2004 Asylum and Immigration (Treatment of Claimants, etc) Act: Introduced new system of appeals with Asylum and Immigration Tribunal; created criminal offence of entering UK without a valid passport. 'Certificate of Approval' from secretary of state required for marriages involving a person requiring leave to remain.

2006 Asylum and Immigration Act: Increased grounds for depriving dual nationals of citizenship; reduced rights to appeals; increased role of employers in preventing 'illegal' working.

The 1905 Aliens Act, passed under a Conservative government, allowed those deemed 'undesirable' to be refused permission to enter Britain. It listed four categories of undesirability: the diseased, the insane, criminals and those likely to be a burden on public funds. Most were rejected on this last ground (Hayes, 2002: 34). Aliens could be expelled if found to be receiving poor relief within a year of entering Britain, guilty of vagrancy or living in unsanitary conditions due to overcrowding. The Act distinguished between refugees and other migrants, with those judged to face persecution excluded from its provisions. The number of expulsions under the Act was limited especially since it allowed for appeals, but mass deportations of German gypsies took place during 1905 and 1906 (Holmes, 1988: 19).

The established Jewish community played an ambivalent role in relation to the implementation of the Act. They provided charity through the Jewish Board of Guardians so that new immigrants would not be a charge on the rates. The *Jewish Chronicle*, which reflected mainstream opinion within the community, reported sympathetically on appeals against deportation. On the other hand, the Jewish establishment sought to distance itself from these migrants, who as well as being impoverished were culturally and religiously different (Holmes, 1988: 47). They gave charity only to those with permission to stay and considered 'deserving'.[3] They were thus the 'self-appointed intermediaries and social policy stop-gaps' (Jones, 1977: 67). Others in the community were more radical, providing support to those deemed 'undesirable' through the Jews Temporary Shelter (Jones, 1977: 87).

The Aliens Act was also used against members of the small Chinese community that had become established first in seaports and later in London, with restaurants and laundries in Limehouse and Poplar. Hostility against the Chinese was related to colonial relations and was exacerbated by the Boxer Rebellion against British rule (Holmes, 1988: 80). It drew on notions of danger and the 'yellow peril'; accounts of Chinese in Britain 'frequently referred to their exotic or potentially provocative habits such as opium taking, gambling and sexual relations with 'white women and girls' (May, 1978: 111). Chinese seamen were also seen as blacklegs. The official journal of the Seamen's Union, *The Seaman*, made continuous attacks on them until it ceased publication in 1909 (May, 1978: 115).

Although they opposed the Act in 1905, the Liberals did not repeal the legislation when they returned to office in 1906 but implemented it in a milder form (Holmes, 1988: 72). This marked the beginning of a consensus on controls in official party policy that continues to characterise British immigration policy making. Labour replaced the Liberals as the main opponent of the Conservatives in the inter-war period, but this consensus has continued. With the outbreak of war in 1914, immigration control took a more draconian form. The 1914 Aliens Restriction Act, passed in single day in response to widespread anti-German sentiment, increased the authority of the home secretary to prohibit entry and enforce the registration and deportation of aliens. It distinguished between 'friendly' and 'enemy' aliens and included powers to remove or restrain the movements of the latter. This distinction was based on country of nationality rather than individuals' own political and social position in relation to that nation. The distinction between aliens and refugees lapsed in the wartime legislation undermining protection for those facing persecution in their country of origin and 120,000 refugees were repatriated during the war (Holmes, 1988: 101).

At the same time, the 1914 British Nationality and Status of Aliens Act confirmed the common status of nationals across the empire and the *ius soli* principle of nationality (Paul, 1997: 11). This legislation also incorporated discrimination against women, who were not able to transmit status through marriage and lost their own status on marriage to an alien. Alien women marrying British men, however, became British, confirming the notion of women as 'subsidiary subjects' to their husbands, reflecting their lack of economic and political rights at the time (Paul, 1997: 12).

With the end of the war, rather than the restrictions against aliens being removed, they were intensified. The 1919 Aliens Restriction Act consolidated the powers of the home secretary over the entry, employment and deportation of aliens already in the UK. These measures, renewed annually and supplemented by Orders in Council of 1920 and 1953, 'remained the basis of official policy on alien immigration down to the 1971 Immigration Act' (Holmes, 1988: 308). With the Russian Revolution of 1917, the Act incorporated an explicitly political dimension, making it a criminal offence for an alien to 'promote industrial unrest' and allowing the deportation of Bolsheviks (Holmes, 1988: 113). Attacks on the black and Asian community in seaports continued, culminating in the 1925 Special Restrictions (Coloured Alien Seamen) Order, which was used to harass black citizens as well as immigrants. Paul (1997: 115) describes this as a form of state-sponsored racism, suggesting that this harassment was not a result of over-zealous implementation but the intention of the legislators.

As controls on entry were extended, emigration was encouraged through the 1922 Empire Settlement Act in order to maintain the British population of the empire. In its first decade, 404,000 UK residents emigrated at a cost to the Treasury of £6.7 million (Paul, 1997: 28). This reflects the importance of the empire to British nationhood, an issue that acquired greater significance in the period of decolonisation.

As the persecution of Jews in Germany increased, many attempted to flee to Britain. They received a hostile reception as a 'common thread of anti-semitism' (Saggar, 1992: 29) persisted across all classes. Advertisements for accommodation in the 1930s often included the phrase 'no Jews' (Holmes,

1991: 34) and the British Medical Association secured an agreement limiting the employment of refugee doctors in 1938 (Holmes, 1991: 31). Official policies capitulated to this sentiment and simultaneously reflected and reinforced it (Holmes, 1991: 32). There was some pro-fascist sympathy in government and the abdication crisis revealed this within the royal family. As London (2000: 12) puts it, official policy was designed to keep out European Jews, and only a few of these would-be migrants were able to enter. They were required to show that they had the means to support themselves, which excluded all but the rich or those supported by charitable organisations (Saggar, 1992: 29). Restrictions on the entry of Jews continued even during the war. The established Jewish community maintained its ambivalence. They took the lead in supporting Jewish immigrants financially but the *Jewish Chronicle* did not oppose the internment of aliens when it was introduced in 1940 (Holmes, 1988: 189), although many of those targeted were Jews.

The war also threw into crisis the status of Irish citizens in Britain. With the partition of Ireland and the formation of the Irish Republic in 1922, Irish citizens became aliens. The six north-eastern counties became Northern Ireland and remained part of the United Kingdom (Sales, 1997). The Irish Nationality and Citizenship Act, passed by the Irish Parliament in 1935, removed Irish people's status as British subjects, which necessitated a special status in Britain, since to treat them as aliens would have inhibited the free movement on which both states depended (Paul, 1997: 95). This problem was compounded when the Irish government declared its neutrality during the war. Irish citizens were perceived as potentially hostile but controls would have been difficult to implement in view of the land border with Northern Ireland, while their labour was needed, especially with wartime labour shortages. Although nominal controls were established, Irish labour continued to be recruited and many Irish people also served in the British Army during the war. Irish people have retained their anomalous status in Britain. They have free movement and full citizenship rights, and as EU citizens are now insiders in the EU project, but have nevertheless faced continuing racism and discrimination (Hickman and Walter, 1997; Tilki, 2003).

Phase 2: post-war immigration and the reconstruction of British citizenship

Many narratives of post-war immigration policy portray it as a process of gradual reduction in the rights of the New Commonwealth citizens in response to popular pressure and the changing needs of the economy. The authoritative handbook of the Joint Council for the Welfare of Immigrants (JCWI, 2006: 5), for example, suggests that it 'was not until the 1960s that racist agitation led the government of the day to consider restrictions on the rights of nationals'.

Cohen also takes this view, suggesting that 'The successful demand for the first post-war controls against black people, the Commonwealth Immigrants Act of 1962, also came from a combination of the organised labour movement and disenfranchised thugs' (2003: 62).

As Solomos (2003: 56) argues, however, it 'seems inadequate to view the state as being purely responsive to popular opinion or economic interests'. The early post-war period was not an 'age of innocence' (Solomos, 2003: 52) and the reconstitution of British nationality was 'the creation of a policymaking elite that manipulated notions of identity and definitions of citizenship and managed public opinion in order to preserve a constructed national identity' (Paul, 1997: vii). This identity was white, and predominantly Protestant (Cesarani and Fullbrook, 1996: 7).[4] Between 1948 and 1962, the 'state was involved in a complex political and ideological racialisation of immigration policy' (Solomos, 2003: 52). This involved not only politicians but also the civil service within the Home Office, which has often represented a conservative force (Pellew, 1989) influencing policy and its implementation.

Britain emerged from the Second World War on the winning side but diminished economically and politically. The United States was the unchallenged superpower and the Cold War dominated international relations for five decades. Decolonisation threatened to weaken further Britain's position as a leading world power. Paul (1997) suggests that British policy making in the post-war period was dominated by the conflicting imperatives of attempting to maintain her superpower status through reconstructing her relations with the Commonwealth and the need for labour to help in post-war reconstruction. In the much-quoted phrase of the 1949 Population Commission Report, the only immigrants welcomed 'without reserve' were to be of 'good human stock and not prevented by their religion or race from intermarrying with the host population and becoming merged in it' (cited in Paul, 1997: 128). Active recruitment took place among the refugees and displaced people of Europe. Around 200,000 stateless Poles were granted settlement in Britain following the war,[5] including veterans from the Polish Army in Exile based in London. The Polish Resettlement Corps channelled ex-service personnel into civilian employment, they gained freedom from controls after three years and were expected to 'become assimilated to British way of life' (Paul, 1997: 82). The Irish, however, continued to be the main source of labour immigration. In spite of labour shortages, government policy encouraged emigration to Australia, as the export of 'British stock' (Paul, 1997: 26) to the empire was seen as essential in maintaining Commonwealth links. It was assumed that these departing UK residents 'would ever be British, while incoming alien refugees would soon be British' (Paul, 1997: 63). This desire to promote British external interests through emigration, represented by the Foreign Office, was in sharp competition with the need for labour championed by the Ministry of Labour (Paul, 1997: 122).

The 1948 Nationality Act

The 1948 Nationality Act reflected these competing imperatives. It gave rights of entry and citizenship to all citizens of British colonies and the Commonwealth. This symbolic universal equality in the common status of British subject was seen as 'a necessary price to pay for the role of parent' (Paul, 1997: 12) and the maintenance of a united Commonwealth. The status of Commonwealth citizen was introduced to appease India and Pakistan who did not want to be seen as British subjects (Paul, 1997: 17). This status, however, opened the way for differential treatment of Commonwealth citizens in subsequent legislation. In spite of this apparent equality, the racialisation of British society meant that this imperial model of citizenship embodied 'a fundamental contradiction between an inclusive legal nationality polity ... and an exclusive constructed national identity' (Paul, 1997: xii). In fact, only men were included fully and the Act continued the unequal treatment of women. Although they were now allowed to retain their own nationality on marriage, they were not allowed to transmit their citizenship.

It was possible to avoid this contradiction while black citizens remained at home and did not assert their rights of citizenship. When Commonwealth citizens attempted to take up these rights within Britain itself, it challenged the precarious balance on which the Act had been based. The arrival of the *Empire Windrush* at Tilbury in Essex in 1948 carrying 492 Jamaicans seeking work was thus of huge symbolic importance. Although they had the right to enter Britain, Prime Minister Attlee described their arrival as an 'incursion' (Holmes, 1988: 257). Paul suggests that there was room in the early 1950s for the government to promote popular acceptance and understanding of colonial migration. Government and officials, however, took a hostile attitude themselves and assumed that others would be similarly hostile. The TUC, for example, was not consulted on their view and their opposition was assumed (Paul, 1997: 123).

The response of the elite 'did not so much follow popular sentiment as actually precede and create it' (Saggar, 1992: 175). There were seven inquiries on colonial migration before 1954 under both governments, but although the first reported that West Indians made an economic contribution, it recommended controls (Paul, 1997: 146). One report summarised the conflicting interests embodied in different ministries. Commonwealth sentiment and economic interest were in conflict with what were perceived as 'the long term social consequences of the presence in this country of large and growing coloured communities that are "difficult of assimilation"' (Paul, 1997: 164). Although 'coloured' immigration was a small minority of total immigration, and far lower than emigration, the debate focused on this group. The language shifted from 'migrant' to 'Commonwealth immigrant', and Commonwealth immigrant became conflated with non–white (Paul, 1997: 134).

Populist moves against Commonwealth immigration did not build up until the late 1950s, when a series of 'race riots' raised the visibility of the issue and shifted the debate to social order and the issue of black–white relations (Saggar, 1992: 100). The Nottingham 'riot' was initiated by an attack on a black man seen talking to white woman and was followed by the Notting Hill riot of 1958. Immigration was not an issue in the election of 1959, although it did bring into the House of Commons several vocal pro-control MPs from Birmingham (Holmes, 1988: 260). As late as 1961, ministers were looking for 'a more forceful expression of public opinion in the hope that it would be seen to have led the way' (Paul, 1997: 165). The threat of controls forced many people to make the decision to migrate and to settle permanently, for fear of being unable to enter at a later date. Immigration in the year following *Windrush* had been modest, with only 2,000 annually from the West Indies, but the numbers more than doubled the between 1959 and 1960 (Paul, 1997: 161). The increase helped tip the balance of public opinion against immigration and pave the way for the imposition of controls in 1962. This 'perverse' result of controls was repeated in Germany in the 1970s in relation to the guestworker system.

The 1962 Commonwealth Immigrants Act

This Act reversed the formal equality embodied in the 1948 Act, differentiating between the rights of British and Commonwealth citizens. Those born in the UK or with a passport issued by a British embassy abroad were given the right to enter freely, while entry became conditional for others. Formal rights thus started to move in line with the constructed identity of Britishness. The racial intent was clear. William Deedes, who was involved in the Act's passage, later wrote that 'the restrictions were applied to coloured and white citizens … though everybody recognised that immigration from Canada, Australia and New Zealand formed no part of the problem' (cited in Saggar, 1992: 105).

Commonwealth citizens wishing to work in Britain were required to gain a work voucher. These were in three categories: A for those with jobs in Britain; B for those with skills; and C for unskilled workers looking for work. C vouchers were expected to be for 'coloureds' and their numbers were capped. The Act also granted powers to immigration offices to question would-be immigrants and to turn them back. No internal controls were introduced, however, so that, once accepted, this was a route to permanent settlement and family reunion.

The opposition Labour Party opposed the Act but failed to repeal it when returned to office in 1964. This signalled a convergence of the Conservative and Labour Parties in favour of immigration control. The election campaign had been soured when the Labour candidate in the Smethwick constituency of Birmingham lost his seat following a campaign in which the slogan 'if you want a nigger for a neighbour vote Labour or Liberal' featured prominently (Holmes, 1988: 177). Fear that immigration would become an electoral liability helped to shift Labour policy on the issue. The agenda of controls, which had been developing at the Home Office throughout the post-war period, also ensured continuity.

Labour's strategy was to tie controls to improving race relations. In the words of Home Secretary Roy Hattersley: 'Without integration, limitation is inexcusable; without limitation, integration is impossible' (Holmes, 1988: 268). Labour's 1965 White Paper *Immigration from the Commonwealth* called for stricter controls, including a cut in the number of vouchers, and a reduction in the rights of dependants, together with measures to promote integration (Solomos, 2003: 59). The document spoke of the 'good sense' of British people and suggested that their 'tolerance' was threatened by the arrival of too many immigrants (Holmes, 1991: 16), language that implies that immigrants are inherently problematic. This hostility, as in the case of Jews at the beginning of the century, was not related to numbers (Holmes, 1991: 84). The emphasis was on the perceived problems posed by this 'non-British' group and the limits to their potential absorption.

Multiculturalism was officially endorsed when Roy Jenkins, home secretary in 1966, described integration 'not as a flattening process of assimilation but as equal opportunity, accompanied by cultural diversity, in an atmosphere of mutual tolerance' (Jones, 1977: 148). Labour also developed the first race relations legislation in 1965, with a somewhat stronger Act passed in 1968 (Gregory, 1987). The attempt to build a new consensus around race relations combined with control was rudely challenged in the late 1960s with the notorious anti-immigrant speeches by Enoch Powell in which he warned of the 'rivers of blood' that would flow if 'coloured' immigration continued. Powell questioned whether 'being British' was compatible with ethnic pluralism and claimed that politicians had betrayed the electorate, in a conspiracy to increase black immigration (Saggar, 1992: 174). Although sacked from his own front bench, Powell received considerable support from sections of his party, the press and the public. This broke the fragile consensus on race relations that had been forged between the two party leaderships, moving it up the political agenda. This was further strained by the arrival between 1965 and 1967 of groups of Asians from Kenya, prompted by the 'Africanisation' policies of the newly independent government. As British passport holders they had unconditional rights of entry.

The 1968 Commonwealth Immigrants Act: the development of patriality

The government responded to the arrival of these British citizens by changing the rules to restrict their rights in a new Commonwealth Immigrants Act. As one commentator put it: 'If the design involved the betrayal of both legal and ethical obligations to British citizens in Kenya or elsewhere, the Labour Government considered it worthwhile' (Saggar, 1992: 109). The Act introduced the concept of 'patriality' that, albeit in coded form, involved a racialised division between Commonwealth citizens. Patrials were defined as:

a) those entitled to citizenship through birth, adoption, naturalisation or registration, or with a parent or grandparent entitled to citizenship, or;
b) citizens of Britain and its colonies who had settled in Britain and resided there for five years.

Only patrials retained the right of abode in Britain. Britishness was thus linked more explicitly to notions of kith and kin. A large proportion of citizens of the white settler states of Australia, New Zealand and Canada had British parents or grandparents, while this was unlikely for citizens of the New Commonwealth. This legislation, and the debate surrounding its passage, suggested how far the consensus had shifted. As Saggar put it, whereas 'six years earlier it had been a shameful betrayal of the ideals of the Commonwealth, virtually all leading politicians now subscribed to the view that the denial of entry rights to British nationals was a necessary and desirable thing to do' (1992: 110).

The 1971 Immigration Act: the end of primary migration from the Commonwealth?

With the return of a Conservative administration in 1970, its victory achieved partly on the basis of the controversy over immigration, a new assault began on the rights of Commonwealth citizens, which aimed 'to bury the immigration issue' (Saggar, 1992: 114) and end primary migration from the (New) Commonwealth. The Act set out the structure of immigration control, appeals, and powers of immigration officers. It introduced powers for the home secretary to make immigration rules that set out the requirements for individuals to be admitted under particular categories of entrant (JCWI, 2006: 10).

The 1971 Immigration Act extended the distinction between patrials and non-patrials introduced in 1968, placing the latter 'on virtually the same footing as aliens' (Paul, 1997: 181). The rights of workers from the New Commonwealth were further restricted as they were allowed to enter for employment only if they had a work permit for a particular job. Work permits carried no right to settlement (Fekete, 1997: 3), thus they were reduced to the status of 'contract labour' (Holmes, 1998: 267). The Act came into force on the day that Britain joined the Common Market (later the EU) and marked a shift towards a policy of recruiting labour from Europe. The dependence on Commonwealth labour continued, however, particularly in health and education. Attempts to 'Europeanise' labour recruitment have increased with Britain's decision to grant free access to the British labour market to the new accession countries in 2004.

As with previous legislation, Labour opposed this Act, but not on principle (Saggar, 1992: 117), and retained it when it returned to office in 1974. The new government sought to rebuild the consensus by tightening immigration controls while legislating to improve race relations. A stronger Race Relations Act was passed in 1976 but enforcement was relatively weak while the immigration control side of the bargain was much stronger. As Jones (1977: 162) suggests, it is easier to be rigorous in controlling immigration since this negative policy is more tangible than the aim of promoting 'good race relations', a distinction that has become more institutionalised with the implementation of 'managed migration' policy.

The 1981 British Nationality Act

The return of a Conservative government in 1979 marked an end to the consensus on race relations. The infamous speech by party leader, Margaret Thatcher in 1978, in which she claimed that British people were becoming afraid of being 'swamped' by people of an 'alien culture', signalled that race would be high on the political agenda, and a series of attacks on multiculturalism followed. The 1981 British Nationality Act reconstructed the basis of British citizenship, extending the link between citizenship and ethnicity established with patriality and closing off the rights of British citizens abroad who were not of British 'stock'. It abolished the status of Citizen of the United Kingdom and Colonies (CUKC), introduced with the 1948 Act, and established three tiers of citizenship of which only the first, now called British Citizens, had the right of abode in Britain. The other two groups, Citizens of Dependent Territories, who held or acquired citizenship in an existing dependency, and a residual group of British Overseas Citizens, had no right of abode. The Act removed the automatic right to citizenship of those born in Britain (*ius soli*), confining this to those whose parents were 'settled' in the UK and not subject to immigration restrictions (JCWI, 2006: 1403).

The 1981 Act also introduced greater scrutiny of marriage. Women marrying British citizens lost the automatic right to citizenship and it became conditional on a stringent set of conditions involving both their own status and the rule that they could be supported without public funds (JCWI, 2006: 1455). Men retained this right until a case brought on the grounds of sexual discrimination ended this discrimination by removing the right from both sexes. The 'primary purpose' rule introduced as part of the implementation of the Act allowed an immigration officer to deny entry to a spouse or fiancé(e) if he or she deemed that the primary purpose of a marriage was immigration. This was applied even where the legality or genuineness of marriage was not in question. The real targets of this policy became obvious in the way in which it was enforced. In 1990, 69% of husbands from the Indian subcontinent were refused entry. In the same period, Australian spouses and fiancé(e)s were allowed to enter freely without facing questioning on the nature of their marriage (JCWI, 1997:13). This rule was abolished in 1997, although scrutiny of marriage has continued in other forms (see Chapter Seven).

The 1988 Immigration Act

The 1988 Immigration Act and the new Home Office practices that followed it made deportation easier and swifter (JCWI, 1997: 6). The rights of Commonwealth citizens were further reduced during the 1980s, when visa controls were introduced, first for Sri Lankan refugees in 1985 and later for visitors from India, Pakistan, Bangladesh, Nigeria and Ghana in 1986 (Solomos, 2003: 67). The Act also withdrew what had been the only unconditional right to family reunion, of long-settled Commonwealth men to bring in their families.

The post-war period thus saw a long diminution in the rights of citizens from the New Commonwealth. Immigration policy was racialised on the basis primarily of skin colour. Despite the rhetoric about the end of immigration, however, immigration from the New Commonwealth continued, although in particular sectors and with growing restrictions on the rights of residence and access to benefits.

Phase 3: asylum takes centre stage

Asylum applications increased in the 1980s, rising from 5,300 in 1988 to 15,600 in 1989 and reaching 44,800 in 1991 (Schuster and Solomos, 1999: 63). This increase came as a result of the growing conflicts discussed in Chapter Four, particularly the destruction of the states of the Eastern bloc. Another important element was that, with primary migration cut off, asylum became the only route by which many migrants could enter. As Schuster and Solomos (1999: 63) suggest, although the percentage increases were large, the absolute numbers were not dramatic, especially in relation to other European states. In 1991, Germany had more than five times as many applications, while the much smaller Switzerland had almost as many, and their numbers continued to grow during the 1990s. This increase was used, however, as evidence of an 'asylum problem' by those seeking further controls. Asylum became a key element in immigration control during the 1990s, although controls on labour migrants also continued to be tightened. Rights to benefits, including Child Benefit, were removed from work permit holders in 1996, and the 1999 Immigration and Asylum Act removed the right to all non-contributory benefits from 'persons subject to immigration control'.

Until the 1990s, Britain had no domestic asylum legislation. The Geneva Convention was ratified in 1954 but no legislation was passed to anchor it in domestic law (Schuster and Solomos, 1999: 57). Most refugees arrived in Britain through organised programmes and their refugee status was already established. They therefore had secure residence and access to a range of citizenship rights, including family reunion. Britain has resisted setting up a permanent settlement programme, preferring to see refugee flows as temporary. These programmes have been ad hoc and relied on local initiatives involving the voluntary sector (Duke, 1996; Duke et al, 1999). The nature of their reception depended on the causes of the flight and its relation to Britain's foreign policy as well as the extent to which they could be seen as future 'insiders'. Hungarians who arrived in 1956 were seen as escaping Communism and were European and therefore assimilable. The Vietnamese 'boat people' in the 1970s were dispersed around the country to avoid concentrations of ethnic communities (Robinson et al, 2003). Chilean refugees from the Pinochet coup were rejected by the Conservative government, but some were accepted under Labour in 1974 (Joly, 1996). As political refugees, they found considerable support among Latin Americans in the UK and those sympathetic to their cause. In the 1990s, a programme for Bosnian refugees aroused little opposition from local communities (Bralo, 2000: 20; Guild, 2000: 84) as they were portrayed as victims of atrocities by Serbia, with whom Britain was at the time in a state of war.

The majority of asylum seekers arriving in the 1990s have been 'non-quota', or 'spontaneous', refugees. They travel independently, often using illegal channels and must make individual claims for asylum. Their status is insecure and has become more so as legislation has whittled away their rights, while a hostile media contributes to creating a negative environment for them.

Box 6.3: UK asylum legislation: key points

1993 Asylum and Immigration Appeals Act: Effectively incorporated Geneva Convention into immigration rules, created processes for dealing with asylum applications. Withdrew rights to secure tenancy in social housing for asylum seekers, who lost right to be considered homeless if any other housing available, 'however temporary'. Benefits for asylum seekers set at 70% of income support.

1996 Asylum and Immigration Act: Withdrew cash benefits for asylum seekers, followed by introduction of 'vouchers' following court judgment that local authorities should provide basic subsistence for 'destitute', while Children Act gave right to support for children and families.

1999 Asylum and Immigration Act: Introduced vouchers for all asylum seekers, organisation of support through NASS. Level of subsistence set below level of welfare benefits; asylum seekers ineligible for benefits, for example Child Benefit. Compulsory dispersal for families and single people; accompanied asylum seeker children do not ordinarily have access to Children Act or welfare benefits, but do have access to to education and health care. Unaccompanied minors remain responsibility of local authorities.

2002 Nationality, Immigration and Asylum Act: Introduced new controls on entry, proposed new induction/accommodation/removal centres for asylum seekers; proposal for separate education in accommodation centres. Vouchers phased out.

Section 55: Support refused for individuals but not families with children if asylum seekers do not make claim 'as soon as reasonably practicable'. Removed 'concession' allowing asylum seekers to apply to work after six months. Detention centres renamed 'removal centres' and targets set for removals.

2004 Asylum and Immigration (Treatment of Claimants, etc) Act: Limited rights of appeal on asylum claims. Electronic monitoring of asylum seekers who 'appear' over 18, restricting their movement, employment and residential occupation. Support can be refused for failed asylum-seeking families with dependent children *deemed to be in a position to leave the UK* if they do not cooperate with removal. Credibility of asylum applicants jeopardised if they fail to show passport on request, use false document, change or destroy a travel document without good reason or do not answer questions from authorities.

2006 Asylum and Immigration Act: New asylum model to exert greater control over asylum seekers, separate procedures for different nationalities. Refugees granted temporary, to permanent, status to be reviewed after five years. Detention or electronic tagging to become 'the norm' for those whose application fails. New processes for considering asylum claims enable the state to exert greater control over asylum seekers. Pilot return of unaccompanied asylum-seeking children.

Legislation on asylum

The government started to respond to the increase in asylum applications in the 1980s, introducing visa requirements for Commonwealth countries where there was refugee-producing conflict and, in response to EU harmonisation, the 1987 Carriers' Liability Act imposed fines on airlines carrying passengers without correct documents. The first Act dealing specifically with asylum was the 1993 Asylum and Immigration Appeals Act. There have been five subsequent Acts and each new piece of legislation has created a different system of support alongside previous arrangements, 'leaving a complex tangle of law, provision and regulation' (Mayor of London, 2004b: 8). The trend has been to separate asylum seekers from society on arrival, with the presumption that most applications will fail. Another aspect of the legislation has been to make status more temporary, thus extending the insecurity even for those granted some form of status.

The 1993 Act ended the right of asylum seekers to permanent local authority accommodation. The 1996 Immigration and Asylum Act extended this by removing benefits from people making their asylum claims inside the country rather than as they entered (in-country applicants) and from those appealing a negative decision. A subsequent court ruling that destitute asylum seekers came under the terms of the 1948 National Assistance Act made local authorities responsible for their support. Adults were not allowed to receive cash but were housed and given subsistence in-kind in the form of 'vouchers' that were exchangeable at designated supermarkets. Check-out operators were empowered to check eligibility and ensure that purchases did not include banned items such as cigarettes and alcohol, thus introducing an element of moral surveillance and exposing asylum seekers to racist abuse from other customers.

This system shifted the costs of supporting asylum seekers from the national benefit system to local authority budgets. The costs were not recouped in full and were concentrated in a small number of boroughs most of which had high levels of deprivation (Audit Commission, 2000a). As the voucher system raised the visibility of asylum seekers, pressure on local authorities for resources, and on the already depleted housing stock, increased. The majority of asylum seekers arriving during the 1990s were based in London (Carey-Wood et al, 1995) largely because of the support networks available within the community. By 1998 many London authorities were dispersing asylum seekers outside London to areas where empty housing was available.

The NASS system

The Labour government elected in 1997 moved further down the road of isolating asylum seekers. The stated aims of the White Paper *Fairer, Faster and*

Firmer introduced in 1998 were the speeding up the processing of asylum claims, controlling entry and reducing incentives for 'economic migration' (Audit Commission, 2000b: 9). The 1999 Immigration and Asylum Act that followed introduced some limited new rights, mainly in relation to appeals (Chatwin, 2001: 7) but gave extensive new powers to the home secretary and extended police powers to search, arrest and detain asylum seekers. The most controversial measures concerned the new support system for asylum seekers. The voucher scheme was extended to all asylum seekers and compulsory dispersal for those needing accommodation was introduced to locations outside London and the South-East. In determining housing need, the secretary of state could not 'take into account any preference for locality or type of accommodation' (Home Office, 1998a) and dispersal often took place to areas without existing communities of fellow nationals. Local authorities' direct role in supporting asylum seekers was replaced by a new centralised agency, the National Asylum Support System (NASS). NASS, however, subcontracts its work to local authorities as well as to private housing providers and voluntary agencies, including refugee organisations.

The immediate motive for dispersal was to relieve the pressure on London local authorities through 'burden sharing'. This 'burden' had been artificially increased by the policy of removing asylum seekers from national benefits. This was in line with European moves towards 'burden sharing' or as it is now called 'sharing the balance of reponsibility' (Geddes, 2000: 29). Linked to this was the aim of reducing social tensions arising from competition for scarce resources and 'visible' concentrations of ethnic minorities (Robinson et al, 2003: 164).

The primary aim of dispersal was deterrence. The White Paper suggested that new arrangements were needed to ensure that 'genuine asylum seekers' were not left 'destitute' while minimising 'the attractions of the UK to economic migrants' (Home Office, 1998a: 3). Studies have shown that migration is not driven by the search for welfare benefits and that 'benefit tourism' is not widespread (Somerville, 2006: 42). Southern European states with low levels of welfare experienced increasing asylum applications as other destinations became more difficult to reach.

The government claims that 'those who are genuinely fleeing persecution' would 'not be overly concerned about whether that support is provided in cash or in kind, nor about the location in which they are supported' (Home Office, 1998b: 5). Official thinking was that 'genuine' refugees would be prepared to undergo a temporary period of hardship since the process would weed out 'bogus' claimants, thus making their own position morally stronger. The ability to move freely within the country of residence is a fundamental civil right, and the restriction of this has echoes in the Poor Laws that controlled the movements of the 'undeserving poor'. The only reference to recognised refugees – the 'deserving' whom the system is designed to separate from the majority of 'undeserving' – was that they must leave the NASS system within 14 days of a decision on their application.

Secure borders, safe haven

In October 2001, Home Secretary David Blunkett announced a 'fundamental reform' of asylum and immigration policy. The White Paper *Secure Borders, Safe Haven*, published in February 2002, welcomed labour migration and introduced proposals to expand the significance of citizenship. This marked the beginning of the 'managed migration' approach that will be discussed further in the next chapter. The bulk of these proposals, however, involved tightening of controls on asylum and 'illegal immigrants'. The main driver of these policies was an attempt to placate those calling for tougher measures. On the other hand, a campaign against the voucher system had won support from a wide spectrum of individuals and organisations – including the largest trade union, the Transport and General Workers' Union – and was influential in its abolition in the subsequent legislation.

The White Paper included measures to segregate asylum seekers further from mainstream society and to promote their speedy removal. It proposed housing them in new 'induction and accommodation centres' while their claims were investigated. It spoke of a *'seamless'* process from induction to removal, which seems predicated on the notion that the majority of asylum applications are unfounded. The speeding-up of appeals to cut down 'barriers to removal' was central to this goal, with targets set for deportations of 'failed asylums seekers' (Home Office, 2002a: 65) and an increase of 40% in the capacity of removal centres (Home Office, 2002a: 66). The right to apply to take up employment after six months was to be removed, thus intensifying poverty and exclusion.

The measures concerning asylum outlined in the White Paper were incorporated in the 2002 Nationality, Immigration and Asylum Act. As the Bill was presented to Parliament, a new proposal was added, to remove the children of asylum seekers living in the proposed reception centres from mainstream education. This followed a statement by David Blunkett that, in language reminiscent of Margaret Thatcher's 1978 speech, claimed that asylum-seeking children were 'swamping' local schools. This measure was condemned by many MPs and organisations including trade unions and children's charities that saw it as contravening the UN Convention on the Rights of the Child (Sales, 2007). Local campaigns against the development of facilities for asylum seekers have prevented the establishment of any accommodation centres.

In November 2002, it was announced that the status of Exceptional Leave to Remain (ELR) was to be abolished. This had given considerable rights to those not considered to meet the criteria for Convention status but for whom return was dangerous, for example refugees from the civil war in Somalia. It was renewable and provided a path to settlement. This extended the temporary nature of protection.

Immediately following the Act's passage on 8 January 2003, under Section 55, those who had not applied for asylum 'as soon as reasonably practicable' after arriving in the UK were deprived of the right to food and shelter. A joint statement by organisations working with refugees (Refugee Council, 2003) pointed out that two-thirds of asylum claims – and 65% of successful claims – are made in-country. Thus even those subsequently deemed 'genuine' refugees had no legal means of support while they awaited the outcome of their case. In November 2005, the Law Lords ruled that Section 55 breached human rights. In a press statement, the organisation Liberty, one of the parties to the case, said: 'Asylum seekers previously placed in a Catch 22 situation in which they couldn't work or receive benefits will now escape this affront to human dignity'.[6]

The 2004 Asylum and Immigration (Treatment of Claimants, etc) Act (Home Office, 2004a) introduced further measures to ensure that an asylum seeker's stay in Britain was nasty, brutish and short. The Act extended exclusion from benefit to those with minor children in an attempt to ensure compliance with removal. It was envisaged that where families did not leave, children of those made destitute would be accommodated in local authority care, a policy described by the Bishop of Southwark as the 'social policy of the workhouse' (Cunningham and Tomlinson, 2005: 256). Regulations under Section 4 of the 1999 Immigration and Asylum Act provide the Home Office with powers to support destitute failed asylum seekers (Section 4 support), under certain conditions, including if they have taken 'all reasonable steps to leave the UK' or if they are unable to leave because of medical reasons or a lack of safe route to return. Meanwhile, the 2004 NHS (Charges to Overseas Visitors) Charging (Amendment) Regulations introduced charges for health care, including primary and hospital care, for failed asylum seekers. Research by the Refugee Council found that these measures were having a serious impact on the health of asylum seekers and that some were being denied care that they 'desperately needed' (Kelley and Stevenson, 2006: 11). Other key changes included (JCWI, 2006: 9):

- a reduction in the right to appeal with the introduction of a single-tier Asylum and Immigration Tribunal;
- the creation of new criminal offences of entering the UK without a valid passport;
- the credibility of asylum applications is jeopardised if applicants do not answer questions from authorities;

- powers to prevent marriage involving a person who requires leave to be in the UK if he or she does not have a 'certificate of approval' from the secretary of state;
- establishing three lists of countries in relation to their 'safety' with different procedures for each group.

A new asylum model

The government's Five Year Strategy for Asylum and Immigration, *Controlling our borders: Making migration work for Britain* (Home Office, 2005a), which was introduced during the general election campaign, included what it called a 'New Asylum Model'. This involved targets for the removals of 'failed' asylum seekers and suggested that detention was to become 'the norm' for those whose application failed, with electronic tagging to prevent absconding. It also proposed new processes for considering asylum claims to enable greater control over asylum seekers. This includes the 'segmentation' of asylum claims into different categories involving different procedures, with fast-track procedures for those detained.

A key shift in the document was the proposal that refugee status, rather than being permanent would be granted on a temporary basis to be reviewed after five years in relation to the safety of the country of origin. This extends even further the period of limbo into which refugees are plunged as they wait for a decision on their case. No justification was given for this decision, which undermines and delays integration even further (JCWI, 2006: 47). The document also stated that it would tackle 'the difficult issue of returning unaccompanied asylum seeking children'. The government began piloting the forcible repatriation of children in August 2006, beginning with 500 Vietnamese children, many of whom were understood to have been smuggled into Britain where they worked in brothels and cannabis factories.[7] Scotland's Commissioner for Children and Young People expressed concern at the proposals, which children's rights campaigners suggest breach the UN Convention on the Rights of the Child.[8] The 2006 Asylum and Immigration Act incorporated those measures that needed legislation, while other measures, such as the segmentation of asylum seekers, have been brought in through new Home Office rules.

Although the Act received royal assent only in March 2006, and many of its provisions are not yet in force, the government announced yet more legislation on immigration and asylum in the Queen's Speech of 15 November 2006. This announced that 'A bill will be introduced to provide the immigration service with further powers to police the country's borders, tackle immigration crime, and to make it easier to deport those who break the law.' As one commentator pointed out, this is the sixth immigration Bill under this Labour government and '[e]ach home secretary comes to office determined to undo, replace or refocus the work of his predecessor. That means vast swathes of government legislation are being overturned and reversed before they are even implemented.'[9]

The trajectory of asylum policy has been to treat asylum seekers with suspicion, as a risk to society rather than as people themselves at risk. Policy has therefore aimed at excluding them from developing connections with mainstream society in order to remove them as easily and speedily as possible.

Phase 4: towards managed migration

In spite of increasing restrictions on migration, at the start of the twenty-first century Britain's economy remained heavily dependent on immigration from outside the EU. Labour shortages were especially acute in both unskilled work such as agriculture labour, processing and domestic labour and in the caring professions particularly in London (Raghuram and Kofman, 2002). A speech in 2000 by Immigration Minister Barbara Roche signalled a major change in immigration policy. She suggested that 'We are in competition for the brightest and best talents'.[10] The 2002 White Paper *Secure Borders, Safe Haven* (Home Office, 2002a) was heralded as a 'new approach to immigration in modern Britain' with immigration welcomed as a source of both economic and cultural enrichment. A Home Office research paper (Glover et al, 2001) spelt out the case for a more open immigration policy. Home Office practice had already started to change in response, with a significant increase in the number of work permits issued to non-nationals (Clarke and Salt. 2003). The announcement of this increase in 2001 went largely unremarked and, with business supporting increasing openness to labour migration, this measure was not opposed by the Conservative Party. These developments mirrored developments at European Union level where 'alongside a dominant discourse of closure ... most member states are developing strategies for the management of migration' (Morris, L., 2003: 78).

With the acknowledgement of the value of economic migration, government policy is increasingly driven by the explicit aim of tailoring it to the needs of the economy through 'managed migration' (Flynn, 2005). Alongside the more rigorous closure against asylum seeking and 'illegal' migration, specific forms of labour migration have been facilitated. In his foreword to the Five Year Strategy for Asylum and Immigration, Prime Minister Tony Blair argued that it contained 'solutions to a difficult issue which are clear, workable and in the best interests of this country ... [and] meet both the public's concerns and our nation's needs' (Home Office, 2005a: 5). Managed migration will be discussed more fully in the next chapter.

The key characteristics of British policy making

This outline of British policy making on immigration reveals some distinct phases as well as some common elements that have run through the history of immigration controls. This section discusses briefly some of these continuities.

Bi-partisanship policy

Since the 1905 Aliens Act, immigration controls have become part of the accepted 'common sense' of immigration policy and discussion of the principle of these controls has been excluded from mainstream debate. A powerful element in maintaining this consensus has been the bi-partisan agreement in the official policy of the major parties on the main elements of immigration control. This reflects the structure of the British political party system and its relationship to the institutions of the state. This structure has ensured that whole areas of policy are kept outside democratic scrutiny and largely outside party politics.

The first-past-the-post electoral system, which ensures that politics is essentially a competition between two major parties, is institutionalised in the notion of 'Her Majesty's Loyal Opposition'. Neither party has been willing to challenge the institutions of the 'constitutional monarchy' in which the hereditary monarch retains some political powers. Both ministers and members of the official opposition belong to the Privy Counsel, chaired by the monarch, which advises on the exercise of prerogative powers. As David McKie in the *Guardian* argued, these powers enable:

> prime ministers and their chosen subordinates to order the country to war, to make treaties, to give up national territory, to staff the commanding heights of political life, the church and the law, to dish out honours to those who deserve them and some who do not, to keep information from courts even when injustice may result.[11]

The latter was exemplified by two court cases in 2003 that found that the Home Office had abused its powers by failing to act on its own policy in relation to Iraqi asylum seekers. The report of the case is dated November 2005 but only came to light on 25 July 2006 when attempts were made to prevent publicity. Keith Best, chief executive of the Immigration Advisory Service, commented:

> It is clear that because this report is a damning indictment of the way in which British officials treat those who wish to come to the UK that there has been an attempt to bury it among other news. … It can be no coincidence that the Home Affairs Committee's report was published on 21 July and received all the publicity during the following few days during which the Independent Monitor's report was slipped in.[12]

The top-down nature of party politics and the premium on party loyalty also stifles debate within parliamentary parties. The party whips are used to ensure that MPs vote in Parliament with their party leadership, particularly when in government, reducing the scope for open debate and dissent on issues of principle. The two-party structure in turn shapes the views that are deemed acceptable for public debate more widely. The BBC, for example, sees the two major parties, Conservative and Labour (sometimes with the addition of the Liberals and where appropriate the Scottish National Party or Plaid Cymru), as representing the different sides in any debate and therefore including a spokesperson from each represents 'balance'. This excludes anyone outside this narrow range of opinion and often back-bench members of the major parties. Thus issues that are not the subject of debate between the main parties often do not become part of public discussion. The process has narrowed discussion on immigration to issues concerning the ability of ministers to manage rather than the principles on which this is based.

This narrow agenda is evident in the trajectory of policy making on immigration, which has involved the deepening of existing agendas rather than changes of direction as a different party has gained office. The 1905 Aliens Act was passed under the Conservatives but when the Liberals returned to power, 'although they were prepared to work the Act as humanely as possible, made no attempt to repeal it or consider the fundamental issue of how the Act might be worked in the future by an anti-alien Home Secretary' (Holmes, 1988: 72–3). The Labour Party has tended to extend rather than restrict the agenda of previous governments. Although it opposed the 1962 Commonwealth Immigrants Act, 'in the summer of 1965, the newly elected Labour Government tightened the screw of control even further' (Holmes, 1991: 54). This process has been even more evident in their policies on asylum. Although when in opposition the Labour Party opposed the more oppressive measures in Conservative asylum legislation during the 1990s, the 1999 Immigration and Asylum Act went even further in restricting rights and there was little opposition to the legislation from Labour members in Parliament.

When in office, Conservatives faced opposition to their policies from the Labour Party, which was freer to raise issues of principle when in opposition. This placed limits on the extent to which Conservatives were able to override human rights considerations. Labour in office faces less opposition from the Conservatives on these grounds[13] and has been able to promote policies unpalatable to its back bench, which few have broken 'party loyalty' to challenge. With its traditional commitment to a more internationalist perspective, Labour has generally been seen as politically vulnerable in relation to immigration policy. Layton Henry argues, however, that attempting to outflank the Conservatives is self-defeating. Appeasement of right-wing demands 'encouraged right-wing conservatives to believe that they had a winning issue which commanded widespread popular support and which could be used against the Labour government' (quoted in Saggar, 1992: 107). The consensus on asylum has thus shifted to the right during Labour's period in office.

Saggar (1992: 9) suggests that the consensus on immigration has embraced the front-bench rather than back-bench MPs or the membership of either party and therefore has shallow roots and is inherently fragile. Each party is a broad coalition of interests that are rarely reflected in official policy or debate. Bi-partisan policies have been constructed and reconstructed around differing notions of party interest and have become increasingly restrictive in recent years. They have also reflected a fear of immigration becoming an electoral issue, since it is seen as uncontrollable and open to exploitation by 'extremists'. Saggar distinguishes four phases in this consensus in the post-war period up to the Thatcher period, in which the parties attempted different accommodations to the relationship between controls and 'race relations'. More recently the consensus has been built on the basis of managed migration and tough measures to control asylum. The opening-up to labour immigration, including to workers of the EU accession countries, was greeted with very little debate as it accorded with the Conservative pro-market and pro-business agenda.

Rules and the power of discretion

Substantial areas of immigration policy remain to a large extent outside democratic scrutiny. White Papers set out the broad goals of policy and specific proposals but not all of these are enacted in formal legislation. The document *Secure Borders, Safe Haven* set out what is called a new approach to labour migration but this was not reflected in the legislation since most of the changes it proposed, such as the speeding up of response to work permit applications, could be made through administrative measures.

Britain's system of law making involves the amendment of previous legislation rather than the setting out of broad principles on which these measures are based. The Acts themselves are therefore largely impenetrable to the non-legally trained although they are published with accompanying guidance notes. As the pace of immigration legislation has increased, it has become more difficult to keep abreast of this complex mixture of laws and accompanying rules. Many immigrants get poor legal advice from lawyers unfamiliar with the intricacies of this specialist area of the law and the rights and opportunities available to their clients.

The 1971 Immigration Act gave the Home Office power to make 'immigration rules' that 'set out the requirements that must be satisfied in order for a person to be admitted to the UK in any particular category' (JCWI, 2006: 10). Rules involve less scrutiny than legislation. They are 'laid before Parliament', and unless there is a call for a debate, they become law straight away. They cannot be amended, only voted down in their entirety, a situation that has happened only once (JCWI, 2006: 11). The Home Office, which is responsible for producing these rules, is a conservative institution, as Jill Pellew (1989), its official historian, has demonstrated. Duvell and Jordan found that NGOs and other public services perceived that the Home Office 'is relatively impervious to change and had a destructive organisational culture' (2003: 305). Their conclusions from a study of Home Office working practices suggested that the culture includes a range of 'assumptions, stereotypes and myths' and that front-line staff and most managers used 'stereotyped views of particular nationals and communities' (Duvell and Jordan, 2003: 315). The notion that a 'culture of suspicion' pervades the Home Office's dealings with asylum seekers is widespread.[14]

The rules also open up wide areas of discretion. These are 'written in a more relaxed and informal way' than legislation and there is thus more room for manoeuvre in interpreting them (JCWI, 2006: 10). Immigration officers interpreted the primary purpose rule extremely stringently in relation to Asian women, often assuming arranged marriages are a means to enter Britain. A transcript of an interview with a young woman from a village in India included 86 questions about the circumstances of her marriage (JCWI, 1997: 39). The RSA Migration Commission's report suggests that decisions are often based on racialised categories. For example, the British Working Holiday Scheme, which allows Commonwealth citizens to stay for up to two years, and to work to support themselves, has been used mainly by people from Australia and New Zealand. The scheme was revised in 2003 to make it more open to people from New Commonwealth countries but this goal was stymied by High Commission staff in African and Asian countries who continued to treat applications with suspicion (RSA, 2005: 37). Keith Best, in the statement quoted on p 154 above, suggested that the whole process of decision making is fundamentally flawed:

> We drew attention to Parliament flouted, fees unlawful and disproportionate compared with Schengen countries, wrongful removal of immigration categories, increased wrongful refusals, unlawful discrimination on nationality and social class, denial of

entitlement of rights of appeal to 46,000, Government inactivity, stereotyping of applicants – the sorry state of how we treat those who want to come to the UK.[15]

Race relations and immigration

Roy Hattersley's famous phrase quoted earlier, in which he linked integration with immigration control, embodies a view that continues to underlie official policy on immigration. Successive governments have seen the 'securing of borders and boundary maintenance as the pre-condition for harmonious social relations in multicultural Britain' (Yuval Davis et al, 2005: 517). The titles of successive White Papers, *Fairer, Faster and Firmer* and *Secure Borders, Safe Haven*, themselves suggest that the two are interdependent. Most recently ministers have sought to respond to the threat from the far right British National Party by showing themselves tough on immigration and 'understanding' the concerns of those who oppose it. The view that new immigration should be restrained has been endorsed by some immigrant communities as they seek to distance themselves from 'undesirable' new immigrants. Holmes (1991: 2) suggests that the Jewish community has promoted the virtue of 'limits along with the notion of tolerance'.

In suggesting that controls are not only compatible, but necessary to good race relations, the government ignores the racism at the heart of its immigration policy. In 2001, Jack Straw, then home secretary, described the new 2000 Race Relations Amendment Act as the greatest piece of anti-discrimination legislation in the world. The Act placed new duties on public bodies actively to promote anti-discrimination in relation to service provision, explicitly excluding immigration officers who were empowered to discriminate against certain national groups. On this basis, journalist Hugo Young described it, in contrast to Straw's claim, as 'the most discriminatory act by the state in the last 35 years'.[16] Young concluded that this attempt to separate immigration policy and race relations is illusory. Jack Straw was himself criticised by the UNHCR for 'fomenting racism' in relation to asylum seekers during this period,[17] a criticism that clearly linked xenophobic discourse in relation to immigration with race relations.

The view that immigration controls are necessary for good race relations takes for granted the notion of a 'racist public' rather than challenging it. By suggesting that numbers should be limited, it accepts the notion that immigrants are a problem undermining the supposed growth of tolerance. This is a view that Hattersley himself, now no longer in office, endorses.

Conclusion

The processes of immigration policy making have displayed some continuities as well as changes in the century since controls were first introduced. The targets of controls have been different but what has remained constant has been the racialisation of particular groups, as well as distinctions on the basis of class and gender that were embedded in the first legislation. In the early period, Jewish refugees were the main focus of controls and they were portrayed as connected with 'filth' and disease. The post-war period saw the focus shift to Commonwealth citizens, who gradually saw their status change from citizens to 'immigrants' as immigration policy made divisions between the Old and New Commonwealth broadly on the basis of skin colour. The focus on asylum from the late 1980s re-introduced the fear of the refugee, as 'asylum seeker' became itself a racialised category in popular discourse and a specific legal status, increasingly segregated from mainstream society through dispersal, detention and removal. The final phase of managed migration, which makes the economic benefits to Britain the main selection criterion for the entry of migrants, might suggest a 'de-racialisation' of immigration policy. This has been only partial, since while the entry of skilled migrants has been opened up to people from across the world provided they have sufficient income and qualifications, unskilled migration has been 're-racialised' as new EU citizens are substituted for workers from the developing world.

Notes

[1] In 1921, with partition, the 26 south-western counties became an independent state.

[2] Women did not achieve full equality in voting rights until 1928.

[3] The expression 'Board of Guardian face' was used by people who immigrated at this time to describe the submissive expression poor Jewish people needed to assume when appearing before the Board.

[4] Formal discrimination against Jews and Catholics was largely ended during the nineteenth century but in Northern Ireland, the local electoral system that favoured Protestants was abolished as late as 1969.

[5] ZPWB website, www.zpwb.org.uk, accessed 7 January 2006.

[6] Liberty, 3 November 2005 at www.liberty-human-rights.org.uk.

[7] Reported in the *Guardian*, 18 August 2006.

[8] Reported in *The Scotsman*, 19 August 2006.

[9] Nick Clegg, 'Guardian comment is free', *Guardian*, 15 November 2006.

[10] 11 September 2000.

[11] David McKie, 'How ministers exercise arbitrary power', *Guardian*, 6 December 2000.

[12] Immigration Advisory Service, www.iasuk.org, accessed 22 August 2006.
[13] The Conservative Party combined with other parties and Labour rebels to ensure the successful opposition to proposals on terrorism that would have allowed suspects to be detained for up to three months without charge.
[14] This term was used for example by Lord Hylton in a parliamentary question in the House of Lords on 17 March 1995. It is frequently used in Briefings by the Refugee Council.
[15] See note 12.
[16] Hugo Young, *Guardian*, 24 April 2001.
[17] Reported in the *Guardian*, 20 April 2000.

Summary

- British immigration control began in 1905 and controls have become an established element in policy.
- The state has not responded passively to immigration control but actively instigated differentiation on national and ethnic lines.
- There have been four major phases of immigration control, with in each case different targets for control.
- The first phase was aimed mainly at Jews fleeing other parts of Europe.
- The second phase began after the Second World War and involved an implicit separation of Commonwealth citizens on the basis of ethnicity through patriality.
- Asylum became the dominant preoccupation of policy in the 1980s, and involved increasing segregation of asylum seekers from mainstream society.
- In the last phase, managed migration, recognition of dependence on labour migration has been acknowledged.
- There has been bi-partisan agreement on the major elements of migration policy between mainstream political parties and much policy making takes place outside the democratic process.
- Governments have claimed that race relations policy can be separated from immigration legislation.

Questions for discussion

- What has been the main driving force in developing Britain's system of immigration controls?
- How far does contemporary immigration policy represent continuity with the past?

• Is a policy of deterring asylum applications consistent with human rights obligations?

Further reading

Holmes, C. (1988) *John Bull's island: immigration and British society, 1871–1971*, Basingstoke: Macmillan.

Joint Council for the Welfare of Immigrants (JCWI) (2006) *Immigration, nationality and refugee law handbook*, London: JCWI.

Paul, K. (1997) *Whitewashing British: Race and citizenship in the postwar era*, Ithaca, NY: Cornell University Press.

Solomos, J. (2003) *Race and racism in Britain*, Basingstoke: Palgrave Macmillan.

seven

Britain's managed migration policy

Overview

This chapter examines the era of 'managed migration' introduced with New Labour, which has attempted to modernise immigration policy as part of a more general policy of managing and monitoring performance in public services. It explores the three major components of managed migration: labour migration that has become more explicitly linked to British economic interest, with increased privileges given to those with skills; controls, which involve both restrictions on entry and internal controls operated by service providers and private sector employers; and an extension in the meaning of national citizenship, acquisition of which has become conditional on language and other tests. Finally it explores the relationship between immigration policy and the promotion of social inclusion.

Key concepts

Managed migration; national interest; measurable targets; cultural change; skilled labour; internal controls; citizenship rights and obligations; British identity; social inclusion/exclusion

Introduction

In 2005, just before the general election, the government introduced a document entitled *Controlling our borders: Making migration work for Britain*, which set out what it called its five-year strategy for asylum and immigration. As its title implies, this contained the most explicit statement yet of the alignment of immigration policy to British interests. Prime Minister Tony Blair said in the foreword:

> This five year plan for our immigration and asylum system is based on three sound principles. It shows how we are going to enforce *strict controls to root out abuse*. It will ensure *Britain continues to benefit* from people from abroad who work hard and add to our prosperity. And, importantly, it puts forward solutions to a difficult issue which are *clear, workable and in the best interests of this country*. I believe it will meet both the public's concerns and our nation's needs. (Home Office, 2005a: 6; my emphasis)

This represented, in more narrowly utilitarian terms, a continuation of the policy of managed migration that had been foreshadowed in Barbara Roche's speech in 2000 in which she acknowledged Britain's dependence on migration. The 2005 statement represented a significant shift from the welcome for 'diversity' contained in the 2002 White Paper. Although it reiterated the government's commitment to the Geneva Convention, refugee status became temporary and conditional. The welcome for labour migration had never been unconditional. Roche had reiterated the importance of regulating entry 'in the interests of social stability and economic growth' (Duvell and Jordan, 2003: 302) and it was regulation that was central to this document.

Labour came to office in 1997 with a commitment to 'modernise' public services and this has been one of the driving forces of its migration policy. The government was determined to be seen as in control of policy, monitoring performance against clearly stated goals. The Blair administration aimed for an *integrated* approach to the governance of migration, with labour migration, controls and citizenship in an 'overarching framework' (Kofman, 2005a: 460). The obsession with targets has led to a focus on measurable goals such as the number of deportations rather than broader objectives.

A hardening of attitudes towards asylum and 'illegal migration' has occurred particularly in the wake of 11 September and the repercussions of the Iraq war. Achieving control in the complex world of migration has, however, proved extremely difficult. Immigration policy involves contradictory interests (see Chapter Five) and within government itself conflicting interests affect the ability of different departments to work in a 'joined-up' way and may even divide actors within a single department. This was exposed in June 2006 when, in response to a tabloid campaign about foreign prisoners who had been released without being deported, the Immigration and Nationality Department admitted that it had no idea how many foreign prisoners were involved. Two departments of the Home Office, the Prison Service and the Immigration and Nationality Directorate (IND), had failed to communicate with each other. Rather than question the agenda behind this press interest and the assumption that foreign prisoners should automatically be deported, the government promised tough action. Blair sacked the home secretary, Charles Clarke, co-architect of the New Labour revolution. His replacement, John Reid, immediately created his own hostages to fortune, denouncing his own department as 'not fit for purpose', and promising a radical overhaul.

A much less publicised scandal emerged the following month when a report for the Citizens Advice Bureau showed the reality of 'managed migration' for immigrants who are subject to it. The report drew attention to the 15-fold increase in the number of failed asylum seekers in receipt of the Section 4 support. Their research suggested that the NASS failed to respond adequately to this increase and during 2005 delay and error in the processing of applications became commonplace, resulting in 'numerous cases of avoidable and shaming destitution' (Dunstan, 2006: 1).

This chapter examines the meaning and implementation of 'managed migration' in Britain. The first section discusses the development of managing migration as a policy aim. The second focuses on the different elements of this policy: first, labour migration and the way in which the promotion of 'British interests' has been linked to those of business; second, the increase in controls, both external and internal with the involvement of an expanding range of individuals and groups in the surveillance of immigration status; and third, the reconstruction of British citizenship to play a more significant role in managing integration. This has embodied a tension between an acknowledgement of difference (multiculturalism) and a concept of Britishness to which immigrants are expected to conform. The final section discusses the relationship between current migration policy and social inclusion.

The goal of managed migration

> The challenge for the Government is to maintain public confidence in the system by agreeing immigration where it is in the country's interests and preventing it where it is not. (Home Office, 2005a: 5)

In this statement from the Five Year Strategy the government firmly linked its credibility to managing migration. The belief that it is both possible and desirable to 'manage' who comes into the country is part of a more general New Labour agenda in relation to public services. This has concerned itself with management through the development of measurable targets (performance indicators) and structural and cultural change within services (Newman, 2001).

When Labour came to office in 1997, there was a widespread perception of a crisis in immigration policy, particularly in relation to asylum. According to Flynn, Labour's drive for reform was a result of the increase in refugee movements and the 'vulnerability of immigration control regimes in the western countries' combined with the increased volume of international travel that made it difficult to check all entrants (2005: 466). Inefficiencies in the processing of applications had created a large backlog, so that some people waited for many years for a decision. Much of this crisis was, however, the result of the policy agenda itself, as asylum became more visible through the policy of creating an apartheid (Mynott, 2002) in relation to social support. Flynn (2005: 465) sees the main goal of policy as the reassertion of the capacity for state control.

Labour initially attempted to promote a more progressive agenda in relation to migration, recognising its contribution to economic and social life. Until 1997, the goals of the Immigration and Nationality Department (IND) of the Home Office had included 'to restrict severely the numbers coming to live permanently or to work in the United Kingdom'. A symbolic break with this thinking took place in 1997 when the first report on immigration under New Labour dropped this in favour of 'to regulate entry to, and settlement in, the UK effectively in the interests of sustainable growth and social inclusion' (quoted in Flynn, 2005: 464). One of Labour's first acts on gaining office was to abolish the primary purpose rule that had been used to discriminate against Asian people wishing to enter Britain for marriage (see Chapter Six). This suggested a shift towards a more positive attitude towards immigration and human rights. The first White Paper, the 1998 *Fairer, Faster and Firmer*, 'sought to identify its overall tone with progressive, anti-racist sentiment and eulogised Windrush' (Flynn, 2005: 473). A more decisive statement of the benefits of immigration was made in the White Paper *Secure Borders, Safe Haven*, published in February 2002, which claimed to be a 'new approach to immigration in modern Britain' and welcomed immigration as a source of economic and cultural enrichment.

By 2005, the emphasis was on Britain's interests to the virtual exclusion of other considerations. The growing emphasis on control represents an approach in which 'issues of asylum and economic migration are subordinate themes in a programme of reform which is aiming at *the comprehensive management of all forms of migration*, whether forced or voluntary' (Flynn, 2005: 464). This shift is reflected in the goals of the IND as promoted on its website:

• **Strengthen our borders**, use tougher checks abroad so that only those with permission can travel to the UK and ensure we know who leaves so that we can take action against those who break the rules.

- **Fast track asylum decisions**, remove those whose claims fail and integrate those who need our protection.
- **Ensure and enforce compliance with our immigration laws**, removing the most harmful people first and denying the privileges of Britain to those here illegally.
- **Boost Britain's economy** by bringing the right skills here from around the world and ensuring this country is easy to visit legally. (IND website, wwww.ind.homeoffice.gov.uk/aboutus/, accessed 1 August 2006)

In spite of the earlier statements of wider concerns, the agenda of control and selectivity has remained throughout the New Labour period. Scrutiny of marriage did not end with the abolition of the primary purpose rule. Labour refused to end the 'one-year rule' under which spouses (mainly women) entering through family reunion are dependent on their partner's status. This has led to widespread abuse of women forced to choose between deportation and staying in a violent marriage (SBS, 1997). As Flynn (2005: 305) suggests in relation to the 1998 White Paper, the mildly progressive elements were 'swamped' in an agenda that emphasised the reassertion of national state control over immigration procedures. It was preoccupied with sweeping away 'outdated and complex procedures that hinder genuine travellers and are vulnerable to abuse' and promoting a 'joined up' integrated approach using administrative and technological resources to promote efficiency (Flynn, 2005: 473).

The 2002 White Paper put a more positive gloss on labour migration but the assumption that good race relations depend on controls on immigration underpins the whole document. Its very title, *Secure Borders, Safe Haven*, embodies this approach. As Home Secretary David Blunkett states in his introduction: 'Having a clear, workable and robust nationality and asylum system is the pre-requisite to building the security and trust that is needed. Without it we cannot defeat those who would seek to stir up hate, intolerance and prejudice' (Home Office 2002a: 4).

The implementation of managed migration

A key element in the new managed migration has been institutional change aimed at breaking down previous ways of working. As Clarke and Newman suggest, managerialism involves 'not just a process of organisational restructuring but a large scale process of *cultural* change' (Clarke and Newman, 1997: 36). New Labour's strategy for improving performance has encouraged professional identities that are performance-orientated and organisation-based (Duvell and Jordan, 2003: 325). The new managerialism has been linked to the privatisation of key functions (Duvell and Jordan, 2003: 304); there has also been huge investment in technology, incorporating major private companies such as Capita in the development of computer systems.

One reason for the narrowing of the policy agenda has been the emphasis on 'measurable goals'. It is difficult to measure the impact of migration policy in general since there is no counter-factual evidence with which to compare it (Somerville, 2006: 23) and it involves many intangibles that are not subject to easy measurement. Policy has concentrated on areas where measurable targets can be found, such as asylum policy with its focus on deportation and detention.

Removals of principal asylum applicants increased by 91% between 1997 and 2005 (Home Office, 2006b: 6). Somerville claims that the prioritisation of this issue achieved 'some success in reducing unfounded asylum claims' that were more than halved and in the speed of completing the decision-making process (Somerville, 2006: 27). The pursuit of targets, however, has implications for the decision-making process, raising questions about the nature of these 'unfounded' claims. The system has created a 'rigid adherence to a timetable for decision-making irrespective of the quality of the decisions' (Flynn, 2005: 481). A report by the UNHCR in 2005 criticised the 'clarity, expertise and fairness of decision makers' on asylum claims.[1] Keith Best of the Immigration Advisory Service claimed that although roughly 20% of appeals are upheld, for some countries this figure is over 50%,[2] suggesting that decisions may be based on arbitrary grounds. Lady Mar, a member of the Immigration Appeals Tribunal, resigned in June 2006, claiming that the decisions were often 'meaningless'.[3]

This emphasis on targets also has implications for working practices within IND. Individual staff face pressure to meet targets on removals. Duvell and Jordan (2003: 316) quote one staff member as saying that 'as long as we are improving our removal stats [nothing else matters]. This is what ministers want.' An immigration department union official claimed in 2006 that the priorities set by the Home Office meant that 'other immigration offences are on the back burner'. Performance targets for senior managers mean that the focus of the organisation is geared towards meeting them. In his words, senior mangers explain to their staff: 'My job is on the line if I don't achieve my target for removing failed asylum seekers. That's the target I am being assessed on and that's the target I am going to put all my resources into'.[4]

This situation became apparent when Home Secretary John Reid announced a new drive to enforce controls in July 2006 (Home Office, 2006b) and called on the public to report 'rogue' bosses who employ illegal immigrants.[5] A report from the BBC's *Today* programme revealed, however, that when employers did report potential employees who came to them with false documents no action was taken by immigration officers who were too occupied in meeting removal targets.[6] It revealed that a survey of the 450 members of the Recruitment and

Employment Federation showed almost half had no confidence that decisive action would be taken against illegal working if they reported it.

In relation to labour migration, there has been an emphasis on promoting a business-friendly environment. The cultural shift has been most obvious in the change in the framework for managing work permits. The old system in which the Overseas Labour Section (OLS) of the Department of Employment dealt with applications had been a focal point for criticism. This section had dealt with applications for work permits on a rule-of-thumb basis 'relying on their own intuition' to determine whether there was a need for overseas workers (Flynn, 2005: 469). In the view of a Home Office official the work permit system existed 'primarily to safeguard the interest of the UK workforce' (Duvell and Jordan, 2003: 332). The system was characterised by delays and the business press was active in lobbying for a more efficient system (Flynn, 2005:470).[7]

As part of the new business-friendly culture, a new department, Work Permit UK (WPUK), was formed within the Home Office, whose goals are to 'provide high quality service, be more pro-active, meet the needs of British businesses' (Duvell and Jordan, 2003: 311). One WPUK manager described the priority as 'ensuring that big companies get the people that they want, that they get their work permits' (Duvell and Jordan, 2003: 312). The management capacity rose from 40,000 a year in the mid-1990s to over 200,000 in 2003 (Flynn, 2005: 465).

Businesses are the customers of this new improved service rather than the individual workers for whom work permits are applied for. The needs and rights of the people subject to the procedures imposed for managing these flows have been much less evident (Demos, quoted in Flynn, 2005: 485); as one official remarked, immigrants are 'just faceless to us' (Duvell and Jordan, 2003: 320). Although work permit applications have been speeded up, in other areas such as family reunion, delays have increased (Flynn, 2005: 482).

The establishment of the centralised body to provide support for asylum seekers, the NASS, involved the creation of a different culture. NASS deals with a group who are now viewed with suspicion and its establishment was part of a policy of deterrence. The aim has been to disconnect 'the performance of these tasks from the ethos of professions like social work and health care and the cultures of local authorities and the NHS' (Duvell and Jordan, 2003: 325). NASS replaced the role of local authorities, which had provided support for asylum seekers until 2000. Many had established asylum teams including social workers and other professionals to specialise in evaluating and providing support (Duvell and Jordan, 2001; Sales and Hek, 2004). These are now sub-contracted to NASS through regional consortia.

The system of legal advice on immigration has also been remoulded with the Legal Services Commission responsible for legal aid (Somerville, 2006).

Organisations providing immigration advice have been required to register, which involves meeting stringent conditions and the payment of a substantial registration fee. Performance targets have been introduced in this area. A general civil contract between the LSC and solicitors and not-for-profit organisations came into force in October 2006 and incorporates a performance indicator for the success rates at asylum and immigration appeals conducted under the contract.[8] Although this system was promoted to prevent poorly performing or dishonest legal advisers operating in this area, it has had the effect of excluding smaller companies, making it difficult for asylum seekers to gain access to appropriate legal advice (interview with immigration advice worker, 2 August 2005).

By staking its credibility on the ability to control and manage migration, the government has made itself vulnerable when it is not able to meet its own performance targets or to provide relevant data. This has led to constant organisational change within the IND. The five-year strategy was the result of a 'top-to-bottom analysis' of the immigration system that Blair had announced in 2004 (Somerville, 2006: 7) in response to criticisms that large numbers of failed asylum seekers remained in the country. Following the controversy over foreign prisoners in June 2006, a new 'root and branch' review was announced of the functions of the IND. This resulted in a new document entitled *Fair, effective, transparent and trusted: Rebuilding confidence in our immigration system* (Home Office, 2006b). As well as outlining further measures to prevent entry, it proposed organisational changes to make the Home Office 'fit for the future'. This requires it 'to change fundamentally the kind of organisation it is, the systems and processes through which it operates, and the way it does the job' (Home Office, 2006b: 14) in order to rebuild the trust of the public. Pay and rewards are to be linked better to 'roles and challenges, in order to create a unified, high-performance business' (Home Office, 2006b: 17).

Labour migration

> We will continue to allow a small proportion of those who come here to settle permanently where there is a clear economic benefit and where they are prepared to integrate socially. … restricting settlement for economic migrants to skilled workers only. (Home Office, 2005a: 8)

The opening-up of labour migration has presented a wider range of opportunities to migrant workers but selectivity in the entry and rights of labour migrants has meant that the impact has been uneven. Members of the European Economic Area (the EU members plus associated states) have free access to the labour market but for others rights have become more stratified

(Morris, 2002). In contrast to the welcome to labour immigration signalled in the introduction to the 2002 White Paper *Secure Borders, Safe Haven*, the most striking aspect of the proposals on employment was their limited nature. The main measures discussed were the Highly Skilled Migrant Programme (HSMP) and the Seasonal Agricultural Workers' Scheme, which had already been introduced through administrative means. Only one new measure was incorporated into the Act that followed – charging for work permits.

The HSMP programme allowed those who met the criteria to enter in order to search for work. It established a system of points based on qualifications, income and experience and aimed to allow 'those at the top of their chosen profession' the choice of settling in Britain (Home Office, 2002a: 43). This included a simplified process of application for inter-company transfers, board-level posts and posts related to inward investment as well as shortage occupations (Morris, 2002: 82). The number of points needed was reduced in 2004, but Kofman et al (2005) argue that it discriminated indirectly against women since they are concentrated in occupations such as the caring professions in which the qualifications and income earned make it unlikely that they would be able to reach the required level of points. Those without skills were offered only short-term stay without the right to bring in dependants, creating a new form of guestworker system.

There are a number of other legal routes to working in Britain (Ippr, 2004). The work permit scheme allows entry to take up a specific post if sponsored by an employer. This requires the employer to demonstrate that no local person is available. In addition, the Working Holiday Scheme allows Commonwealth citizens to stay for up to two years, and to work to support themselves for one year of this. The main users have been people from the Old Commonwealth, whose shared language and similar education systems facilitate employment in Britain and who have been a major element in the workforce in public services. There have also been specific schemes for domestic workers who have been allowed to enter as part of a family settling in Britain.

The five-year strategy signalled a change in policy, later outlined in *A points-based system: Making migration work for Britain* (Home Office, 2006c). It proposed to replace 'more than 80 existing work and study routes' with five tiers:

- **Tier 1**: highly skilled, for example scientists or entrepreneurs.
- **Tier 2**: skilled workers with a job offer, for example nurses, teachers, engineers.
- **Tier 3**: low-skilled workers filling specific temporary labour shortages, for example construction workers for a particular project.
- **Tier 4**: students.
- **Tier 5**: youth mobility and temporary workers, for example working holiday-makers or musicians coming to play a concert.

These tiers are based on absorbing existing schemes rather than any clear rationale of what is an economic migrant (Somerville, 2006: 38). The 75 points required for Tier 1, which replaces the HSMP, would exclude many professionals such as social workers who are unlikely to have sufficient earnings to qualify. Thus they will enter through the second tier, which necessitates a work permit. These can now be renewed for up to five years, after which permanent settlement may be granted. Overseas domestic workers are to be treated in a similar way to work permit holders, an improvement in their current position. The other tiers allow only temporary settlement. The youth mobility tier includes measures to ensure that stay is temporary. Non-EU students are automatically granted permission to take up part-time work on entry, a policy designed to attract more of this highly skilled group, and they may work for a year on completion of their studies.

Britain's policy towards accession countries, which differed from those of most other EU states in opening up the labour market immediately,[9] envisaged that workers from the accession states would replace unskilled immigrants from outside Europe. This has created new 'underclass' in hospitality, agriculture, food processing and domestic labour, where demand for labour is high. Immigration from these states has far exceeded official projections. In spite of their freedom to take up employment, A8 workers are required to register with a newly established Worker Registration Scheme. The official purpose of the scheme was 'to monitor the impact on our labour market of workers from the A8 countries'. It is widely believed that large numbers of workers fail to register, including those who have continued in informal employment. The Association of Labour Providers describes the scheme as costly and inefficient and the official figures as 'implausible' (ALP, 2005: 1). The government expected 15,000 annually, but the figures for August 2006 showed that 427,095 had registered with the scheme since May 2004 (Home Office, 2006a). The massive difference between the actual and expected numbers demonstrates the government's inability to plan and manage migration and led to renewed debate about the status of citizens from Romania and Bulgaria, which joined the EU in January 2007. The government announced in October 2006 that they would not have immediate access to the labour market as had A8 citizens, but would be confined to existing schemes.

As migration from the A8 countries has become legal through EU membership, their labour market situation has changed. As well as new entrants, many moved from illegal work to legal work after 2004. This group are now able to demand employment rights and the minimum wage and to become involved with trade unions (interview with TUC official, May 2006)[10]. They thus create a gap at the lowest end of the labour market for more precarious workers (interview with representative of the JCWI, May 2006)[11].

One response to labour shortages would be to speed up the entry of refugees into the labour market. Until 2002, asylum seekers were allowed to apply to work after their application had been in process for six months. Only the main applicant was allowed to apply. This 'concession' was revoked in 2002, in spite of a vigorous campaign on this issue from human rights activists and some employers' groups calling for them to be allowed to work immediately on entry.[12] The government has insisted on 'managing' the process of entry to the labour market and keeping economic migration and asylum rigidly distinct. It has been 'disinclined to admit that asylum-seekers might be enterprising, and indeed seeks to confirm this prejudice by withholding rights to employment and business activities' (Flynn, 2005: 480). It has, however, had to surrender some of its decision making in this area as an EU directive of 2003, allowing asylum seekers to work after one year, came into force in February 2005.

'Managed migration' involves attempts to control workers in the interests of business, which are increasingly conflated with the national interest. Different categories of migrant are expected to slot into prescribed categories. Within this framework, 'the migrant's duty is to be useful, first and foremost, to established business, and only after that to him/herself' (Flynn, 2005: 481). The emphasis on managing migration numbers has been separated from managing its broader impact. For example, the immigration of Polish workers has been encouraged but the impact on housing, education and other services has not been prepared for. A report by Slough Council stated that the government had failed to take account of new arrivals in its financial assessment for councils, on which much of local finance for services depends. Over the past 18 months it claimed that 9,000 new National Insurance numbers had been issued in Slough, of which just 150 went to British nationals.[13] Similar problems were reported in Crewe, when an employment agency based in the town opened an office in Warsaw that brought 3,000 new migrants within the space of a year to a town of 48,000.[14] Managed migration is concerned with labour rather than the needs of the people who are the bearers of this labour. Migrants are expected to 'manage' on their own, while the task of responding to their needs falls to local service providers and to networks of friends, family and communities.

Controls

We will require economic migrants to have sponsors … who share responsibility with us to ensure they leave at the end of their time in the UK.

…

There will be a new drive to prevent illegal entry, to crack down on illegal working and a tough policy of removals for those who should not be here. (Home Office, 2005: 6)

> We will 'export our borders', increasingly checking overseas people's eligibility to come here before they travel. (Home Office, 2006c: 8)

Controls on 'unwanted' migration have been central to the government's agenda and the most public face of managed migration. Increasingly this has conflated asylum seekers with 'illegal migration' so that reducing applications has been a priority (Somerville, 2006: 14). Figures for April–June 2006 showed that asylum applications had fallen by 15% compared with the previous quarter, to 5,490 (Home Office, 2006a). A range of measures have been put in place, including tighter controls over entry, which made it difficult to make an application as well as punitive systems of social support for asylum seekers, internal surveillance and detention and removals. Controls have often taken precedence over other goals. For example, the government's response to trafficking focuses on combating crime rather than supporting victims (UNICEF, 2004). Penalties introduced in the 2002 Nationality, Immigration and Asylum Act for not having proper documentation give an incentive to hide the method of entry and deter trafficked people from cooperating with the prosecution of abusers.

Controls on entry

Considerable investment has gone into preventing entry, through extending border controls and the use of more advanced technology. The five-year strategy in 2005 planned to 'fingerprint visitors who need visas, and those planning longer stays, before they arrive' and later biometric visas were promised 'to establish who people are and whether they are entitled to enter' (Home Office, 2006a: 8). This 'new focus on identity management' is to be combined with risk assessment to target activity on high-risk routes and traveller profiles. An 'authority to carry' scheme is proposed under which carriers will not have authority to carry people until this check has been made. This extends the involvement of non-nationals within the private sector in immigration control.

Enforcing removal

Deportation and detention have become 'essential' instruments in the 'ongoing attempt to control or manage migration to Britain' (Bloch and Schuster, 2005: 491). The number of people in detention for immigration purposes increased to 2,540 in the quarter to June 2006, of whom 1,825 were asylum seekers (Home Office, 2006d). Unlike an arrest warrant, the warrant to detain an asylum seeker, an IS91, can be completed by any immigration officer on behalf of the minister of state without further authorisation. It contains a checklist of 14 factors that may have been taken into account in the decision to detain, and officers are requested to tick any that apply (JCWI, 2006: 914). Campaigners suggest that that there is evidence that immigration officers tick these boxes arbitrarily without checking whether they apply.[15]

Detention centres were renamed 'removal centres' in 2002, 'apparently in an attempt to show people that if their asylum claim failed they would be removed' (Mayor of London, 2004a: 62) and as part of 'normalising' the process of deportation. There are now 10 of them operating in Britain. The 2002 Act introduced targets for the deportations of 'failed asylum seekers' (Home Office, 2002a: 65). In the quarter up to June 2006, 5,070 failed asylum seekers were removed, of whom 38% were classed as 'voluntary returns' (Home Office, 2006a) although the notion of voluntary needs to be judged within the context of the hostile climate towards asylum seekers. It is planned to reach a 'tipping point' in which more failed asylum seekers are removed than make 'unfounded claims' (Home Office, 2006b: 9). The government has increasingly seen human rights legislation as a barrier to British policy and counterposed to supposed 'British interests' and has attempted to remove barriers to deportation and removal, including a challenge to the European Court judgment of 1996 that people cannot be removed to countries that are considered unsafe. It has sought to develop 'memoranda of understanding' with governments of unsafe states to ensure that people can be returned 'in accordance with the obligations of the European Convention on Human Rights' (Home Office, 2006c: 11). It is also planned to make deportation the presumption for foreign national prisoners.

An area of particular concern is the detention of children. According to official figures, 40 children under 18 were detained under immigration law on 25 September 2004 (Home Office, 2005a: 9) and they have continued to increase since then (Owers: 2006). Detention of minors represents a breach of the UN Convention on the Rights of the Child (Lumley, 2003: 4).

The conflation of terrorism and asylum has been one of the most corrosive elements in recent discourse. The 2001 Anti-terrorism, Crime and Security Act (Home Office, 2001) empowered the secretary of state to order indefinite detention without trial of foreign nationals suspected of involvement in terrorism. Their numbers are small relative to those detained under immigration legislation, but many have spent many years in prison.

Internal controls

The home secretary suggested in the document *Fair, effective, transparent and trusted* that removals must use 'the best of the public and private sectors' (Home Office, 2006a: 2) and managed migration has involved an ever-widening range of people in carrying out controls. The exclusion of 'undesirable aliens' from welfare has been a key element in immigration policy since the 1905 Aliens Act (Humphries, 2002; Cohen, 2003), but asylum and immigration policy in the 1990s made welfare even more central as it set up a parallel system of social support for asylum seekers and tied entitlement to benefits more tightly to immigration status. In 1993, the government initiated an 'efficiency scrutiny' to ensure greater cooperation between the Home Office and other departments in detecting 'illegal immigration' (Cohen, 2003: 143) and this was followed by the development of employers' sanctions and greater involvement of a wide range of services in scrutinising immigration status (Owers, 1994).

This scrutiny often went beyond legal requirements as service providers, unsure of the legal position, attempted to cover themselves by refusing to take on clients who might not be entitled to services. The British Medical Association's ethics committee responded to the over-zealous behaviour of some doctors' surgeries by informing their members that 'all asylum seekers have the right to be registered with an NHS doctor and therefore there is no obligation or expectation for doctors to check the immigration status of people registering to join their lists' (cited in Coker, 2001: 38). This situation changed with the charging for health care of failed asylum seekers and other categories of immigrant introduced in 2004. Social services departments became the main agents for the provision of subsistence to asylum seekers following the 1996 Act, which removed benefits for in-country applicants. This involved making decisions about eligibility on the grounds of immigration status rather than need. This requirement led to a focus on establishing the credibility of the client's claim and thus to a relationship built on suspicion rather than trust. A social worker described their role as 'inquisitors' and as 'intrusion into people's lives'. She described the process:

> It's like a mirroring of what has happened to a lot of asylum seekers
> ... they have had to tell lies, to use their wits to survive, to get out
> of the situation that they have been in and come to this country.
> Then the social services department continues the interrogation.
> (Sales and Hek, 2004)

With the implementation of NASS, social workers and other professionals have become part of regional consortia operating the dispersal system. As Dunkerley et al (2006) found, this has intensified the ethical dilemmas they face. They quote one social worker as saying: 'We do have families that have been refused [asylum] and they have become overstayers. We have to report them to NASS. They will say they have to leave and we say we are not going to evict them because they will be on the street' (Dunkerley et al, 2006: 87).

Employers have also been tied into enforcement of sanctions against 'illegal working' and ensuring that temporary workers leave when their contract expires. The five-year strategy proposed the 'use of powers to demand financial bonds from migrants in specific categories where there has been evidence of abuse, to guarantee their return home' (Home Office, 2005a: 6); it also promised 'on-the spot fines for employers who collude with illegal immigration'. In *Fair, effective, transparent and trusted*, the Home Office proposed that employers be supported to ensure that they have 'robust systems in place' but penalised if they employ people illegally (Home Office, 2006b: 10). Members of the public were urged to report 'rogue' employers to Crimestoppers. The prioritisation of the removal of asylum seekers has, however, meant that this form of enforcement has been limited.

Incorporating the voluntary sector

A key aspect of recent immigration policy has been the cooption and incorporation of the voluntary sector through offering them an explicit role in service provision (Zetter and Pearl, 2000: 676). This has involved both refugee agencies (RAs), formal organisations with charitable status that work on behalf of refugees, and refugee community organisations (RCOs), often informal organisations run by and for refugee communities (Sales, 2002b). As refugee and asylum policy has become more repressive, the conflict between the government agenda and that of these agencies, which have been established to campaign and work for migrants' rights, has intensified. This issue was raised in particularly sharp form in relation to the deliberately punitive NASS system.

The establishment of NASS created a dilemma for voluntary sector agencies working with refugees and asylum seekers about the role they would play in the new structures (Bloch and Schuster, 2002: 411). The government planned that these agencies would play a key role in the provision of services in the new dispersal areas. Some voluntary agencies argued that involvement in the implementation of 'a system that is directly antagonistic to the interests of refugees' (Cohen, 2003) would give it legitimacy. Others, led by the Refugee Council, the largest agency working with refugees in Britain, favoured working with NASS, arguing that their expertise, knowledge and values would make the system more tolerable for the clients than if it were left to private, profit-making companies. The Refugee Council took the lead in 1999 in forming an Inter Agency Partnership (IAP) of agencies contracted to NASS.[16]

Regional consortia were established in dispersal areas to manage accommodation and subsistence for asylum seekers. These are local authority led but involve 'partners' including private landlords, registered social landlords and other service providers as well as refugee agencies. The role of these consortia was, however, strictly determined by central government policy and the key characteristic of these regional bodies is that they have 'responsibility without ownership' (Harrison, 2003).

Staff from refugee agencies act as 'reception assistants', providing advice and information to dispersed asylum seekers. They assist with filling in applications for support, which involve detailed information about such things as the method of transport used to enter the UK. This information is clearly sensitive, in view of the widespread clandestine entry. The answers provided on this form can prejudice the credibility of an asylum claim if they conflict with those given in the asylum application. Thus refugee agency workers are required to ensure that the applicants answer as truthfully as possible and to probe them on their stories. This makes it difficult for an asylum seeker to distinguish their role from that of an immigration officer.

Involvement in these contracts has wider implications for the independence of these organisations. It creates an organisational interest in the continuance of the system, since jobs and even the future of the organisation itself may become dependent on the contracts. The size of these contracts is considerable, with approximately £23 million received for asylum support in 2004–5 (Refugee Council, 2005b). It involves an accommodation to the culture and expectations within the partnership and acquiescence in the decision-making process in relation to the eligibility of asylum seekers for support that can lead to the eviction of 'failed' asylum seekers. The shift from a rights-based approach to a more professionalised involvement in providing contracted services also has implications for their campaigning role (Griffiths et al, 2005). The Refugee Council retains its campaigning role and has developed a strong critique of recent government legislation but this is a difficult tightrope to walk. Asylum seekers find it difficult to distinguish the role of voluntary agencies from the official NASS bodies, and tend to see the organisation as part of the general oppressive 'NASS system' (Hynes, 2007). Botero et al (2006) found that many refugees are reluctant to have further involvement with these organisations when they leave the NASS system on completion of their asylum claim.

Citizenship

The third arm of the managed migration project involves strengthening the meaning of citizenship. The White Paper *Secure Borders, Safe Haven* promoted the idea that citizenship was more than the formal acquisition of status and accompanying rights. It involved attaining a sense of belonging to the nation. It proposed 'citizenship ceremonies' for 'celebrating the acquisition of citizenship'.

One of the triggers for the increased concern with citizenship was the 'race riots' in some cities in the north of England during the summer of 2001.[17] These gave opportunities for the racist British National Party (BNP) to organise both at street level and within electoral politics. A report into these events suggested that white and Asian people were leading 'parallel lives' (Cantle, 2001) and called for the building of 'community cohesion'. Referring to the riots, the White Paper argued for the need to rebuild a sense of 'common citizenship' (Home Office, 2002a: 10). This necessitated some common understanding of what it means to be a 'British citizen'. As Blunkett stated in his introduction: 'To enable integration to take place, and to value the diversity it brings, we need to be secure within our sense of belonging and identity and therefore to be able to reach out and to embrace those who come to the UK' (Home Office, 2002a: 4).

The White Paper located the essence of British identity not in British history or institutions but in the 1988 Human Rights Act, enacted to bring European legislation into British law. It argued that the Act 'can be viewed as a key source of values that British citizens should share. The laws, rules and practices which govern our democracy uphold our commitment to the equal worth and dignity of our citizens' (Home Office, 2002a: 30). Universal and democratic values are thus seen as inherently 'British'. The 2002 Nationality, Immigration and Asylum Act added a new 'citizenship pledge' incorporating these values (below in italics) to the existing Oath of Allegiance that new citizens make:

> I [swear by Almighty God] [do solemnly and sincerely affirm] that, from this time forward, I will give my loyalty and allegiance to Her Majesty Queen Elizabeth the Second her Heirs and Successors and to the United Kingdom. *I will respect the rights and freedoms of the United Kingdom. I will uphold its democratic values. I will observe its laws faithfully and fulfil my duties and obligations as a British citizen.*

Those wishing to become British citizens are required to pledge allegiance both to the hereditary monarch and to democratic values. The ambiguity in this juxtaposition reflects the continuing limits to democracy embedded within the British state, not least the role of the monarchy itself. Appropriately in these circumstances, the first citizenship ceremony, in the London Borough of Brent in 2004, was attended by the heir to the throne, the Prince of Wales.

This ambivalence is evident in official constructions of national identity. The government claimed that 'British nationality has never been associated with membership of a particular ethnic group' and that people are not excluded from citizenship 'on the basis of their race or ethnicity' (Home Office, 2002a: 10). This account of British identity belies its racialised construction that was discussed in Chapter Six. The ethnic basis for *formal* citizenship status is relatively recent but exclusion on the basis of ethnicity and religion has been central to British national identity and to the rights enjoyed by British residents. British identity was forged during the nineteenth and twentieth centuries through the experience of empire, in which Britain ruled many of the countries from which contemporary immigrants originate. This tension is apparent not just in relation to immigrants but in the meaning of British citizenship for many who are themselves British citizens. It was not, for example, lack of acquaintance with British values or the English language that brought young British-born Asian men onto the streets in violent conflict with both the police and white gangs during 2001. Young suggests it was the reverse, as the 'widespread cultural inclusion followed by structural exclusion' (2002: 15) created the conditions for protest.

The government's uncritical adherence to particular understandings of British history and identity does not provide the basis for the inclusion of groups who have been historically excluded from the notion of British nationality and who continue to experience social and cultural exclusion. Research by Hussain and Bagguley with British-born Asian young men suggests that 'Britishness' and 'Englishness' are seen as racialised identities, while citizenship as an identity is not. Their respondents were able to draw on it as part of their own identity (Hussain and Bagguley, 2005: 409). Those born in Britain feel that their citizenship is their 'natural right' because they were 'born here' (Hussain and Bagguley, 2005: 411) but do not feel part of a common culture, first language, or robust set of values shared by British citizens (Hussain and Bagguley, 2005: 414). They have a strong feeling that they belong but perceive that the dominant white population do not fully accept that belonging (Hussain and Bagguley, 2005: 421). These negative experiences, however, enhanced the young people's sense of the importance of Britishness in relation to the rights of citizens.

The development of the modern British state has also been intimately tied to the development of Protestantism, and despite 'the pre-eminence of *ius soli*, full belonging was predicated upon belonging to the national church: Anglicanism and Englishness were fused together' (Cesarani and Fullbrook, 1996: 7). This has impacted on political rights, which have been 'restricted due to the confessional nature of the state' (Cesarani and Fullbrook, 1996: 7) affecting both Jews and Catholics during the nineteenth century. Religious discrimination in relation to formal citizenship rights largely ended in the nineteenth century, although in Northern Ireland, the local electoral system, which favoured Protestants, was abolished as late as 1969. Elements of that tradition remain, however. Under the 1988 Education Act all state schools are required to carry out a 'broadly Christian' daily act of worship, while the hereditary monarch, to whom new citizens must swear allegiance, is also head of the (Protestant) Church of England.[18]

The 2002 White Paper stated that 'it will sometimes be necessary to confront some cultural practices which conflict with these basic values – such as those which deny women the right to participate as equal citizens' (Home Office, 2002a). The difficulties of reconciling diversity with democratic values and women's rights have long been acknowledged by feminist anti-racist campaigners who have struggled against the acceptance of sexist practices in the name of 'traditional values' (Kofman et al, 2000). The White Paper, however, conflated the issue of forced marriage with arranged marriage in the public mind, combining a statement opposing forced marriages (Home Office, 2002a: 99) with the expression of a preference for marriage partners coming from the UK rather than abroad. Blunkett chose to make repeated statements about forced marriage during the consultation period of the White Paper, thus reinforcing the stereotype that arranged marriages were forced. This served as a cover for proposals that displayed a 'disturbing suspicion of the genuineness of marriage' (Yuval Davis et al, 2005: 519) and placed the whole issue of marriage with people living abroad under scrutiny, restricting the right of British citizens as well as non-citizens to choose a partner from any part of the world. The White Paper restated the significance of the probationary year for those entering through family reunion as a 'safeguard against abuse' and indeed extended it to two years, although it produced no evidence of this abuse.

Since 2002, there has been a hardening of the attitudes toward citizenship and criticisms of multiculturalism from a number of quarters, including from Trevor Phillips, the chair of the Commission for Racial Equality, the organisation established to promote it. It has been suggested that multiculturalism has 'gone too far' and that there is a need for a set of shared beliefs and values within the public sphere.[19] The attacks on multiculturalism may have been exacerbated by the rather mechanistic and insensitive way in which it has sometimes been implemented (Hewitt, 2005: 125–6). Hewitt concludes from a study of the area of south-east London in which Stephen Lawrence was murdered that some white people experienced themselves as 'having an invisible culture, of being even cultureless' (2005: 126). This 'backlash' has taken place in the context of a political centre ground, which is shifting further to the right with the abandonment by the Labour Party of traditional class-based politics and has been attractive to those living in areas that have lost many of their traditional male jobs. It has been most in evidence in areas that have relatively few immigrants or people from minority ethnic communities and thus little everyday social interaction with them.

This retreat from multiculturalism has become more strident in response to the growth of support for the BNP in certain local areas and the terrorist outrages in London in 2005. In contrast to the celebration of diversity promoted in 2002, official constructions of British identity have become more narrowly constrained as 'British values' are perceived by some to be under threat. The idea of a people 'at the end of their tether' is contained in the claim in the five-year strategy that the 'tradition [of] tolerance is under threat' (Home Office, 2005a: 5). Repeated demands have been made for Muslim 'community leaders' to pledge allegiance to Britain and to declare publicly opposition to terrorism.

This has been coupled with a growing concern with the obligations of citizenship. As the 2002 White Paper suggested, 'those coming into our country have duties that they need to understand and which facilitate their acceptance and integration' (Home Office, 2002a: 4). Demands are placed on new citizens that current citizens may find difficult to comply with. Many would, for example, have difficulty in taking an oath of allegiance to the monarchy. In 2005, a 'good character' test for citizenship was introduced in the Immigration and Nationality Bill (Home Office, 2005b), which extended the notion of loyalty.

New citizens are now required to 'prepare for citizenship' through passing tests in language and 'knowledge of the UK'. The language test involves reaching English as a Second Language (ESOL) level 3 in English or Welsh and includes understanding, speaking, reading and writing. Language is central to the enjoyment of the rights of citizenship and to participation in society and therefore to becoming full citizens. The ability to learn a new language, however, depends on age, gender, class and previous level of education and is particularly difficult for some groups (Sales, 2002b). The grounds for exemption, except for those over 65, are stringent. Knowledge of the UK is assessed through an on-line test involving 24 questions based on *Life in the United Kingdom: A journey to citizenship* (Home Office, 2004b).[20] These questions cover a wide range of issues, some of which are quite obscure, and most current British citizens would be unlikely to pass without considerable preparation.[21] In 2007, language and citizenship tests were extended to those applying for indefinite leave to remain. These tests therefore exclude potential citizens, and the most vulnerable are most at risk of failing. The importance of citizenship status, however, has increased as immigration statuses and the rights attached to them become more stratified.

Inclusion, exclusion and immigration policy

The borders across which migration is managed are becoming more numerous and complex and no longer confined to the physical frontiers of a country. They run between workers with particular skills, age groups, gender, ethnic groups and in different stages of the migration process and between 'genuine refugees' and 'bogus' asylum seekers. The path to citizenship is policed by new requirements, including language tests, 'knowledge of British society' and the possession of 'good character', placing the onus on immigrants to conform to what are claimed to represent core British values.

This raises contradictions between the promotion of inclusion, which has been at the centre of New Labour policy (see for example MacGregor, 1999;

Hills and Stewart, 2005), and the exclusions promoted by immigration policy. Social exclusion is a highly contested concept. It refers to various processes that prevent individuals and groups from participating in the rights that members of a social and political community would normally expect to enjoy. For migrants these include both formal exclusions (for example ineligibility for certain forms of benefits, restrictions on political participation) and informal processes, such as the impact of poverty or poor language skills on the ability to access services. Levitas (1998) identifies three discourses, which she calls **redistributive** (where poverty is seen as inhibiting social participation and the exercise of full citizenship), **social integrationist** (which emphasises integration through paid work) and **moral underclass** (which stresses moral and cultural causes of exclusion and notions of the 'undeserving' poor).

The predominant inclusionary discourse under New Labour has been social integration through paid work and the building of 'cohesive' communities. Labour-market policies for those accepted as refugees aim to integrate them 'more fully into UK society' (Home Office, 2002a: 37), but this route has been denied to asylum seekers, who are increasingly perceived in terms of a moral underclass. The Social Exclusion Unit, in its 2004 report, identified asylum seekers as at 'high risk' of exclusion (SEU, 2004: 25). They fall into all four dimensions of exclusion identified by the Centre for the Analysis of Social Exclusion (Burchardt et al, 2001: 31). These exclusions are not accidental but a result of policy. Politicians have manufactured a 'moral consensus' against asylum seekers through the use of language such as 'abusive claimant' (Morris, 2002: 91) that denies the legitimacy of their rights to be included. Furthermore, while spending on immigration control escalates, the funding for refugee integration is less than one per cent of the spending on asylum (Somerville, 2006: 45). This differential indicates that exclusion of the one rather than the integration of the other has been the priority.

According to Young (2002: 8), the 'underarching discourse [of the White Paper *Secure Borders, Safe Haven*] is social inclusion'. Indeed, the aim of promoting social inclusion is seen as applying not merely to new immigrants but to British citizens, including 'white working class communities whose alienation from the political process, along with their physical living conditions and standards of living, leave them socially excluded' (Home Office, 2002a: 10). This document, however, which remains the most wide-ranging official statement of immigration policy, promotes the social inclusion of the deserving while placing stronger boundaries of exclusion around those deemed undeserving. Their inclusion into mainstream society is denied either permanently (through deportation) or temporarily (until they have won a right to remain). This is particularly apparent in relation to asylum seekers.

Basing inclusion and cohesion on the exclusion of others raises fundamental contradictions at a number of levels. First, the subjection of asylum seekers to a punitive and stigmatising regime on entry to Britain produces profound dislocation and anxiety to people already experiencing severe loss as a result of exile. The experience of detention or forced dispersal prevents people from forming the links with communities that are part of the process of building a new life or from becoming part of 'cohesive' communities. Dispersal involves multiple exclusions through poverty, separation from community and difficulties in accessing services (Hynes, 2007). This delays the process of integration, which should begin on arrival (Refugee Council, 2004). For children, this problem is more intense as what may be a relatively short time for an adult can seem like a lifetime for a child, representing a significant part of their childhood (Refugee Children's Consortium, 2002: 1) and such delays have a long-term detrimental effect on their development. The policy introduced in 2005 of granting only temporary stay to those with refugee status prolongs the limbo that refugees experience while they are awaiting a decision, making it more difficult for them to put down roots.

In 2006, it was announced that free ESOL classes for adult asylum seekers were to be axed. The government claimed that the resources saved would be used for those whose applications had been successful. This move, by depriving people of the chance to improve their language skills will make it more difficult for them to pursue their asylum cases successfully. It also delays the process of integration for those granted settlement, who are the supposed beneficiaries of this process. The Children's Society warned that denying parents the chance to learn English would harm children since it would make parents more dependent on them for translation. Children, it reported, are forced to engage in inappropriate scenarios for example interpreting results of sensitive medical tests relating to rape or torture (Children's Society, 2006).

The denial of access to any form of income to asylum seekers who made their claim in-country (Section 55) represented a particularly extreme form of exclusion. Following the court hearing that declared this illegal, a spokesman for the organisation Liberty, which was a party to the case, said that the government policy towards 'those fleeing murderous regimes who seek a safe haven in the UK' had been to force them to 'beg, steal and prostitute themselves or face starvation in the streets'.[22]

Second, the increased scrutiny of these newly racialised groups feeds xenophobia, making all those who are visibly 'different' liable to have their rights questioned. The denigration of asylum seekers and of the concept of asylum itself, combined with policies that exclude asylum seekers ever more tightly from participating in society, undermines the basis for building cohesive, inclusive communities and 'feeds into and nourishes this racism' (Cohen, 2003: 46). The third and starkest form of exclusion is the detention and deportation of 'illegal entrants' and failed asylum seekers. This raises the contradiction between the exclusion inherent in immigration controls and a 'universalist commitment to the moral equality of humanity' (Cole, 2000: 2), which will be discussed in Chapter Nine.

Conclusion

Labour's managed migration policy raises the 'liberal paradox' discussed in Chapter Five. It juxtaposes the philosophy of the market and economic competitiveness that requires access for employers to the global labour market with 'social democracy's more traditional interests in training its own workers and maintaining generous social and labour protections' (Papademetriou, 2003: 44). Labour has attempted to resolve this apparent contradiction by imposing an increasingly tight and selective regime of controls on entry, while operating a more market-oriented labour-market policy. Social inclusion has been more and more narrowly defined, with the main route out of exclusion seen as through incorporation into the paid labour market rather than through broader notions of social justice and equality. Certain groups, particularly asylum seekers and those who enter through clandestine means, are denied routes to inclusion. At the same time, migrants are expected to conform to more prescriptive rules both in relation to the conditions of their stay and, for those seeking citizenship, in the notion of Britishness that they are expected to embrace.

Notes

[1] BBC Radio 4, *File on Four*, 21 June 2005.
[2] BBC Radio 4, *File on Four*, 21 June 2005.
[3] Reported in the *Observer*, 23 July 2006.
[4] BBC Radio 4, *Today*, 17 August 2006.
[5] Reported in the *Daily Express*, 26 July 2006.
[6] BBC Radio 4, *Today*, 17 August 2006.
[7] At a conference in October 2001 on 'The Business Case for Immigration', organised by the United Kingdom Race Equality Network, business leaders expressed concern at delays in gaining work permits for employees.
[8] Legal Service Commission website, www.legalservices.gov.uk/, accessed 1 August 2006.
[9] The Republic of Ireland and Sweden were the only other EU states to do this.
[10] Interview for 'Polish migrants in London and European enlargement: social networks, transience and settlement', research project funded by the ESRC, 2006–7, carried out by Louise Ryan, Rosemary Sales and Mary Tilki., Middlesex University.
[11] See note 9 above.

[12] The British magazine *Personnel Management* launched a campaign in 2001 to ease the restrictions on asylum seekers. The Industrial Society also condemned these restrictions in a report produced in 2002 entitled 'Poor reception, refugees and asylum seekers: welfare or work?'.

[13] Reported in the *Guardian*, 8 August 2006.

[14] Reported on BBC *Newsnight*, 20 January 2006.

[15] Bob Hughes, www.ncadc.org.uk, accessed 24 August 2006.

[16] The other agencies involved are Refugee Action, Migrant Helpline, Refugee Arrivals Project, Scottish Refugee Council and Welsh Refugee Council.

[17] See the first report from the government's Community Cohesion Unit, launched in 2003.

[18] The Archbishop of Canterbury has insisted that the next coronation will be Christian rather than multi-faith (report in the *Guardian*, 3 February 2003).

[19] See, for example, the writings by David Goodhart in, inter alia, *Prospect* magazine and the 'Euston Group'.

[20] This is priced at £9.99 and the test costs £34.

[21] A colleague, whose first language is English and who gained a PhD in Britain recently, failed this test at the first attempt.

[22] Press statement by Liberty, 3 November 2005.

Summary

- The New Labour government has attempted to modernise immigration policy on the basis of performance targets and cultural change in relevant departments.
- The focus on targets has led to an emphasis on measurable goals rather than more 'intangible' elements of policy.
- Immigration policy has become more narrowly focused on the 'national interest'.
- Managed migration involves a framework for labour migration, controls and citizenship.
- There has been increased differentiation in the entry and rights in relation to skills and country of origin.
- Controls have been extended geographically, in the use of technology and through the incorporation of wider groups in their implementation.
- The meaning of British citizenship has been extended with citizenship ceremonies and the notion of 'British values', but has become more difficult to acquire through the establishment of language and other tests.
- Immigration, and particularly asylum, policy conflicts with the goal of promoting social inclusion.

Questions for discussion

- Whose interests should immigration policy take into account?
- What responsibilities do (and should) service providers have in relation to immigration controls?
- What are the values on which British identity and British citizenship should be based?

Further reading

Duvell, F. and Jordan, B. (2003) 'Immigration control and the management of economic migration in the United Kingdom: organisational culture, implementation, enforcement and identity processes in public services', *Journal of Ethnic and Migration Studies*, vol 29, no 3, pp 299–336.

Flynn, D. (2005) 'New borders, new management: the dilemmas of modern immigration policies', *Ethnic and Racial Studies*, vol 28, no 3, pp 463–90.

Kofman, E. (2005a) 'Citizenship, migration and the reassertion of national identity', *Citizenship Studies*, vol 9, no 5, pp 453–67.

Morris, L. (2003) 'Managing contradiction: civic stratification and migrants' rights', *International Migration Review*, vol 37, pp 74–100.

eight

Living with immigration policy

Overview

This chapter explores immigration policy from the point of view of the people who are subject to immigration controls. It is based on the experiences of migrants as told to researchers and campaigners for migrant rights. The stories illustrate different aspects of living with migration policy and are mostly based on Britain. These include the risks people take to travel to Britain, the insecurity experienced while waiting for a decision on an immigration or asylum status and the implications of the increasing differentiation of social rights, for example the separate support system and dispersal for asylum seekers. Many of those whose stories are told have fought long campaigns to remain in this country, some of which have been successful, and some are still awaiting an outcome, while others have been deported.

Key concepts

Insecurity, limbo; dependence; loss of status; unaccompanied minors; trauma; campaigning

Introduction

This chapter looks at some of the human stories behind the policies discussed in earlier chapters. It discusses the experiences of people subject to immigration control and the impact it has on their lives. Many people become involved with immigration policy on a regular basis: immigration officers and lawyers and, increasingly, service providers, who are required to scrutinise immigration status as well as people who become involved in campaigns for migrants' rights. The focus here is on those who are the target of immigration policy, for whom it can make the difference between security and insecurity; the ability to settle and being socially and economically excluded; and in some cases between life and death. Immigration control involves a process in which those most affected by decisions may have little influence over them and have no part in making the broader policy agenda within which these decisions are made. They may receive little information about the reasons for these decisions and may wait months or even years during which their lives are placed 'on hold'.

The chapter concentrates on the direct impact of immigration policy itself rather than on more general issues involved in settling into a new society. The diversity of experiences of immigration policy has increased as civic stratification has widened the gap between different groups in relation to their rights and security of residence status. Those with skills deemed highly valuable gain secure status and may face only minor inconvenience as their visas and permission to work are negotiated, often by an agency or through their own company. For the unskilled, immigration controls may dictate where they work, how long they stay and whether their family is able to join them. The ease with which people are able to negotiate immigration controls also varies by nationality. As well as the formal rules that have, for example, made nationals of the EU A8 accession countries insiders in relation to the British labour market, the application of discretion means that informal processes of discrimination persist. For people of the Old Commonwealth, for whom a temporary period of work in Britain has become an accepted rite of passage, the process of getting a working holiday visa is generally simple (interviews with social workers from Australia and New Zealand, June 2004)[1]. Workers with similar skills from the New Commonwealth have, however, found their applications viewed with suspicion by embassy staff and this route has been effectively barred to them (RSA, 2005). For asylum seekers the process they undergo while waiting for a decision on their application has become deliberately punitive. Many experience periods of detention and the fear that they will be returned to the country from which they fled is ever present.

Not all stories are negative. Communities in remote villages as well as the more culturally mixed large cities have shown themselves willing to engage positively with migrants and to support them in their struggles to make a life in Britain. Migrants themselves, often including children, have been active in these campaigns and resisted attempts to deport or imprison them. Although controls are being ever more vigorously enforced, these campaigns have sometimes been able to make the authorities change a decision. This chapter uses interview material from research projects as well as other sources including literature from campaigns. The names used here are pseudonyms unless the names are in the public domain. These stories are by no means unusual or particularly extreme. They have been chosen to illustrate particular aspects of immigration policy and its impact on people's lives. Similar stories can be heard from the thousands of people who live with immigration controls.

Covert entry

> We were on a big boat and it was night time and the storm began, and then the waves started. ... The sails broke down and the ship started rocking. The boat was a small lifeboat, and everyone was squashed in and it was terrible. I remember lots of small kids, one was crying for his dad. His hands were tied to his dad as they were trying to get in, so the dad he let go of the rope so his son could get in, and the boy was crying because [his father] had died. One lady was dead on the boat next to me, loads of people died. We had no food or water and people were starving and thirsty. (Quoted in Hek et al, 2001: 11)

This description of his journey to Britain by a young Kurdish boy now attending a school in London illustrates the dangers that some people face in order to reach a country where they hope to find safety. With legal means of entry closed, even to those fleeing persecution and danger, more are forced to enter clandestinely, often relying on smugglers. One group of Afghan men who arrived in Dover in 2002 had all paid several thousand pounds to agents. They had not chosen to come to Britain, but this was where the agent had brought them. One described the journey:

> We were all men, it was too difficult for women to travel this way. We came in small inflatable boats and often we did not eat for several days. It was very dangerous, many people drowned on the way. In Yugoslavia the police set dogs on us and they bit into our flesh.

They had undergone this expensive and hazardous journey to escape danger. As well as the general situation of insecurity and abuse of human rights in Afghanistan, some had faced individual persecution. During the same period Britain was promoting voluntary return programmes to Afghanistan, offering cash and other incentives, as well as forcible deportation (interviews, Dover, 17 October 2002)[2]. Some people do not survive these journeys as the case of the 'Dover 58' illustrated. These 58 would-be Chinese migrants were found dead in the back of a container lorry in Dover in 2000 after being deprived of air during their journey to Britain.

For some, clandestine entry is less hazardous. Polish migrants who were not entitled to work in Britain before 2004 without a work permit mostly worked in the informal sector. They were able to cross borders fairly easily, developing strategies to avoid suspicion from immigration officers, presenting themselves as tourists rather than workers (Sales, 2006). One young man described the strategies he used: 'When I came here in January the immigration officer kept me for 25 minutes, asking everything, but this time I was smart, I booked my ticket for Sunday, so that he couldn't check on things' (young man, focus group, London, 2 October 2004)[3].

Waiting for a decision

Insecurity

> It took ten years to get refugee status and for all that period I could not leave the UK. I was in a sort of house arrest. I could not make any plans for the future. (Interview with African refugee, June 2004)[4]

One of the most difficult aspects of living with immigration control is the uncertainty created by the long wait for a decision on an asylum application or on leave to remain. People are not able to settle and may feel that they are living in limbo, unable to get on with their lives. Michael, quoted above, was a political activist from an African country. His fight for refugee status took so long because the British embassy in his home country insisted that the country was safe, in spite of reports by human rights organisations of widespread human rights abuse. During this period he remained in a state of insecurity, with the ever-present threat that he would be returned to a country where he had already suffered persecution and imprisonment and where he feared for his life. Another story, told by Mehmet, a Turkish asylum seeker interviewed in London illustrates the day-to-day uncertainty and fear that many live with. At the time of the interview, he was still waiting for a decision on his asylum claim:

> We keep getting six months' extensions to stay and this is how we are living. For four years now we have been getting extensions and now if suddenly they were to say you have to go back it would be very difficult. Orhan [son] is only 14 and the little one was only four months when we came here.

> Two years ago they sent a letter to the solicitor saying that I should go to Stansted airport to talk things through. When I arrived,

the immigration officer had all my documents, the ticket was all ready to send me back on the plane. The friend who came with me used to work with the solicitor so he was able to explain that I was seeking asylum as a political refugee. I had not been refused at that time. My friend said if you send him back on this plane, he will be detained. He managed to convince the immigration officer that they couldn't do this legally. (Interview, 2000).[5]

The uncertainty of the parents' status may affect the children. A teacher in London described the impact of this uncertainty on some of her pupils:

For many of them they don't know if they will stay or go. We have one kid here whose family have been here six and a half years. They still have no decision and have an extension until July. It's so unsettling they've moved about so much. The boy was sleeping on the concrete floor with one blanket, and the mother and the younger child had a mattress between them. They had no cooker or anything. Well they had been told that they were not entitled to anything. (Hek et al, 2001: 24)

Chronic uncertainty can lead to mental health problems, as they did for Mehmet's wife, Fatima: 'Fatima is having treatment for depression because every day she fears that somebody will send a letter or someone will knock on the door and take me away. She has been on anti-depressants for a long time.' For asylum seekers, this anxiety is a repetition of the trauma that led them to flee (see for example Silove et al, 2000). Moses Kayiza, who fled Uganda due to the persecution of gay people there, described the experiences in Britain that led to a breakdown in his health:

When I first arrived in the UK I thought things would get better. I felt that the UK would be a fair place as it was a more civilised and democratic country where human rights would be respected more than in Uganda. However, the constant grind of refusal after refusal in the asylum process as well as the way asylum seekers are treated in the UK wore me down both mentally and physically. This impacted on my fragile mental health after my experiences in Uganda. Eventually I was detained in hospital under the provisions of the Mental Health Act. (National Coalition of Anti-deportation Campaigns (NCADC), 11 August 2006)

Mental health problems may not appear immediately on arrival. Ahmad, a Kurdish refugee from Turkey, began to show symptoms of depression only after he was granted refugee status:

> For those first two years life was very very hard. I didn't earn any money. After two years, I got my decision. I found a good job, I earned good money. My wife and children joined me. Life was easy. But I got sick with depression. I went to the hospital, and they gave me medicine. (Interview, 2000)[6]

He explained that while he was in London on his own he just carried on, but once his family were able to join him and he was emotionally more settled he started to get symptoms of depression. When he was no longer preoccupied with the day-to-day struggle for survival and security, he felt ready to face the traumatic experiences he had undergone. It was almost as if he 'relaxed' into the depression.

Loss of social status

The loss of status as a result of being unable to work and dependence on benefits can be a major source of distress. Two refugees who had high-status jobs in their country of origin explained how they felt. Joe had been a journalist in an African country. When he arrived in Britain he claimed asylum and applied for support from NASS, which proposed to disperse him to Sheffield. He was unwilling to go since he had read media reports that refugees had been attacked in the city. He refused to leave London but, deprived of official support, he had to fend for himself in finding accommodation and food. He become dependent on people he met in places where refugees congregated, such as international call centres. Although they were casual acquaintances, they allowed him to stay with them and he spent months sleeping on sofas in overcrowded conditions:

> Initially I felt like an outsider, unwanted, completely depressed. It was a very sombre experience, very difficult to cope with. No food, nowhere to sleep, no way to get a job. I have always worked for my living … I became someone who was always receiving from others and that was a very difficult experience for me. (Interview, June 2004)[7]

Once he had acquired refugee status, he was able to enrol on a postgraduate course. He has financed his studies by working as a security guard, an occupation in which many educated Africans now find work. He has been unable to find employment as a journalist because of his lack of work experience or references in Britain. In spite of his secure immigration status, he remains deskilled. Michael, already mentioned earlier, had worked as a manager in his home country and found the change of status very difficult at first:

> We had our own house, we had people who were working under us … My son found it difficult to see us living in this way, becoming servants and cleaning for other people. He could not accept it. But I was prepared to do anything because to me taking money without working is not acceptable.

The scrutiny that migrants face as they try to establish their status is another aspect of this loss of status. People face questioning not only from immigration officers but, as internal scrutiny of immigration status has extended, from more and more service providers. In a research project on the work of an asylum team in a London borough, members of refugee community organisations complained of the way asylum seekers were treated by front-line social workers. Typical comments were 'they ask all sorts of unnecessary questions' and 'they feel interrogated like criminals'. Another said: 'Refugees are interviewed as if by immigration officers or police officers. If you have a gold ring, they tell you you are not destitute. The staff members don't want to treat people properly' (quoted in Sales and Hek, 2004: 69).

The psychological importance of being free of this kind of scrutiny was emphasised in a focus group of young Polish migrants, which took place soon after EU accession.[8] Before May 2004, when coming to Britain for work they had had to use strategies to deceive immigration officers and convince them that they were visiting as tourists. One young man described his feelings now when travelling between London and Poland: 'I feel that what has changed is travelling home and coming back here. When I came back from my last holiday it was so much easier, I wasn't asked all those questions, I didn't have to go through that terrible process.' As one young woman said: 'We used to feel like rats who had to scurry around and keep out of sight. Now we are free to move about openly. I feel a great freedom, now. I feel like a normal human being.'

Unaccompanied minors

Asylum seekers under the age of 18 arriving alone (unaccompanied minors) are a special case in British immigration law. Children who enter with a parent or an adult deemed by the authorities to be responsible for them are dealt with as part of the family in relation to their asylum application and are supported through NASS and subject to dispersal. Unaccompanied minors, however, have remained the responsibility of local authority social services departments, which are obliged to provide care and accommodation under the 1989 Children Act.

Unaccompanied minors must make an asylum claim in the same system as adults (see Chapter Four). If they lose their case they can remain in care, but face deportation when they reach the age of 18. Uncertainty about their asylum claim thus dominates their lives and undermines their confidence about the future (Kohli, 2001: 31). Asylum-seeking children have no automatic right to legal advice; winning an asylum claim depends on establishing 'credibility' and without proper advice and support, children can jeopardise their claim by failing to present their case within the terms required.

Mahdi Hidari from Afghanistan, who came to Britain as an unaccompanied minor in 2002, is a member of the Hazara tribe, who are persecuted in Afghanistan. He fled Afghanistan after he was detained and ill-treated by the Taliban. His asylum hearing took place when he was 16 years old and he attended alone without any accompanying adult. In spite of his history of persecution, the adjudicator took the view that Mahdi was not a 'credible witness' and rejected his claim. He later appealed but despite 'compelling' evidence his appeal was refused.[9]

Without proper representation, minors may be given misleading advice by people on whom they rely, which can damage their case. Miri,[10] an orphan from Vietnam, came to Britain in 2005 at the age of 15. Family members had paid for her to travel with an agent. On arrival, the agent advised her to tell the immigration authorities that she was aged 19, although she has no idea why. In spite of this claim, social services recognised that she was a minor and took her into care. She attended classes in a voluntary centre for refugees. Her teacher descried her as 'a brilliant student. She spoke no English when she arrived but she is speaking it really well now, and she was my best student in maths.' Five months after Miri arrived, she was arrested and detained in Yarl's Wood Detention Centre from where she was deported to Belgium where she had made a brief stop on her way to England. Under Dublin II, as an unaccompanied minor, she should not have been deported because she had made no asylum application there (see Chapter Five) and her case demonstrates some of the problems with that agreement. Her teacher, who visited her in the detention centre, described what happened:

> The immigration authorities insisted on basing their decision on her original claim that she was 19 even though she clearly looked only 15, and she even had a birth certificate confirming her age as 15. She was utterly distraught. Even the staff at the centre were embarrassed because they could see that she was too young to

be held there. She did not want to go to Belgium and knew no one there.

For unaccompanied minors, the formal transition to adulthood at 18 is particularly daunting. As well as coping with the usual problems of growing up, they lose their entitlement to care and may lose their right to remain in Britain. Rather than looking forward to their eighteenth birthday, they may dread its approach (Dennis, 2002: 15). They are expected to find their way in an adult system, often provided with a minimum of information. Those who have already lost their claim to asylum face immediate deportation. If the claim is outstanding as they reach this critical age, they face dispersal and the loss of friends and support networks (Stanley, 2001: 5). Some young people choose simply to 'disappear' rather than face dispersal, a risky choice that can lead to crisis, destitution and homelessness (Mayor of London, 2004a: 21). Mahdi from Afghanistan lost his accommodation and subsistence from social services on reaching 18 but was saved from destitution by the support of friends.

Roy Ekundayo Ajala came to Britain from Nigeria when he was 11. He joined his parents, who were already in the country, after he had been abused by his uncle in Nigeria. He travelled on a false passport but had no idea at the time that he was being brought in illegally. In Britain, Roy's father also abused him physically and sexually and his mother colluded in the abuse. He and his brother were taken into care. He made an asylum application in his own right but his application was refused on the grounds that he did not fit the Geneva Convention categories of persecuted groups. Roy received treatment for depression. When he reached 18, he became homeless, unable to work or claim benefits and faced deportation. In the eyes of the law, he had changed from a vulnerable child in need of protection into an adult requiring removal. With the help of friends, Roy launched an appeal to remain. Speaking on a video for a campaigning organisation, he described how he felt as he waited for his case to be decided. His words illustrate the problems of the rigid adherence to the notion that 'adulthood' begins at 18 in the case of asylum seekers:

> I keep saying to myself, when am I ever going to relax and just take it easy, to come home to a family, say goodnight to somebody. Half of the time I'm talking to myself. … I want somebody to take some of the load. … I've got the feeling I've got to grow up too fast. I'm already 18 and all I want is to be a child, just for someone to come and look after me, but that's not possible. One thing I keep asking is who am I in society, who am I in the community … But I am a strong man that's one thing I definitely know I am.[11]

Separation of families

Separation from family members can be the most difficult price imposed by immigration law. Metaphors of the nation often characterise the state as protecting the national home from outsiders (migrants), with the territorial boundaries of the state enclosing the private space of the nation (Bhattacharya, 1997). In claiming to maintain the integrity of the national home, states can violate the private life of those deemed 'outsiders'. Immigration law may prevent, or impose heavy conditions on, family members joining people living in Britain or deny the right of partners to live together in Britain.

The primary purpose rule discussed in Chapter Six prevented many spouses and fiancés from the Indian sub-continent from entering Britain, causing 'great hardship' (JCWI, 1997: 13). Cases were often decided on the basis of the entry clearance officer's assessment and tended to use western notions of romantic love to judge whether a marriage was 'genuine'. Thus 'arranged marriages' became conflated with marriages of convenience to secure settlement in Britain. In the case of Zuber and Khatija Latif, which began when this rule was in force, their marriage was based on love. They nevertheless had to fight a long campaign to prevent their separation.

Box 8.1: Zuber and Khatija Latif

Khatija was born in Britain and Zuber in India. They met while they were both students but both sets of parents objected to the proposed marriage since they came from different religious groupings. Khatija's parents held her captive in their home for several months, subjecting her to mental and physical abuse in an attempt to force her to marry a 'suitable' husband. She escaped and later married Zuber, but he remained under threat of deportation for many years. His leave to remain had run out while she was being held by her family and the marriage for which Khatija suffered so much was treated as 'suspicious' by immigration officials. They insisted that if they wanted to live together, they should both go to India, a country with which Khatija had no ties and where Zuber was estranged from his family due to his marriage. The stress of this long period of uncertainty, combined with the estrangement from her family, meant that Khatija became severely ill with depression. Zuber was finally given leave to stay in November 1999, after 12 years in Britain.

(Information supplied by Zuber and Khatija Latif.)

The rules governing the rights of various categories of refugee may also separate families. If they enter together they can claim asylum as a family, with the husband as the main applicant. If they enter alone, they may be separated from family members not only while they wait for a decision, but after a decision has been made. Only those granted full refugee status are entitled to bring in family members and this extends only to dependants (spouses, minor children and in some cases older parents). Many Somali women who entered Britain in the 1990s came alone, often having become separated from their husbands and other family members during the civil war. Unable to meet the conditions for refugee status since they were not considered to have faced individual persecution, they were granted the secondary status of Exceptional Leave to Remain. This did not give them automatic rights to family reunion, which was conditional on four years' residence and having adequate housing and income to support the other family member(s), a condition that it was almost impossible for them to meet. Many subsequently managed to regain contact with family members but were unable to bring them in. Interviews with Somali women in London revealed that, for most, family separation was the worst problem that they had to cope with. Many had suffered brutality and lost family members in horrific circumstances. This separation deepened the losses they had already endured and made it difficult to put down roots and to plan a future (Sales and Gregory, 1998). As one woman put it, 'I don't feel complete without my husband.'

Families are defined narrowly in immigration law and generally only spouses and dependent children are allowed to enter as part of family reunion or under EU labour mobility rules. This can cause separation from the extended family, which can be particularly difficult in periods when family members are in need of care (Ackers, 1998). Turkish-speaking refugees in London, for example, were often deprived of the support of their own mothers during the birth of their children, leaving them isolated in an unfamiliar system (Hoggart et al, 2000).

Dispersal

Dispersal was introduced specifically as a punitive measure to deter asylum claims. By controlling the movement of asylum seekers and cutting them off from networks of support, this system creates multiple exclusions (Griffiths et al, 2005). It prolongs the period of limbo before they are able to rebuild their lives.

Dispersal involves a lottery for individual asylum seekers who may be located in an area with which they have little connection and where the development of community organisations is weak. The implementation of the policy was led by the availability of housing rather than the original plans of 'clusters' of language and ethnic groups (Hynes, 2007). This housing was generally 'unpopular' and 'hard to let' and concentrated in deprived areas. The Audit

Commission (2000a) in an early review of dispersal found inadequate support structures outside London, both from statutory and voluntary services. Subsequent research has shown that access to services remains uneven and limited (BMA, 2002, 2004; Rutter, 2003). Lack of community structures also deprives asylum seekers of practical help such as interpretation, and the lack of social support exacerbates isolation and depression. For people with particular health needs, dispersal can be dangerous. The National Aids Trust (2006), for example, found serious concerns about the health of asylum seekers with HIV.

Some dispersal areas had previously had no significant minority ethnic populations and the sudden arrival of asylum seekers has meant they have been highly visible and vulnerable to racist attacks.[12] The removal of the 'concession' that allowed asylum seekers to apply to take up employment after six months meant that they often had little to do and with no money to spend they were often forced just to 'hang around'. This enforced idleness increases their visibility, revealing their lack of work and dependence on benefit (Boswell, 2001).

Many people have left the NASS system rather than face compulsory dispersal, often returning to London where they have friends and networks of fellow nationals. Joe, for example, was able to survive with no state support with the help of friends. Single men have generally found it easier to survive outside this system than women, particularly those with young children. Dunkerley et al quote a nurse who describes how the inflexibility of the system put the life of a pregnant woman and her unborn child at risk:

> We had one woman who was dispersed and she was in the late stages of pregnancy and she was actually due the next week. And they told her if she didn't get on the train, she'd miss the house here. She thought her other children needed to be in a house rather than a bed and breakfast hotel in London. So this woman she had a miscarriage. (Dunkerley et al, 2006: 85)

Detention

Detention has been an increasing element in the treatment of asylum seekers, with the numbers detained passing 2,500 in June 2006. Detention or imprisonment is highly stressful and even more so for immigration detainees for whom it is generally a prelude to deportation. Between April 2005 and 31 January 2006, 185 people in immigration removal centres self-harmed to the extent of requiring medical treatment, and three killed themselves.[13]

Her Majesty's Inspector of Prisons, Anne Owers, in a report of a visit to Yarl's Wood Immigration Removal Centre (IRC) raised 'significant concerns about aspects of safety in the centre' and stated that removals were being carried out without proper planning or warning to the people involved (Owers, 2006:

5). She was particularly concerned at the detention of children and suggested that 'there was no evidence that children's welfare was taken into account when making decisions about initial and continued detention'. There were 32 children held at the time of the visit, seven of whom had been there for more than 28 days. In an earlier report on the Dungavel Detention Centre in 2003 she had raised similar concerns:

> We are separately concerned about the welfare and development of children within a locked-in custodial setting, where there is a high level of insecurity, and without the freedom to engage with wider society and establish other social and cultural relationships. It remains our view that, however conscientiously and humanely children in detention are dealt with, it is not possible to meet the full range of their developmental needs. (Cited in Lumley, 2003: 6)

Owers interviewed 13 children detained at the centre in 2006 and 'their comments and fears illustrate potently the distress of detained children and their anxieties about their current and future situation' (Owers, 2006: 14–15). Some spoke about the intimidating nature of the process by which they were brought into detention:

> When they came to the house like an earthquake the way they knock. I think there were ten of them spread all around our house … The way they look at you is like you are a criminal … My two hands were cuffed in front. (Aged 13)

> I was sick on the van. But they would not stop the van even to be sick or for fresh air. (Aged 10)

Some described staff as friendly but most found the situation intimidating:

> The officers are tall and scary – their shoes are big and noisy. (Aged 10)

> This morning they shouted at us, I don't know why. My six year old brother was frightened, we're not criminals. (Aged 10)

Parents from 16 families with children held at Yarl's Wood went on hunger strike on 27 July 2006. After speaking to some of those involved, Nellie deJongh of the National Coalition of Anti-Deportation Campaigns reported that they could no longer take life behind the wire. Their main concern was for their children and they did not understand why they were being incarcerated indefinitely. One parent said:

> It is like they have put us in a small box, with the intention of forcing us to go back to our countries which are not safe. As I am on medication that I need to take with food I have stopped taking any medication. We are tired of being treated less than human beings, the ill treatment of our wives and children must stop. They deserve to be treated with human dignity.[14]

In the same month it was reported that some breast-feeding mothers had been detained in the centre separated from their babies. One, a Vietnamese mother married to a British citizen, was snatched from her Birmingham home. A last-minute reprieve allowed her to challenge the decision to deport her. The other, a Turkish asylum seeker, was detained although she was married to a refugee and therefore entitled to be in the UK. She later described her feelings: 'I have had terrible experiences in Turkey but this was worse. I thought constantly of my son. I cried all the time. It has taken my son some time to settle down after my return.' Both women have subsequently been released. When the cases were raised by Lord Avebury, the Home Office minister claimed that officials had mistakenly ignored Home Office procedure.[15]

Deportation

The renaming of detention centres as Immigration Removal Centres in 2002 signalled the intention that detention was aimed at facilitating faster deportation – or in the new, more clinical, phrase 'removals' – of failed asylum seekers and others whose cases for remaining in Britain have failed. The New Asylum Model allows for the fast-tracking of the process for nationals of particular countries, reducing the time spent in considering individual applications. The National Coalition of Anti-Deportation Campaigns reports that while deportations took up to six months to arrange in 2005, by 2006 they could be completed in a few days. They also claim that the pressure to meet deportation targets is leading to more women and children being deported, since women are seen as easy targets, 'always at home and not likely to put up a fight'.[16]

The prioritisation of removals brought an increase in their numbers, which exceeded 2,500 for the first time in the quarter up to June 2006. The largest number, 690, were deported to Iraq, with 265 deported to Afghanistan. Iraq remained highly dangerous in this period, with a monthly toll in 2006 of several hundred civilian deaths due to the conflict. A report by Human Rights Watch dated May 2006, posted on the UNHCR website, described rising insecurity in Afghanistan as the Taliban are again resurgent while attacks on civilians that constitute 'serious violations of humanitarian law' are widespread.[17]

As the government attempts to develop 'memoranda of understanding' in order to deport people to countries where human rights abuses are known to be widespread, serious concerns are raised about the safety of some of those returned to countries that the Home Office now deems safe. Muhammad Osama Sayes was forcibly returned to Syria after his asylum application failed. He received a 12-year jail sentence from the 'notoriously unfair' Supreme State Security County that convicted him of being a member of the banned Muslim Brotherhood in a trial that fell far short of international standards. According to Amnesty International, 'This is a glaring example of what happens when countries like the UK fail to offer protection to asylum-seekers: incommunicado detention, unfair trials, draconian jail sentences and a real risk of torture' (quoted in the *Guardian*, 2 July 2006).

Mary[18] was involved in political activity in support of the opposition in Uganda. According to a report in the *Guardian*, she left the country after being kidnapped, raped and tortured, first by the insurgent Lord's Resistance Army and then by the Ugandan Defence forces. She was refused asylum and faced deportation with her daughter Ella. She has been treated by the Medical Foundation for the Victims of Torture for Post-Traumatic Stress Disorder and epilepsy caused by the beatings she received in captivity. The Home Office says that 'depression and mental illness cannot amount to inhuman and degrading treatment even when a condition deteriorates on return'. Expert opinion from Dr Ben Knighton, an academic specialising in East Africa, testified to human rights abuses in Uganda and the likely fate of returned asylum seekers:

> The pattern is very simple. A failed asylum seeker, with a deportation certificate, arrives at Entebbe airport and is handed over to one of the security organisations. If suspected of political dissident activities, the person is taken to a safe house for questioning. Rape, for young women, is inevitable. Children over three – Ella's age – are taken from their mother and put in an orphanage. Detention can last weeks, or months; a number of people have 'disappeared' from custody.

The fear of deportation can lead people to desperate action. Ramazan Kumlaca was awaiting deportation to Turkey when he hanged himself in Campsfield House IRC in Oxfordshire on 27 June 2005. He was born in Turkish Kurdistan and feared that his life would be in danger if he were returned. Ramazan was only 18 when he took his own life because he was 'in despair at his impending removal from the country'.[19]

Poverty and destitution

Immigration law restricts access to benefits and other services for different categories of migrant, creating poverty and social exclusion for those unable to find adequate employment. Dependent spouses are unable to claim benefits in their own right in their first year, making them financially dependent on their partners. For asylum seekers who are banned from paid employment in their first year, the social support level is set below normal benefit levels. Many work in informal, often highly exploitative, work although finding such employment has become more difficult with dispersal outside London.

Poor accommodation exacerbates the effect of low income. A survey of asylum-seeking families in London found serious problems of damp, disrepair, infestation, security, safety and overcrowding (Mayor of London, 2004b: 16–17). The child of an asylum-seeking family interviewed in school described the conditions in which his family of six lived:

> We live in a little flat. We only have two rooms, and in one the little ones are sleeping. My little brother and sister, my other little sister and my mum, and sometimes my older brother until he got his flat, so there are about six of us. There is no space. There is one living room and the kitchen and there's a lot of us trying to do our homework. Sometimes the little ones are noisy and chat. But my mum always tells them to shut up and get on with your homework. (Hek et al, 2001: 16)

Asylum seekers have found it difficult to access services. Over half in the London survey had no information about how to register with a doctor or enrol a child in school (Mayor of London, 2004b: 16–17). They often have poor language skills and do not understand that they should register with a doctor. A member of a Chinese community organisation explained:

> Two people came to see us yesterday. One had severe stomach ache and the other chest pains. They are both young people, they must be in their early 20s. ... Their language skills are very poor. Nobody explained to them in Chinese that they need to register with a GP so when you get ill you can go to see a GP and be referred to hospital. We need to encourage them to be more proactive rather than waiting till it's too late and they say 'I don't know where I can seek help'. (Director of Chinese community organisation, 8 December 2006)[20]

'Failed asylum seekers'

Asylum seekers lose their NASS support when their appeal fails. Israfil Shiri, a gay man from Iran, was evicted by NASS following the Home Office's rejection of his appeal. Denied a home and benefits and without the right to work he became totally destitute. He was unable to get access to the medication that he needed and was unable to eat without bleeding and vomiting. On 23 August 2003, he walked into the offices of Refugee Action in Manchester, doused himself in petrol and set himself on fire. He died 10 days later. As the flames were put out, he screamed that he did not want to die and he did not want to be sent back to Iran. The court returned an open verdict rather than suicide.[21]

Failed asylum seekers can claim Section 4 support under certain circumstances (see Chapter Six). A report for the Citizens Advice Bureau (CAB) revealed serious concerns about the operation of this support (Dunstan, 2006). Daniel, an elderly Kenyan, was granted this support following the intervention of the CAB after four months in which his claim had been lost and mishandled by NASS. He was now receiving £35 per week in the form of Luncheon Vouchers and lived in accommodation provided by a private landlord contracted to NASS:

> On the kitchen floor, a plastic bowl slowly filled with water leaking from a hole in the ceiling. In the bathroom, Daniel showed us the two sources of this deluge: a cracked sink and broken toilet bowl. In his bedroom, where paper peeled from damp, mouldy walls, he pointed out another: the water tank in a cupboard. Around both this cupboard and Daniel's bed – for which he had been given a thin duvet but no sheets or pillowcases – the carpet was sodden. (Dunstan, 2006: 3)

The charging of failed asylum seekers and other migrants for health care from 2004 has also led to severe hardship. A Refugee Council report on this new policy includes the following cases:

> E, a young woman from China was turned away several times by her local NHS trust, who told her that unless she could pay them several thousand pounds upfront, they would not support her through the birth of her baby. She gave birth at home, with no medical care, and then both she and her baby had to be admitted to hospital with serious health problems relating to the traumatic birth. Once discharged, the hospital continued to send E bills,

which frightened her so much she fled her home. The whereabouts of her and her child are not known.

H is Rwandan, and when he came to Refugee Council he was living on the street and destitute. He had bowel cancer and a colostomy bag from a previous operation. Not only had the Trust refused to provide care without advance payment, his local GP was refusing to register him. (Kelley and Stevenson, 2006: 12)

People may not seek medical help for fear that their status will be reported and they could be deported. The manager of a Chinese community centre in London described the case of an illegal worker who had sought help.

We had a young man, 28 years old, who went to work in this factory. He had hand cut off and all they did was take him to hospital, stick a bandage over the stump. Because of the shock they found that he had diabetes and also HIV. And then he received a letter, through the hospital from the Home Office saying that he should get out of the country. ... He came to us asking for help to find a doctor. (Director of Chinese Community Centre)[22]

Many children find it difficult to gain access to adequate schooling. Dennis (2002: 7) reports that nearly half of the children participating in a survey had not been offered a school place. The imposition of targets and league tables for children's performance in national examinations has exacerbated this problem, making some schools reluctant to admit asylum-seeking children, who are seen as potentially costly in resources and who may not achieve in examinations without support. Some children spend long periods being educated through voluntary projects, rather than in mainstream schools.

The inability to attend school can be serious for children who may already have faced interrupted schooling and be struggling to learn the language, making it difficult for them to catch up. Schooling is also important socially. According to the BMA, research indicates that 'the most beneficial event for a refugee child can be their becoming part of the local school community, with its attendant benefits of learning and making new friends' (BMA, 2002: 9). Jill Rutter, an expert on refugee children's education, argued that 'for refugee children, inclusion within mainstream education has special significance. Attending school may be a therapeutic and normalising experience for a child whose recent life experiences have been far from normal' (Rutter, 2003: 9). The proposal in the 2002 Nationality, Immigration and Asylum Act to educate asylum-seeking children living in accommodation centres separately was condemned by a large number of MPs and by the largest teachers' trade union, the National Union of Teachers, and many children's charities.

Refugee children's experience in schools has often been positive. Schools are recognised and valued by most refugee communities, unlike other agencies, such as social work, which may be unfamiliar and be treated with suspicion. An Ofsted report in 2003 found that '[M]any asylum seeker pupils make good progress in relatively short periods of time and almost all made at least satisfactory progress. The combination of their determination to succeed and the strong support of their parents provided a potent recipe for success' (cited in Mayor of London, 2004a: 44). Many schools, especially in large cities, have developed specific policies to support refugee children. Research in two London schools showed that in the school where there was a greater commitment to this, students felt comfortable about talking about their own experiences and identifying themselves as refugees. Fewer reported bullying, and they did not feel stigmatised as refugees (Hek et al, 2001: 28).

Young asylum seekers

Unaccompanied minors are the responsibility of local authorities which must provide them with care and accommodation. There is a great deal of good practice (Hek, 2002; Kohli and Mather, 2003) but breaches of human rights legislation routinely occur, particularly in the treatment of older teenagers, placing them at risk of abuse (Cemlyn and Briskman, 2003). Age is crucial in determining the treatment they receive but many do not have correct documentation and may not know their correct age. There is no reliable medical test and children may be held in detention if their age is disputed (Barnardo's et al, undated). Even for those whom the authorities accept are minors, age affects how they are cared for by social services. Many social services departments are reluctant to treat older teenagers as 'children in need'. They are 'often treated with suspicion at worst and at best are assumed to be too "street wise" to need "looking after"' (Morris, J.,2003: 40) in spite of a court judgment in 2003 (the 'Hillingdon judgment') that reiterated local authorities' duty to support all unaccompanied minors under Section 20 of the 1989 Children Act.

Most children aged 16 or 17 are supported under Section 17 of the 1989 Children Act, often in unsuitable and poor quality bed and breakfast accommodation (Mayor of London, 2004a: 15). Some children have been placed in hostels with adults who take drugs or have mental health problems (Mayor of London, 2004a: 16). Many are housed outside the borough and experience problems in gaining access to legal advice, interpreters and support networks and may face hostility from the local population (Mayor of London,

2004a: 25). Younger children may be accommodated in children's homes or with foster parents. A young man interviewed in a London school was living with an English family but did not feel comfortable with this. He did not speak English well enough to communicate with them properly and he felt that they did not make any effort to get to know him or to find out about his background: 'At home everyone is speaking English and I don't understand them. They don't know about me. It's difficult' (Hek et al, 2001: 17).

Campaigning

Some of the stories discussed earlier have been the subject of local or national campaigns, some of which are continuing. These have involved large organisations such as trade unions and national campaigns, as well as friends, neighbours, fellow students and colleagues. They have taken place across Britain, in rural areas as well as large cities. In 2006, villagers in the Shetland Islands off Scotland's north-east coast came together to support a Thai man facing deportation who had come to Britain at the age of 10:

> Shetland's close-knit community is furious about plans to deport a 23-year-old Thai man. Sakchai Makao may be a convicted criminal, but after 13 years on the islands he is one of them. A group of friends established a fighting fund to prevent the deportation. One night, with hundreds of the crowd in tears, a friend sent round buckets and the crowd produced more than £2,300. (*Guardian*, 19 June 2006)

The crime for which Sakchai was convicted dated back to February 2002 when, aged 20, he set fire to a car and a portable building belonging to a local fishmonger, causing damage estimated at more than £40,000. Nevertheless, the proposal to deport him, at the height of a media furore about released foreign prisoners who remained in Britain, incensed the local community. At the other end of Britain, in Weymouth in the south-west of England, the Kachepa family, who fled from Malawi to seek asylum, won huge local support in their campaign against deportation (see Chapter One).

Some of these campaigns have been successful. Zuber and Khatija Latif campaigned vigorously for many years, speaking at public meetings and lobbies about Zuber's case while pursuing legal appeals. The family gained all-party support from their local council, Hackney, as well as from local individuals and organisations. The Conservative mayor, Councillor Joe Lobenstein, made an urgent appeal to the home secretary to allow the family to stay in the UK. The support of all these groups was seen as important in Zuber's successful appeal. Following his discharge from hospital, friends and supporters helped

Moses Kayiza to develop a campaign to stop his deportation, supported by the Transport and General Workers' Union, Manchester City Council and thousands of individuals. Moses won his appeal in 2006. Roy Ekundayo Ajala, who was threatened with deportation to Nigeria, also waged a successful campaign to remain in Britain. The Kachepa case shows, however, that even high-profile support may not be enough to protect vulnerable people. The family were deported soon after the general election in 2005.

Schools have often been the focus of campaigns, as pupils resist the removal of friends and classmates. A report on a campaign based in a Rochdale school to save six children from deportation described it as the latest in a 'string of locally-organised campaigns against the removal of children from schools ... [where they have] become part of the community' ('School fights pupils' deportation', BBC News, 6 June 2005)[23]. A few months after the interview with Mehmet, he received a letter saying that he was to be deported at the end of the week. The family, with the support of the children's school, organised to halt the deportation. Teachers and pupils wrote letters to the Home Office describing how well they were settled and the severe impact that losing their father would have on them. Mehmet was finally given leave to remain.

Muyeke Lemba from Angola led a successful campaign to stop the deportation of her family with the support of her school and local organisations. She was 15 when, with friends Mansanga and Feliciana Nanga, who were also at risk of deportation, she spoke at public meetings in her local London Borough of Hackney and to a 1,000-strong audience of the full conference of National Union of Teachers as well as on radio programmes. She described her experience for a campaigning website:

> The government had sent a letter to my Dad saying we have to leave the country ... I took it very seriously and was very upset, we all suddenly became closer to each other ... People who knew our case were so supportive, they wrote petitions, letters to the Home Office, we had meetings, and people from different coalitions helped ... I was able to take care of the campaign and school work.

Her teacher, Angela Sibley, described how Muyeke and her friends grew in confidence during the campaign:

> At the beginning they were very anxious. In the end it wasn't a problem, because even though they were nervous, they had a strength and determination. Even though they were very shy and lacking in confidence they had this drive that, if something was

necessary and right to do you just got on and did it. I think it's a survival mentality that people develop if they've been through hard times. (From Schools against Deportation website)[24]

Mahdi Hidari from Afghanistan has received support from staff and students at Canterbury College where he is studying IT. He was detained in July 2006 pending deportation but was released on bail when supporters provided him with a bail address and sureties. They have set up a campaign to fight against his deportation. At the time of writing his fate is uncertain

Conclusion

Migrants have shown themselves able to win support from a wide variety of individuals and groups, including some unlikely sources. Government policy attempts to deprive asylum seekers of their humanity, making them faceless numbers rather than human beings. The existence of these campaigns demonstrates the continuing possibilities of solidarity between people. They also help to explain the government's determination to keep asylum seekers apart from society through dispersal and the removal of asylum-seeking children from mainstream schooling. As the government's focus on numbers and targets drives the system towards greater dehumanisation, the human faces behind these numbers sometimes refuse to disappear.

Notes

[1] Interviews for 'SMILING' project, funded by European Commission, 2003–4.

[2] Interviews for 'Professional capacity of Afghans in the UK' project, funded by Refugee Action and International Organisation of Migration, 2002.

[3] Focus group, for 'Polish migrants in London and European enlargement: social networks, transience and settlement', research project funded by the ESRC, 2006–7, carried out by Louise Ryan, Rosemary Sales and Mary Tilki.

[4] Interview for 'SMILING' project, see note 1 above.

[5] Interview for 'Civic stratification, social exclusion and migrant trajectories in three European cities', project funded by the ESRC, 1999–2001.

[6] See note 5 above.

[7] Interview for 'SMILING' project, see note 1 above.

[8] See note 3 above.

[9] NCADC, www.ncadc.org.uk, accessed 23 August 2006.

[10] Information supplied by teacher, 7 June 2005.

[11] http://tv.oneworld.net/article/view/104576/1/, accessed 23 August 2006.

[12] For example the *Manchester Evening News* reported an attack by nine people on a Kurdish asylum seeker in Salford, in which his leg was broken (*Manchester Evening News*, 25 April 2005).

[13] Figures supplied by NCADC, January 2006.

[14] NCADC, www.ncadc.org.uk, August 2006.

[15] Reported in the *Guardian*, 18 August 2006.

[16] Reported in the *Guardian*, 9 June 2006.

[17] www.unhcr.org, accessed 24 August 2006.

[18] The story is reported in the *Guardian*, 23 August 2006. In December 2006, it was reported that a Home Office official, who is also a leading activist in Uganda's ruling party, has been suspended following allegations that he has blocked asylum applications from Ugandan nationals (*Guardian*, 18 December 2006).

[19] 'In memory Ramazan Kumluca', Bob Hughes for Campaign to Close Campsfield, Monday, 22 July 2006, www.ncadc.org.uk, accessed 24 August 2006.

[20] Focus group with Chinese community organisations, London.

[21] *Institute for Race Relations News*, 26 October 2004.

[22] See note 20 above.

[23] http://news.bbc.co.uk, accessed 7 May 2006.

[24] www.irr.org.uk/sad/haggerston/hagg.htm, accessed 7 June 2005.

Summary

- Immigration policy affects people's lives both before and after their arrival.
- Many migrants risk their lives in order to enter Britain and other western countries.
- The period of waiting for a decision on immigration or asylum status creates anxiety and insecurity as people are unable to rebuild their lives.
- Unaccompanied minor asylum seekers face particular problems at the age of 18 when they are deemed to move from being 'children in need' to adults who may be dispersed or deported.
- Migration policy frequently separates families.
- Immigration detention has become routine and frequently includes children, violating international obligations.
- Asylum policy has led to poverty, destitution and difficulty in accessing services.
- Many people risk their lives rather than face being sent home.
- Migrants have led many successful campaigns against immigration controls.

Questions for discussion

- How does uncertainty of immigration status impact on people's lives?
- Does contemporary asylum policy meet international obligations in relation to the rights of children?
- What prompts 'ordinary' people to become involved in supporting migrants' right to remain?

Further reading

Kelley, N. and Stevenson, J. (2006) *First do no harm: Denying healthcare to people whose asylum claims have failed*, London: Refugee Council.

Mayor of London (2004a) *Offering more than they borrow: Refugee children in London*, London: GLA.

National Coalition of Anti-Deportation Campaigns (www.ncadc.org.uk).

Rutter, J. (2003) *Working with refugee children*, York: Joseph Rowntree Foundation.

nine

The future of immigration policy: immigration controls, immigration and citizenship

Overview

This chapter draws together some of the key ideas in the book and then explores the basis of different views on migration policy. It focuses particularly on the arguments for the abolition of immigration controls, and examines these from the point of view of their ethical, economic and social implications. The chapter discusses the tensions between universal values, which make exclusion on grounds of place of birth unjustifiable, and the need to define entitlement to social and political rights. It suggests that this could be resolved by making residence rather than place of birth the relevant criterion. The chapter ends by suggesting that a debate is urgently needed that questions the 'taken for granted' agenda of controls.

Key concepts

Human rights; consequentialism; nationalist; cosmopolitanism; universal values; liberal paradox; migration without borders; post-national citizenship

Introduction

This chapter both draws together some of the ideas developed in the book and discusses alternative views of immigration controls. For the past century, the imperative of maintaining strict control on entry has been an assumption of policy making that has been taken for granted in Britain and increasingly in other developed countries. The practical and ethical problems associated with immigration policy, however, demand that this view is questioned rather than accepted as obvious. The chapter firstly summarises some of the issues discussed in earlier chapters. It then examines in more detail the approaches to immigration that were outlined in Chapter One. Finally, the case for open borders is discussed, including arguments from ethical, economic and social perspectives.

Current immigration policy making

Managed migration has become the dominant policy of states in the developed world. While markets in goods encompass every corner of the world and global communications bring visions of opulent western lifestyles to the poorest places on the planet, the ability to exercise mobility is becoming increasingly selective. Inequalities in the global economic and political system and the conflicts these generate have precipitated international movements on a scale that matches the mass migration associated with the industrialisation of the major powers in the nineteenth century. Governments in the rich countries attempt to separate out 'wanted' from 'unwanted' migrants, competing for skilled workers, who are given privileged entry and rights of settlement, while the poor are blocked from entering the most desirable destinations. New hierarchies are developing based on skills, wealth and country of origin. For example, as Polish people move to Britain in search of work, their place in Poland is taken by people from Ukraine and other states to the East whose economies are unable to provide them with an adequate living. Meanwhile, emigration from Britain exceeds immigration for long-term settlement[1] as British people seek better lives elsewhere.

Individual states remain the most powerful determinant of policies on immigration and citizenship even though globalisation of trade and investment, together with the development of regional and international policy-making institutions, erodes national sovereignty in other areas. Immigrants, by challenging the permeability of national borders and boundaries, have become the visible symbol of globalisation and the insecurities that it brings in its wake. Through managed migration and the re-forging of notions of national citizenship, nation states are attempting to reassert control over their borders and to redefine the boundaries around the nation.

State rhetoric in relation to immigration policy presupposes a 'natural' and unchanging nation around which borders are constructed. In practice the 'nation' rarely accords with the geographical or legal borders of the state. Still less do the borders bequeathed by colonialism in Africa, Asia and the Middle East reflect national, ethnic, geographical or historical entities. These arbitrarily imposed boundaries are at the root of much current conflict in these regions. The shifting contours of British and EU citizenship in the post-war period illustrate the distinction between borders and boundaries around the nation, such as for example the distinctions that were made between citizens of the Old and New Commonwealth, including the former and excluding the latter. The tension in current policy between the acknowledgement of diversity and the attempt to develop a particular notion of British identity reflects this confusion.

The complexity of contemporary migration flows is breaking down the dichotomies between countries of emigration and countries of immigration, between temporary and permanent migration and between forced and voluntary migration. Immigration policies, however, force people into particular statuses that may not reflect individual migratory strategies. Managed migration sees immigrants as atomised individuals, whose migration can be controlled through rules imposed by immigration countries. In attempting to gain the benefits of migration and rid themselves of its costs, these policies treat migrants as units of labour rather than as human beings with needs, aspirations and social relationships.

Although policies towards economic migration are driven by narrowly constructed notions of national self-interest, the major states continue to adhere to the Geneva Convention on Refugees, which is based on humanitarian principles. Increasingly strict control of national borders, however, has restricted the possibilities of claiming asylum. The low recognition rate for asylum applications may suggest unfounded claims or reflect the narrow criteria on which these decisions are made and the sometimes arbitrary quality of decision making. The Geneva Convention definition, which requires claimants to prove a well-grounded fear of persecution based on their membership of particular groups, excludes many people who face imminent danger if returned. National and international preoccupation with return and the increasingly temporary status accorded to refugees constitute a potential threat to their safety and the principle of non-refoulement.

While states attempt to restrict entry, the development of settled migrant communities has forced them to develop policies towards incorporation and to define paths towards citizenship. As citizenship and its associated rights have been opened up for some groups but not for others, the rights of different categories of migrant status have become increasingly stratified.

The recurring 'crises' at the British Home Office illustrate some of the problems involved in managing migration. The 'headline' figures of deportations and asylum applications are amenable to measurement, but governments have shown themselves signally unable to provide figures, or even rough estimates, for other aspects of migration policy. For example no data is kept on exit, so there is no way of knowing how many migrants remain after their visa has run out or when their application has been turned down. It has been officially acknowledged that large numbers remain illegally; an official estimate in 2005 placed this figure at 430,000 (Somerville, 2006: 32). The controversy in August 2006 over the much greater than expected numbers of people from Eastern Europe registering with the Workers' Registration Scheme showed not only how widely the government had underestimated the extent of this migration,[2] but also the lack of available information on those migrants who had not registered but were nevertheless living and working in Britain.

Meeting targets is costly in financial and human terms. Huge sums are spent on staff and technology to deter and detect migrants. A widening group of public and private service providers are required to check immigration status. This surveillance itself has potentially perverse results, as it conflicts with other goals that require free movement of people, goods and information. The cost to migrants is huge. It is borne by those who travel in dangerous conditions, live in insecurity and fear and are denied social rights and by those who are detained and expelled. Many incur a huge financial cost in payments to smugglers but the cost to their psychological health as a result of insecurity, separation from family and home, and loss of status may be greater. Some pay with their lives as did the 'Dover 58' in 2000.

The current debate on immigration policy

Migration has been high on the political agenda of most developed states for several decades. Public debate has been characterised by the narrowness of boundaries around what is considered legitimate. This flows from the 'peculiarities' of immigration policy (Sciortino, 2000) and its relationship with the construction of national identity and national security. In Britain, the nature of the policy-making process and the bi-partisan consensus on the need for controls that has prevailed for much of the century since 1905 have served to restrict debate. The opening-up to economic migration by western countries in the twenty-first century has not been matched by a corresponding openness in the terms of the debate.

Public discussion of immigration since the late 1980s has been dominated by asylum, which has often been confused with immigration in popular perception (Lewis, 2005). Gibney (2001: 7) suggests that the end of the Cold War shifted asylum policy from 'high politics' (matters of national security) to 'low politics' (matters of day-to-day electoral politics, including employment, national identity and the welfare state). Asylum seekers are increasingly projected as competing for jobs and resources, rather than as victims of persecution. The focus on maintaining tight controls and on 'bogus asylum seekers' and 'benefit scroungers' has fed the perception that immigration is inherently dangerous and unwelcome, undermining support for those forms of immigration that governments consider welcome.

This restrictive policy discourse on immigration and asylum is not just a response to real or imagined public hostility, but creates and nourishes this type of sentiment. As Saggar (2003) argues, the 'race card' thesis has come to be accepted uncritically as an element in British politics. The history of the development of immigration controls suggests, however, that the racialisation of immigration policy was not a response to popular pressure, but arose out of the racialisation of the state itself. Gibney claims that political elites believed that controlling asylum was the key to electoral victory and that the 'roots of restrictive asylum policies' lay in this perception (2001: 7). This view ignores the role of these political elites in setting the agenda. Immigration policy itself, for example by excluding asylum seekers from mainstream society, has helped create the 'problem' of asylum and made it visible.

The 'securitisation' of migration in the wake of the terrorist attacks of 11 September in the US and Britain's 7 July shifted asylum back to the 'high politics' of national security. Border controls have become 'naturalised' in the United States as the notion of 'homeland security' suggests the need to protect the national home. The PATRIOT Act was aimed at silencing debate in the name of protecting the nation against terrorism. In Britain, terrorist attacks have brought measures to impose greater control not only over immigration but also over British citizens suspected of responsibility for 7 July and the alleged plot to destroy aircraft in August 2006. There have been repeated conflicts between the government and the judiciary over the implications for human rights legislation of the detention of suspects and the deportation of alleged terrorists. In an echo of earlier colonial administrations, the government has attempted to involve Muslim 'community leaders' in controlling 'their' communities and ridding them of potential terrorists in their midst. This unequal 'partnership', however, does not allow discussion of the key issue that is widely perceived, not just by Muslims, to be at the root of these outrages: British foreign policy in relation to the Middle East and the 'war on terror'.

In spite of the conventional wisdom and opinion poll evidence that there is overwhelming support for immigration controls, the reality is more complex. Public opinion is formed in the context of a wider political discourse. The restrictive agenda has given little space for more positive views on immigration. In Britain, politicians, while attempting to combat the growth of support for racist parties in some areas, have legitimised their rhetoric through claiming to sympathise with their concerns about immigration. The national press has predominantly supported this position. Local newspapers, however, have often given more sympathetic coverage to these issues (Lewis, 2005), reporting, for example, instances where local people have come together to defend the rights of neighbours and friends. The majority of academic research and commentary has been broadly 'pro-migrant' and critical of current policy making. A growing number of groups campaign for migrant and refugee rights, including major refugee and immigration voluntary agencies, religious groups and individual anti-deportation campaigns. Trade unions have in general changed from hostility to immigration to becoming advocates of migrant and refugee rights, often campaigning for individual members, as they did in some of the cases discussed earlier. These local campaigns suggest that when people have real social contact with immigrants and asylum seekers, they often reject the idea that they do not belong.

The practical and ethical failures of contemporary policy have led some to challenge the basis on which it is constructed. The idea of an amnesty for irregular immigrants was debated briefly within Parliament in 2006 before being summarily ruled out by ministers. The case was made by the think tank the Institute for Public Policy Research (Ippr, 2006) and has been supported by other voluntary agencies and trade unions including the largest trade union, the Transport and General Workers' Union.[3] Amnesties, which have been widely used in other EU countries, challenge one of the assumptions at the heart of managed migration policies, namely that those who flout controls should not be allowed to benefit from this. Another challenge to accepted wisdom came from the Countess of Mar, a cross-bench (independent) peer who was for more than 20 years a member of the Immigration Appeals Tribunal. She told the *Observer* newspaper:

> If I had my way, what I would say to these folks is come to our country and you are very welcome if you find yourself a job and accommodation within six weeks, if you keep our laws and don't demand health service treatment immediately, and after so many years you can come into the system – and if you can't do that you get sent back immediately. (*Observer*, 23 July 2006)

The case for open borders is being made more widely from a range of perspectives within academic and popular campaigning literature (eg Cole, 2000; Hayter, 2000; Harris, N., 2002; Cohen, 2003). A report from a UNESCO research programme in 2003 summarised the arguments for Movement without Borders (MwB). It described this scenario as morally desirable in relation to human rights and argued that its '[u]nfeasibility should not be uncritically taken for granted' (Pecoud and de Guchteneire, 2005: 1).

Views about immigration control

The variety of views about immigration policy reflects the different interests of individuals and groups in relation to migration flows as well as different political and ethical stances. The typology developed by Ruhs and Chang (2004) outlined in Chapter One provides a useful framework for discussing different approaches to immigration control. They suggest that conflicting positions are divided in relation to two key issues:

- Whose interests are most important in immigration policy making, those of the migrant-receiving nation or those of migrants?
- Should attention focus on the consequences of migration or on individual rights regardless of their possible consequences?

The first concerns the degree of 'moral standing' accorded to non-citizens (Ruhs and Chang, 2004: 83). Ruhs and Chang distinguish between nationalism at one end of the spectrum, which would give non-citizens minimal rights, and cosmopolitanism at the other, which favours equal rights for migrants and citizens. The second issue concerns the degree of 'consequentialism'. From the 'consequentialist' point of view, the real or assumed impact of migration is what should decide policy. The 'minimally consequentialist' position is concerned with the consequences of policy for individual rights rather than with their actual outcomes for individuals or communities. Ruhs and Chang use these distinctions to develop four 'ideal type' positions:

- **consequentialist nationalists** are concerned with the impact of migration on the nation;
- **consequentialist cosmopolitans** are concerned with the global consequences of migration;
- **rights-based nationalists** place the rights of nationals above those of migrants;
- **rights-based cosmopolitans** place the rights of migrants on an equal footing with nationals.

An extreme version of the consequentialist nationalist position is articulated in this statement by David Coleman of Migration Watch. Discussing claims that free movement of labour might double global GDP, he suggests that: 'speculations are ... irrelevant to the UK case. The imagined increase in global GDP per head accrues entirely to third world countries, to some extent at the expense of first world incomes' (cited in Kearns, 2004: 2–3).

Managed migration policies reflect consequentialist nationalism as states seek to gain the benefits of migration while avoiding its (real or perceived) costs. The consequences that they estimate, or assume, tend to conflate the interests of the nation with the interests of particular groups. Harris (1996) uses a consequentialist cosmopolitan position to argue for the free movement of labour on the grounds of its potential to expand global income and welfare.

Bob Rowthorn is a 'rights-based nationalist' who opposes migration on the grounds that nations 'have the right to shape their own collective future as they see fit, and to resist developments that undermine their identity and sense of continuity' (cited in Kearns, 2004: 3). Rowthorn argues that immigration will harm the interests of British workers in relation to wages and employment. This argument has been used to criticise Britain's open-door policy for A8 nationals, which some have argued reduces wages for unskilled British workers who compete with them for jobs.[4] As Ruhs and Chang point out, the interests of different groups within a nation are not uniform and those focusing on the interests of workers are likely to favour a lower level of immigration than those favouring business interests. They suggest that the widespread policy of 'benign neglect' over illegal immigration is, in effect, based on an ethical framework of 'employer-rights-based nationalism' (Ruhs and Chang, 2004: 88).

The UN Declaration of Human Rights is an example of 'ethical cosmopolitanism' and its obligations may clash with the state institutions that are the guarantors of these rights (Ruhs and Chang, 2004: 84). A number of individuals and non-state organisations argue for open borders on ethical and political grounds (Cole, 2000; Hayter, 2000; No Borders Campaign). Cohen argues that this is a fundamental principle and that arguments in support of migration based on the (assumed) benefits that migration brings are problematic because 'if the facts were to go against them (and facts change) then their argument against controls would disappear' (2002: 248). Campaigns to prevent deportation are a practical demonstration of this position, although they often deploy consequentialist arguments about the skills and contribution that particular individuals offer to society.

Most positions on migration are placed at various points within these spectra rather than at the extreme ends. Ruhs and Chang themselves, while sympathetic to the cosmopolitan case, suggest that freer entry for migrants should be restricted to temporary stay since they argue it is politically unrealistic to expect a greater degree of cosmopolitanism from national electorates. This position was adopted by the Migration Commission of the Royal Society of Arts, which argued that the separation of labour migration from residence and citizenship rights represented a step towards a more open migration policy (RSA, 2005). Others deploy both rights-based and consequentialist arguments in support of particular positions. The think tank Ippr, which has been influential in pushing for more open immigration policies, has based its arguments on both aspects (Spencer, 1994, 2003; Ippr, 2006). The Ippr's Sriskandarajah (2006) grounds his argument for maintaining Britain's open door to Eastern European labour primarily on what he see as its positive consequences for the British economy and public services but he also suggests that it is important to maintain this policy in order to build 'a more progressive, prosperous and cosmopolitan society'.

Migration without borders

The strengths and weaknesses of these positions can be highlighted by examining the arguments about whether immigration controls are justified. The case for abandoning controls has been made on the basis of two different types of argument, those based on human rights and those based on social justice (Seglow, 2005). Both are cosmopolitan according to the typology discussed earlier, but the primary focus of the first is the individual migrant and of the second (the consequentialist position) the broader society. They draw on two different notions of rights: individual rights and collective social rights. These are not, however, mutually contradictory. The anti-racist argument is based predominantly on the human rights of migrants but relates this to a broader concern that border controls perpetuate racism and reinforce the interests of dominant classes in society. This distinction is contained in the UNESCO report (Pecoud and de Guchteneire, 2005) that examined the ethical, economic and social dimensions of the case for MwB and this framework is used in the following discussion.

Ethical arguments

The ethical argument against immigration controls is based on the notion that there is no moral justification for dividing people into the 'included' and the 'excluded' and that common humanity rather than membership of a particular national group is the key moral imperative. The negation of this 'common humanity' – by ceding greater rights to some than to others – is grounded in racism and always morally arbitrary. The UN Special Rapporteur of the Commission on Human Rights made clear in 2002 that the UN Charter of Human Rights applies to all people regardless of status, so governments have a duty to respect human rights of people within their territory 'without distinction' (Cole, 2007: 1). A number of arguments have, however, been made to support the privileging of nationals, which have drawn on moral justifications.

Borders and nation states

Some supporters of immigration control suggest that borders have a moral force and draw on an 'automatic assumption about the overlap between the boundaries of the state citizens and "the nation"' (Anthias and Yuval Davis, 1992: 20). State boundaries are seen as dividing culturally and historically distinct communities. Rowthorn, for example, claims that nations 'are historical communities' (cited in Kearns, 2004: 3) that have the right to exclude others. He makes the arbitrary claim that the 'native population of Britain', which he identifies as the population with the moral claim for excluding outsiders, consists of 'anyone not a post-war immigrant or descendant of one' (Rowthorn, 2004: 20).This notion of the British people not only excludes migrants without legal status in Britain, but citizens and their descendants settled for many decades, and is thus far narrower than that assumed by most mainstream commentators. Lane challenges this privileging of national membership, arguing that: '[t]he assumption that membership of a national group somehow naturally brings with it an entitlement to economic advantage if that national group has been lucky or clever in the past is not itself morally obvious' (2004: 11).

The boundaries around the people considered to belong to the 'nation' rarely coincide with the borders of the nation state. Membership of the 'nation' may not be lost when people leave the state or gained as they enter. Patriality, for example, meant that Britishness was transferred by people who had left the country to their descendants who might never live in the UK. Likewise *Aussiedler* were able to transfer their belonging to the German nation when living outside Germany, while at the same time Turkish people may remain non-citizens even after the third generation of residence in Germany. Britain's post-war immigration policy involved the gradual differentiation of rights for different categories of British citizen. The development of the European Union and EU citizenship has also brought shifting legal and social meanings of the 'included' and the 'excluded'.

This argument for exclusion also depends on a notion of the 'national interest', which tends to be conflated with the interests of the powerful. Formal membership of the nation theoretically applies to all citizens but political and economic power are unequally distributed. Moreover, the rights of citizenship have been won through processes of internal struggle as well as through shifting boundaries around the nation. Marshall (1950) discusses the extension of civil, political and social rights in Britain and the tensions between universal citizenship and inequalities based on social class. His account does not address the gendered nature of citizenship rights (Pateman, 1998) and that women have had to struggle for full inclusion in the nation, for example winning political rights belatedly as a result of the struggles of the suffragettes. The ability to exercise citizenship rights also varies with age and has shifted historically as well as varying between countries. The acquisition of rights is not a one-way process. Groups can also lose citizenship and their inclusion within the nation, as did the Jews in Nazi Germany and more recently the Tutsis in Rwanda.

Culture and belonging

A related argument for exclusion is that nations embody a 'common culture' that could be threatened by immigration. Western states are currently attempting to promote notions of national identity by setting down values that they claim are common to the existing nation and to which would-be immigrants are expected to subscribe. In countries of immigration such as the United States the myth of nation building has been based on immigration, although this has always been selective on grounds of nationality or social class and acceptance has been conditional on the adoption of 'American values'. The British government's attempts to define national identity have been ambivalent, drawing on values that are identified as British while seeking to acknowledge past immigration. In the White Paper *Secure Borders, Safe Haven*, it welcomed diversity, creating a new fiction, or 'imagined community', of the British population based on a multi-ethnic citizenship. This undermines any moral justification for exclusion based on traditional racialised or cultural notions of belonging to the nation.

Seglow (2005: 9) argues that individuals have an interest in access to a 'secure cultural context' that can provide them with 'a sense of meaning, orientation, identity and belonging'. National identity is, however, only one element of an individual's identity. People draw their 'cultural context' from a range of relationships, institutions and local, national and international networks. The cultural context in which one lives one's life is continually transformed by economic and social change. For example mining villages had to remake their sense of community in the wake of pit closures. Former migrants and their descendants become part of the cultural context of the present generation. The East End midwife quoted in Chapter Six felt threatened by Jewish immigrants but her own cultural context at the beginning of the twentieth century included the Irish migrants whose arrival an earlier generation had feared.

For Londoners in the twenty-first century, multiculturalism has become their cultural context and was celebrated in the city's successful Olympic bid. Jordan and Duvell (2003) argue that it is the middle class who are perceived as benefiting from multiculturalism and immigration, which provides access to restaurants and cheap cleaners, while working-class people see their living standards threatened by migrants. This raises the divisions that constructions of 'national' cultures attempt to transcend. As they suggest, immigrants can become the scapegoat for processes over which the disadvantaged have no control and that arise from inequalities of wealth and power rather than immigration itself.

Exclusion of non-contributors

A further morally based argument for exclusion privileges citizens because of the contributions they make to society and national prosperity. The ability of migrants to contribute through work and the payment of taxes, however, depends on their migration status, and their status as outsiders is thus 'determined by morally arbitrary factors' that exclude them from the formal labour market (Cole, 2007: 5). Asylum seekers, for example, are prevented from seeking employment and therefore forced into dependency on benefits. The issue of the extent to which migrants contribute economically is discussed further later. The concern here is with the conflation of an assumed failure to contribute in this way with a lack of moral worth.

This argument is akin to Thatcherite discourse against 'benefit scroungers' in which moral worth is predicated on contribution rather than need. This type of logic also calls into question the rights of groups of citizens, such as older people, the sick and some disabled people, who may not be able to contribute economically through employment. Cohen, in rejecting the search for 'facts' to demonstrate the contribution of migrants as an argument to justify their inclusion within the nation, is asserting the principle that all have rights, regardless of their economic, or indeed their moral, worth.

New Labour has also drawn on moral arguments to justify exclusion of certain groups, arguing that the breaking of the rules is unfair to existing citizens. For example in the White Paper, *Fairer, Faster and Firmer*, it suggested: 'In fairness to those who have followed the rules and to deter others who might consider abusing the system, we must be able to identify and deal appropriately with those in the UK without authority' (Home Office, 1998a: para 11.1).

In both these cases the 'rules' that are themselves the product of a morally arbitrary policy process are given a special ethical status. These rules change frequently to exclude and include different groups, as the example given below, when 'failed asylum seekers' lost their entitlement to free health care, illustrates.

Social justice

The 'liberal paradox' (see Chapter Five) provides the strongest moral argument in favour of controls. As Benhabib puts it: 'Universal human rights have a context-transcending appeal, whereas popular and democratic sovereignty must constitute a circumscribed demos which acts to govern itself' (2004: 19).

This suggests that there is a potential conflict between allowing free movement of people and maintaining liberal democracy, which is seen as a precondition for the promotion of policies of social justice. This conflict is at the heart of much of the philosophical debate on immigration although it tends to be little discussed by those advocating free movement from other perspectives. Rawls (1971) based his theory of social justice on the notion of equal rights, but ruled out its application on a global scale, thus abandoning universal values in favour of localised social justice for its citizens. Walzer (1983) argued that communitarian values imply a moral imperative on the part of the state to care for citizens. Boundedness, however, is necessary for welfare and other social rights because the state needs to be able to decide who is included in membership. In this view, the moral duty to care for citizens overrides universality.

John Reid, when health secretary, used a version of this argument to justify withdrawing free health treatment from 'failed asylum seekers'. He argued that they were: 'effectively stealing treatment from the people of this country. I am not talking about emergency treatment, matters of life and death. I am talking about routine treatment that causes the people of this country, who are legally and morally entitled to it, to have to wait longer' (quoted in Cole, 2007: 3). As Cole comments, the 'moral aspect of the argument has to do the work because before this change, asylum seekers were legally entitled to free treatment'. The argument for exclusion was based not on the assumption that they had not contributed but was based on the idea that they had no right to be included in 'the people of this country'. Reid suggests here that using national resources to support these 'outsiders' harms the interests of those who are part of the nation.

While the 'liberal paradox' raises a significant moral dilemma, the ways in which states restrict their membership cannot be justified through any consistent set of moral principles. Indeed Reid in the example above is attempting to justify a new form of exclusion. Cole (2000) suggests that liberal values are, by definition, universal and make no distinction between people of different nations. Any criteria for distinguishing between members and non-members in order to restrict the basis on which rights are granted must therefore conflict with liberal standards. Carens (undated: 1) argues that 'although democracy presupposes a demos, membership in the demos is not something that the demos itself is morally free to grant or withhold as it chooses'. He links this to the tension within liberal democracy, the 'democratic paradox', between 'the notion that normative legitimacy must be derived from the democratic will of the people and the notion that there are independent standards of morality' (Carens, undated: 2). The democratic will might want to impose solutions that are themselves undemocratic in that they undermine democratic rights for some groups, as when Jews were excluded from membership of the German nation by a regime that came to power through an election. Immigrants and their descendants could similarly be excluded by a democratic vote within a state.

In practice, states use a combination of justifications for the ways in which they categorise potential immigrants and exclude certain groups, including those based on morality and national self-interest as well as assumptions about who is included based on history and myths about nationhood. Managed migration bases decisions on whether to admit migrants on their usefulness to the country of migration. A wider moral argument is attempted in relation to asylum, where 'genuine refugees' are separated from 'bogus' asylum seekers. The criteria for these decisions and the way they are implemented, however, mean that many people in desperate need are rejected as the stories in Chapter Eight illustrate. Furthermore, the boundary between members and non-members can only be created and policed in an illiberal way in practice and in theory (Cole, 2005: 11). This policing involves the erosion of human rights, which not only affects those subject to the decisions but corrupts the wider society. Immigration officers and others involved in this policing are required to deny the reality of human stories in order to meet targets in relation to detention and deportation. This bureaucratic indifference has been nourished in the wider society through a discourse that has systematically placed the rights of nationals above those of others, so that even the words 'asylum' and 'human rights' have become terms of abuse.

The economic argument

Economic arguments for migration are based on the expected or assumed consequences of migration rather than on moral principles. They are based on the impact for groups (in countries of immigration and emigration) rather than individuals and depend on evidence. As Kearns (2004) points out, however, facts may be disputed and the relevance of particular facts depends on the argument that is being made. People choose facts selectively depending on their position in the spectra discussed earlier and the argument that they wish to promote. Those taking a pro-immigrant stance may focus on the extent to which immigrants provide useful services while advocates of restricting migration may focus on the resources that they use. Migration Watch, for example, claimed in August 2006 that if legal immigration to Britain were to continue at its projected rate, it would lead to a requirement of about 1.5 million extra houses in the period 2003–26.[5] This figure was based on an extrapolation of existing trends, taking no account of other relevant factors such as, for example, the extent of emigration and the availability of empty housing.

The data on which estimates of economic impact are based are patchy and may simply be unavailable. Some relevant evidence is not collected routinely or systematically. It is known, for example, how many A8 citizens have registered with the Workers' Registration Scheme but not how many of those who have not registered are working, either informally or as self-employed, and how many others are out of the labour force. The headline figure represents a cumulative total over two years rather than the number registered at any one time, since people are not required to de-register when they leave. Migrant labour tends to be disproportionately concentrated in the informal sector, so that its contribution does not find its way into the official data. Quantitative data do not take account of intangible costs or benefits. Disentangling the impact of immigration from other changes is difficult and requires assumptions based on value judgements. Official data reflect the existing distribution of resources and wealth so that the benefits of the work of a nurse for example may be valued much lower than those of an entrepreneur who can command a higher income within the market.

The costs and benefits of migration affect countries of immigration and of emigration. Neoclassical economic theory suggests that the impact of unrestricted migration would be positive since controls represent a barrier to the operation of the free market preventing labour from moving to areas where it is most in demand and thus most productive. Hamilton and Whalley argued in 1984 that liberalisation of the world labour market would double world GDP (cited in Pecoud and de Guchteneire, 2005: 10). Global markets are not, however, the perfectly competitive markets assumed in neoclassical theory. Moreover, different groups may gain or lose as a result of immigration. For example, this scenario envisages wages being equalised on a global level, which implies that they would fall in high-wage countries. The next section does not attempt to make judgements on these estimates but points to some of the relevant costs and benefits.

The country of immigration

Immigration may impact on the labour market, welfare provision and social infrastructure. Its overall impact on national income is almost always positive as migrants contribute to employment and spending, but the distribution is uneven. 'Managed migration' policies, like guestworker systems, attempt to maximise the economic benefits of migration to the host country. British government policy in relation to the A8 countries, for example, allows employers free access to their labour power but limits the access of these workers to welfare benefits. Those unable to work must either return home or become destitute.

The impact on individual labour markets may be to reduce wages and increase unemployment for domestic workers. This is the case against migration made by Rowthorn (2004), who suggests that immigration disproportionately affects the low waged and unskilled with whom they compete for jobs. The impact depends on the extent of regulation, including for example the enforcement of minimum wage legislation and whether migrants become part of collective bargaining agreements. Trade unions in Britain are actively recruiting new migrants, and A8 workers, for example, are becoming increasingly aware of their rights in the labour market (interview with TUC official, London, May 2006)[6]. It also depends on the extent of competitiveness or complementarity between the jobs of migrant and domestic workers. Research on migrants' incorporation into the labour market suggests that they may create their own niches, which do not compete directly with domestic workers (eg Anderson,

2001). British firms have recruited bus drivers from Eastern Europe and agriculture is dependent on migrants as local people have been unwilling to take on this low-paid and seasonal work. At the other end of the spectrum are those who carry out skilled work where there are shortages such as in social work, health and IT (Raghuram and Kofman, 2002), although recent changes to the National Health Service have meant that some of these workers are no longer required.

Economic arguments in relation to wages and employment often assume that there is a fixed demand for labour. While wages may go down in certain sectors, at least in the short run, the expansionary effects of migration may shift the whole demand for labour outwards. Migration may also expand the domestic labour force as, for example, migrant labour in the domestic sphere enables more women to enter employment (Tacoli, 1999).

The impact on welfare depends on the age profile and other social characteristics of migrants as well as their formal entitlement to welfare services. Labour migrants tend to be young and without dependants and therefore net contributors to welfare through taxation. With settlement and family reunion or family formation they will make more use of welfare services. Some immigrants may find it difficult to access services, and extra resources may be needed to facilitate access such as interpreting and health advocacy. Sudden increases in migration may have implications for services such as schools, as in the example of Slough quoted in Chapter Seven. Migration may also impact on the social infrastructure, for example the availability of housing, and affect rents and house prices. Temporary migrants tend to live in private rented accommodation, often sharing with fellow nationals, and may not necessarily compete with the mainstream market. They may contribute to the provision of new and renovated housing. Polish builders, for example, have been much in demand in Britain due to shortages of skilled workers (Garapich, 2005).

Migrants also contribute directly to welfare services. Migrant workers in Britain, especially women, have been disproportionately concentrated in welfare both in public services and within the domestic sphere (Kofman et al, 2000). This has increased as populations have aged in the more developed countries and demand for services has increased while labour shortages have developed in these areas.

Opening up the labour market to all migrants would reduce the reliance on the informal sector and increase contributions from taxes. A study by the Ippr (2006) calculated that regularising the status of the estimated 430,000 irregular migrants in Britain would produce a potential income of at least £485 million per annum, and that it is more likely to be around £1 billion.

Another significant cost associated with migration is the direct and indirect costs of immigration control. These include border controls and the cost of detaining and deporting people whose right to remain is questioned. The

National Audit Office estimates the cost of the enforced removal of a failed asylum seeker as around £11,000 (quoted in Ippr, 2006: 12). Controls also involve substantial costs in the time spent by others in checking immigration status, for example by human resources departments and hospitals, which are obliged to ascertain eligibility for treatment.

Countries of emigration

Migration, as suggested earlier, may be a form of aid from the poor to the rich, as the costs of reproducing labour are borne by the country of origin while the country of immigration gains the educated, productive worker. This is particularly relevant where migration takes place from poorer to richer countries. The term 'brain drain' has been used to describe this process in relation to skilled workers. This may have serious consequences in the case of medical doctors, whose emigration after expensive training can leave poor areas short of trained health workers (Mesquita and Gordon, 2005). There is thus a moral case to be made against the unrestricted export of health workers from poor countries (Cole, 2007). The British health service has instituted a code of conduct to prevent the active recruitment of health workers from certain African countries. Restrictions on the exit of workers, however, would challenge fundamental rights enshrined in the UN Declaration of Human Rights. This right has generally been violated only in times of war and by Eastern bloc countries during the Cold War. Some governments have attempted to recoup payments for the training received but these are difficult to enforce and may push individuals into a decision to move permanently in order to avoid these payments. Restrictions on the entry of individuals would be unlikely to promote positive benefits to the country of emigration since they would not impact on the conditions in the country of emigration. They would not necessarily prevent people leaving, but they might be forced to move to less attractive locations.

These arguments tend to be based on the assumption that people move permanently. More recently, the discussion of brain drain has moved to 'brain circulation' or 'brain gain' as people have been able to take advantage of a temporary move to gain experience and then return to their country of origin. The IT industry in India, for example, has been built on skilled workers returning from the US (Aneesh, 2000). Immigration controls make this kind of circulation more difficult, as the difficulty of negotiating entry forces people to decide between permanent stay or returning. An important element in the picture is remittances, which are increasingly recognised as an element of aid.

The economic implications of migration are complex and dynamic, with short-term implications superseded by longer-term developments. The 'benefits' and 'costs' are distributed unequally and many are unknown and unknowable. Policy makers use economic arguments selectively. Managed migration, for example, is based on the notion of securing the economic benefits of migrants for the 'nation'. Asylum policy, however, involves huge financial and other costs to secure the political goal of controlling borders. Allowing asylum seekers to work legally would be economically beneficial in reducing the cost to the welfare budget but would conflict with the goal of removing them as fast as possible. Similarly, the NASS system involved major new costs in managing dispersal, but its main purpose was to deter asylum seekers rather than to save resources.

The economic results of migration are dependent on migration policies themselves and the legal status of migrants. These policies are made on the basis of wider sets of values, which also frame the way in which the economic implications of migration are assessed. Economic arguments cannot therefore be the prime basis on which to judge immigration polices.

Social effects

Pecoud and de Guchteneire (2005: 13) suggest that the social dimension has had less attention than the ethical and economic aspects of MwB as a result of the 'near-impossibility' of predicting and evaluating the numerous consequences. These social effects overlap with the issues discussed earlier and concern the broader impact on society.

The key issue that tends to be raised is about numbers. Scenarios of 'huge and unmanageable migration flows' (Pecoud and de Guchteneire, 2005) are often evoked, overwhelming welfare services and social infrastructure and undermining social cohesion. This draws on the idea of 'thresholds' of tolerance discussed in Chapter Five. The issue of acceptance of migrants has, however, generally had little to do with their numbers and much more to do with their perceived difference. Only 492 people were aboard the *Empire Windrush* when it landed in Britain in 1948 but the prime minister described this as an 'incursion'. At the same time, other migrants from Europe were being actively recruited into the British labour market. The most hostile reactions to asylum seekers have often been in areas where their numbers are small but highly visible due to a pre-existing assumed monoculturalism. Hostility is not confined to new migrants or to non-Europeans. The Portuguese community in rural Boston in the east of England, which has long been involved in agricultural labour there, continues to experience racism and xenophobia.[7] Home Office figures released in 2006 as the government was promising yet more tough measures against asylum showed that there were only 25,715 asylum applications while over 400,000 people from the new EU countries of Eastern Europe had registered to work in Britain since 2004 (Home Office, 2006d).

Although MwB would represent a major reversal in the policy of the past century, there have been examples of borders being removed that provide some idea of the possible results. Post-war immigration, when Commonwealth citizenship allowed free entry to Britain, was at first limited, and increased significantly only with the threat of controls. The opening-up of free movement within the European Union increased mobility, but the overwhelming majority of people have remained in their home countries, in spite of significant initial differences in national incomes between the richer nations and the poorer Mediterranean economies. Free movement from the new Eastern European member states has produced a greater proportionate increase in mobility, largely due to the greater differences in economic opportunities and the dislocation of their societies during the transition to market economies. This movement has been concentrated on the three EU states that allowed this free movement. There was an initial surge in movement to Britain but the majority returned home soon afterwards (Sales, 2006). The number of people from these states now living in Britain is unknown but there was a reduction in the numbers registering with the Workers' Registration Scheme between the first two quarters of 2006, suggesting that the rate of new arrivals may have peaked (Home Office, 2006a). The freedom of movement allowed through the EU means that most are temporary migrants, who return frequently to their home country and do not have long-term plans to remain. As other EU states open their borders to these workers over the next few years some may experience similar patterns of migration. Some plan to do so earlier than required by the terms of the Accession Agreement because of the economic benefits they see accruing to those countries that have opened their doors.

Large-scale migration clearly has consequences for welfare services and for other key social resources such as housing, as suggested earlier, but the impact is complex and cannot be measured by crude extrapolations. New migrants, especially the young, single and temporary migrants who are likely to be encouraged by MwB, tend to be net contributors to welfare. The diversity of migrants may present an immediate challenge to welfare professionals (Vertovec, 2006), for example those attempting to care for patients from countries for whose language there are no interpreters available. Migrants, however, if given a free choice, tend to move to areas where they have existing connections and where they may be able to speak the local language.

The claimed impact of migration on 'social cohesion' has also fed demands for restrictions. Speaking at the launch of the British government's new Commission on Integration and Social Cohesion on 23 August 2006, the Communities Minister Ruth Kelly said that 'There was a danger of white Britons becoming alienated by the pace of social change ... [and if they did not participate in the benefits which arose from this they could] begin to believe the stories about ethnic minorities getting special treatment and to develop resentment' (*Guardian*, 24 August 2006). Immigration policy feeds this sense of separateness, or alienation, through excluding groups of people from citizenship rights and questioning their right to belong.

The abolition of controls could have positive effects on social cohesion, removing the presumption that immigrants are unwelcome and to be viewed with suspicion, which is at the root of much of the hostility towards immigrants. It would also allow them rights to participate in society and become part of cohesive and open societies. It would also remove the need for migrants to be 'irregular' and allow them to live and work openly, removing some of the opportunities for exploitation and abuse. As Tony Woodley, the general secretary of the Transport and General Workers' Union, claimed in calling for an amnesty of irregular migrants:

> Workers worried about their immigration status are among the most exploited in our workplaces. Global criminal operations extort their money, while in the workplace unscrupulous employers can intimidate them without fear of reproach. The only way to end this exploitation is to end the isolation these workers experience. (*Independent*, 31 March 2006)

Citizenship rights in a borderless world

One of the thorniest issues in relation to the argument for open borders has been the question of how social justice could be promoted in a border-free world. If everyone is free to enter, on what basis could belonging be established and how could citizenship rights be allocated? Cohen (2003), an advocate of free movement, suggests that the abolition of border controls would mean that the welfare state would need to be fundamentally restructured but he does not suggest how this would be done. The Migration Commission established by the Royal Society of Arts to discuss the future of migration policy argued in favour of free mobility but attempted to separate the issues of settlement from entry to work. They argued that the issue that people feared was settlement not work and thus free movement should be allowed on a temporary basis. The report does not, however, specify what citizenship rights would be accorded to these temporary workers, or how the temporary nature of their migration would be enforced. The suggestion that family reunion should be denied to temporary workers conflicts with established human rights principles in relation to the right to family life as contained for example in the UN Convention on Human Rights.

Cole (2007: 1) suggests that 'the exclusion of migrants of any status from any welfare system cannot be ethically justified, because the distinction between citizens and migrants cannot be an ethical one'. He argues, however, that the 'liberal paradox' produces a fundamental contradiction between freedom of movement and the maintenance of social provision, suggesting that there are two possibilities:

- we have complete freedom of movement, which under current conditions would make it impossible for liberal states to deliver goods and resources to members – this means there are no liberal *states*, or:
- exercise membership controls, which violates the central principle of liberal morality – this means there are no *liberal* states (Cole, 2005:10).

The exclusion of migrants from a welfare system may not be ethically justifiable, but neither is the destruction of the conditions for welfare provision. This paradox must be overcome if a policy of open borders is to be feasible either politically or ethically. There needs to be some way of allocating rights to migrants without undermining the very basis on which these rights are established. In the foreseeable future this will mean through the national state, so the categories on which nation states base membership would have to change fundamentally.

The problem may not be as intractable as Cole's statement of the problem suggests. In practice, migrants have been incorporated into aspects of social citizenship within the country of settlement. The extent and nature of this incorporation has depended on the particular welfare state regime, migratory history and tradition of conferring citizenship, as well as on the citizenship status, class, length of stay and gender of the individual migrant (Kofman et al, 2000). Faist (1995:178) argues that social citizenship, unlike political and civil citizenship, defies 'clear cut institutionalised criteria' and therefore the boundaries between citizens and non-citizens tend to be blurred. Some rights are acquired through employment, for example work-related benefits and workers' protection. Some are dependent on eligibility, which is not determined primarily by nationality (for example to social housing and unemployment benefits). Non-citizens are also entitled to some civil rights when visiting or residing in other states, for example to protection from assault and against arbitrary arrest, the right to fair trial and so on. Migrants may therefore be able to acquire rights through residence and participation, thus decoupling rights from nationality.

Robin Cohen suggests that it may be legitimate to ask intending adult migrants whether they intend to obey the laws of the society. This would, he suggests, create a moral equivalence between a politician's demand for exclusion and an immigrant's claim for inclusion (Cohen, 2006: 210). This is, however, merely a statement of the existing position. On entering another state one implicitly agrees to obey these laws, however different they may be from those from which one has come. All within the state, whether citizen, resident or visitor, are legally bound by that state's law, and have a right to its protection.

The conditions for accessing citizenship rights

Basing rights on residence provides the possibility of developing an ethically just way of overcoming the 'liberal paradox'. For Carens, 'length of residence is the key moral variable' (undated: 1). He argues that some legal rights ought to be enjoyed by everyone physically present within the boundaries of the state, and most others ought to be enjoyed by anyone who lives there for an extended period. Residence implies a commitment to a society and allows people to develop relationships with neighbours and fellow workers that are not just economic. People who live in a society over an extended period become members of that society and moral claims to legal status flow from membership (Carens, undated: 10).

Some rights are inalienable and cannot be removed from residents. These include health care, and schooling for children, a fundamental right outlined in the United Nations Convention on the Rights of the Child (UNCRC). Carens suggests that it may be necessary to distinguish between residents and 'health tourists', particularly in the intermediate period where differences in health provision may attract migrants. Payment could be claimed through reciprocal agreement for visitors, as is the case within the European Union. The charging for health care in the name of preventing 'health tourism' is costly in terms of bureaucracy and its implications for both patients and those who care for them and these costs may outweigh the revenue gained. Most people do not travel for this reason, preferring to be treated at home where they have the support of friends and family. Depriving people of health treatment also has negative implications for public health and social cohesion (Spencer, 2003: 23). It may discourage people from seeking treatment for contagious diseases.

Immediate access to the labour market would prevent the dependence on benefits that some migrants, particularly asylum seekers, are forced to endure. The freedom to live openly would reduce the incentive to work in the informal sector, allowing people to take up employment more appropriate to their skills and aspirations. It would also reduce the incentive to produce false documents, a practice that undermines safety as employers are unable to check qualifications, references and where appropriate, police checks.[8] Access to other social rights such as public housing and cash benefits related to employment could be attained after a period of residence in the same way as is required for nationals. Child Benefit, on the other hand, is a key measure in combating child and family poverty (Bennett, 2006) and should be available to all with children.

MwB would allow migrants to gain important civil rights that are violated by immigration controls. These include freedom of movement, both within and across national boundaries, and the right to live where one chooses and with whom one chooses. It would end the process of immigration detention, which is outside the normal judicial process, allowing people to be detained without trial and without having committed a crime.

Political rights have generally been reserved for citizens and have thus been the last right that immigrants have acquired. Migrants may engage in informal activity and are increasingly involved in trade unions but the difficulties and delays in the acquisition of citizenship mean that many are denied formal political participation in their country of residence even after many years of settlement, and the principle of 'no taxation without representation' is regularly flouted. There have been, however, some exceptions to this that suggest that wider forms of membership are possible. EU citizens have been allowed to vote in both local and EU elections in other member states though not in national elections. Some states also allow their own citizens to vote in national elections even though they are not resident. Voting in elections requires some form of local registration and to do this implies some level of membership of the society in which one resides. The granting of voting rights for some groups of non-citizens in some elections suggests that it is possible to separate voting rights from citizenship so that they are linked to membership of the society in which one lives.

Asylum

Some writers have suggested that MwB could harm the interest of asylum seekers and leave them unprotected (Zolberg et al, 1989; Castles, 2004a). Zolberg et al (1989: 271) suggest that open entry for all refugees would not help the neediest victims of violence who are not able to travel outside their region. While this is true, their plight would not be helped by a continuance of the present system of placing barriers to entry for those who are able to travel. They suggest limiting the number of prospective beneficiaries through a ranking principle based on the immediacy and degree of life-threatening violence (Zolberg et al, 1989: 270). A reform of the present system on this basis would not, however, overcome the major ethical and practical problems that it produces, since it would continue to involve intensive scrutiny of individual case, and presumably the removal of those deemed not to be a priority.

A system based on freedom of entry and residence could, on the contrary, provide better protection. For 'genuine refugees' under the Convention definition, the ability to enter a country and remain freely and to work may be the most important rights that they need, removing the dangers of clandestine entry, the insecurity caused by the fear of detention and return and the stigmatisation of being segregated in a punitive system while their application is processed. It would deter people from claiming to be refugees if their primary motive was economic, reducing the number of asylum claimants. Refugee-determination systems currently use up huge resources while spending on refugee integration is comparatively trivial. Allowing free entry would mean that only those in need of specific support (for example through mental or physical disability) would need to register as refugees and consideration of their claims could be based on their needs rather than on a scrutiny of the veracity of their claim to be refugees. The removal of the period of limbo would be of particular importance for refugee children, for whom delays in settlement can have long-term detrimental effects.

The acquisition of citizenship

The acquisition of citizenship denotes membership of a society as well as a series of important rights. The granting of citizenship is always discretionary rather than a right, and in some states, including Britain, has become increasingly conditional on fulfilling obligations, for example language and citizenship tests and the introduction of a 'good character' condition. As it expands in importance, through for example citizenship ceremonies, and rights become more stratified according to migration status, so more people are potentially excluded.

Carens suggests that citizenship should be granted on the basis of the length of residence alone; membership and belonging is in the place where one is based and this, he suggests, is the only morally acceptable determinant (undated: 6). The most important condition for citizenship is currently length of residence, but different countries have different lengths and all involve several years. This means *legal residence*, so periods spent informally do not count and it can be many years before people can apply for citizenship. Opening the borders would remove the distinction between legal and illegal residence, and allow people to register their residence – and possible future citizenship status – immediately. Citizenship could be acquired after a short period when people had had a chance to settle and decide whether they wished to remain on a more permanent basis. Other conditions are unreasonable and discriminatory since existing citizens are not required to fulfil them. Although knowledge of the local language, for example, is important for the exercise of citizenship, restricting it to those able to pass a test denies citizenship status to those who are likely to be the most vulnerable, marginalising them further.

Towards post-national citizenship?

Migration has necessitated the opening-up of citizenship, and states increasingly recognise continuing transnational links through allowing dual citizenship. Migration also challenges the nature of national citizenship itself. National citizenship, while claiming to be grounded in universal values and above cultural difference, develops in the context of a particular national state and reflects that state's history and particular construction of national identity (see Chapter Five).

In France, this universalism is based on the adherence to a secular public sphere in which religious and ethnic belonging are seen as private matters. In Britain, this tension is more visible. The Church of England has a special constitutional position with the monarch at its head, and 'broadly Christian' acts of worship are compulsory in all publicly funded schools.[9] Religion is also integrated into the school system through 'voluntary-aided status', which gives majority control over the management of the school system to a voluntary body in return for a minimal financial contribution. The majority of voluntary-aided schools are Church of England, with a smaller number of Catholic and Jewish schools. Some Sikh and Muslim schools have recently opened.[10] This process is being extended through the development of 'academies', many of which are run by religious groupings, including the Church of England. National citizenship thus embodies privileges based on religious belonging.

Although citizenship is claimed to be equal, it also reflects the experience of the powerful within society. It involves individual rights but individuals have specific, and different, characteristics that mean that their ability to exercise these citizenship rights varies. Political freedom, for example, is meaningless if one does not have time to participate because of employment or childcare commitments and one cannot pay the fare to attend a meeting. Social rights have been essential for full participation in society (Marshall, 1950). These rights are based on particular conditions such as income or family responsibilities and thus include or exclude particular groups. Being a school governor or a local councillor, for example, is contingent on being able to take time off work without losing one's job, a situation generally confined to professional occupations or public sector jobs. Women have had to fight for inclusion as citizens. These struggles have involved both the demand for equal treatment, for example in relation to voting rights and pay, and for the recognition of particular social rights such as maternity leave.

Citizenship thus involves a tension between the universal and the particular and between individual and group rights. The tension between equality and difference has been at the heart of much debate around citizenship, particularly from a feminist perspective (Walby, 1990; Lister, 1997). These issues are also relevant to the incorporation of migrants into new forms of citizenship. Multicultural citizenship needs both to remove the inequalities that privilege particular forms of national identity and at the same time allow space for the expression of particular identities. It thus needs to recognise both equality and difference, or individual rights and group rights. Castles (2000) suggests four principles that should underlie multicultural citizenship:

- equality of citizenship rights;
- recognition that formal equality of rights does not lead to equality of response, resources opportunities or welfare;
- mechanisms for group representation and participation;
- differential treatment for people with different characteristics, needs and wants.

The third of these principles is apparently the most contentious. Habermas argues that democracy in a multicultural society means guaranteeing social and cultural rights for everyone rather than just for members of specific groups, which would remove the 'false contradiction between the individual and a bearer of collective identity' (cited in Castles, 2000: 144). This issue is, however, fraught with problems since it raises the question of which groups are considered significant and on what basis they should be represented. The response in Britain to demands to end the religious discrimination embedded in the school system has been to open up voluntary-aided status to Muslim and other faiths, increasing the separation of children on a religious basis. Ironically, as the government launched its review of multiculturalism in the name of 'integration and community cohesion', it made it clear that discussion of the religious basis of schools was not within its remit, although it might consider initiatives such as allowing children from these separate schools to play football together.[11]

There is an increasing trend in Britain to conflate religion and ethnicity, leaving little space for other, non-religious, forms of identity and practice. Multicultural citizenship, especially when based on religious belonging, runs the risk of essentialising and freezing cultural differences within the boundaries of supposedly homogeneous ethnic groups. Feminists have criticised the patriarchal nature of multicultural policies, which often institutionalise a conservative and male 'community leadership' as the interpreters and defenders of cultural norms (Yuval Davis, 1997; Kofman et al, 2000). Respect for 'traditional values' too often leads to a lack of intervention to protect against the abuse of rights, particularly in the case of women and children (Sales and Hek, 2004; Meetoo and Mirza, 2007).

A renewed citizenship cannot overcome national privilege by attempting to grant some of the privileges of the majority religion to a small number of other religious groupings who claim to speak for wider communities. It requires a more fundamental democratisation of the state itself to rid it of these undemocratic features. In the British case this would include abolishing the special position of the established Church of England and the hereditary monarchy at its head. The ending of state support for religious schools would help to create a social environment in which children from different faiths and from secular families could mix on equal terms. Community cohesion can only be achieved in a situation of equal rights for individuals and groups. Group rights – for example to practise religion, to observe particular national and religious holidays and to speak one's own language – need to be placed within the context of a secular framework that allows membership and the terms of membership to be chosen freely.

Returning to Castles' characteristics of multicultural citizenship, while the third characteristic may appear the most radical, it is in fact the first that has proved most difficult in Britain and that most urgently needs attention. Equality of citizens would involve dismantling the national particularity of citizenship and removing the privileges to particular national or religious groupings that they embody. This would involve a more thorough-going confrontation with its national history and the basis of national identity.

Conclusion

The arguments in this book suggest that there is an urgent need to review the basis of immigration policy. Current policy is based on the premise that immigration is a problem to be curtailed as far as possible and managed in the name of the 'national interest'. In practice, the people who are seen as 'immigrants' and thus the objects of these controls have always been specific groups rather than immigrants as a whole and those targeted for exclusion at any one time have rarely represented the majority of immigrants in numerical terms. Government policy is not simply a response to the real or imagined fears of the public. It has invariably played a major role in creating fear and fomenting xenophobia. Through constructing immigration controls it has created and sustained divisions and legitimised the racist attitudes that demand ever-further controls.

Migration controls impose a huge cost. This includes the financial cost of the human and technological resources deployed to restrict entry and to detect those who are deemed to be illegally present. More important is the social cost of a system that divides people on an ethically arbitrary basis and that enforces these divisions through means that undermine human rights. The process depends on the systematic denial of information, for example on the safety of the states to which migrants are deported, and creates a bureaucratic indifference to the fate of those involved. As the immigration officer quoted in Chapter Seven suggested, migrants become 'faceless' rather than human beings. This situation corrupts not just those involved but also the society whose interests it claims to protect.

Demands for the abolition of controls are widely seen as utopian and politically unfeasible. The current situation, however, is unsustainable in both practical and moral terms. Ever-more fevered efforts to control migration take us further down the path towards a dystopia in which every migrant is distrusted, a distrust that extends to citizens who appear 'different', and the tightening of national borders creates heavier boundaries between groups. It should not be taken for granted that an opening-up of this system would provoke uniform hostility. Campaigns for migrants show how individuals and communities can respond when the human dimensions of controls are presented to them. As Vertovec (2006) rightly points out, it would be naive to suggest that simply by virtue of living near to each other, people from different communities will become neighbours and overcome tensions. The recent examples of Rwanda and Bosnia point to the dangers of this view. Real engagement, through schools and other local institutions, as well as through individual relationships, does offer the possibility of breaking down the divisions that immigration controls help to maintain.

A more open public debate on immigration would be risky and no doubt open up possibilities for giving voice to reactionary sentiments. Governments, however, have the responsibility to 'give citizens the confidence that the risks are not life threatening and are worth taking' (Spencer, 2003). Only by opening up and examining the real social and human implications of migration controls can we move behind the narrow agenda that is doing so much damage to individuals and society.

As this chapter was being completed in the week leading up to Christmas 2006, an email appeal to immigration minister Liam Byrne (see *Box 9.1*) arrived from Ilengela Ileo, a refugee from the Congo. Her story, and her appeal to the minister's humanity, encapsulate many of the points that this chapter, and the book, have discussed.

Box 9.1: Ilengela Ileo

I arrived in the UK three years ago as I fled my country because of my family involvement in politics and was separated from my brother and sisters. Up to now we do not know their whereabouts as all the efforts made to trace them have not been successful and there are very slim chances to find them alive. My only remaining family, my mother and little baby sister, are here in the UK and have the right to remain here legally.

During this past three years, when I was going through my legal battle to remain in the UK, I have integrated into the community by not only going to learn the language but have acquired other different skills. I have also volunteered regularly at the Coventry Refugee Centre as an asylum caseworker for the last three years. … I am an active member of the Potter's House Church in Coventry and these are the reasons why I call Coventry my home.

A campaign group has been formed to support my application to remain here. They have submitted over 2,000 signatures and personal letters to the Home Office in support of my application. This shows me that I belong to this city and people genuinely care about me.

... I do know that you are not Santa to perform miracles but I am appealing to you not only as the Minister for Immigration but also as a father and human being with a heart to allow me to remain in the UK. ... As a father, how would you react if your child was to be sent to a death sentence knowing that you do not have the power to stop it? This is the feeling my mother is living with every day.

Source: NCADC News Service, 20 December 2006.

Notes

[1] Analysis of official figures reported in the *Guardian*, 23 August 2006.

[2] The government estimated an annual inflow of around 15,000 in 2004.

[3] Former minister John Denham argued this case in the *Guardian*, 26 July 2006.

[4] See for example the article by Jackie Ashley in the *Guardian*, 31 July 2006.

[5] www.migrationwatch.org.uk, accessed 2 August 2006.

[6] Interview for 'Polish migrants in London and European enlargement: social networks, transience and settlement', project funded by ESRC.

[7] In August 2006, a film based on the experience of a Portuguese woman living in the town was due to be played at the local railway station, but the plan was abandoned at the last moment when sponsors withdrew following local pressure (reported in the *Observer*, 27 August 2006).

[8] A recruitment agency manager in the care sector raised this problem in a report on illegal employment for the BBC's *Today* programme, 17 August 2006.

[9] Schools may apply to a local body, SACRE, to have separate services for different religions. This, however, means that children meet separately and do not participate in whole-school assemblies. Many schools attempt to resolve this by basing assemblies on 'ethical' rather than specifically religious themes.

[10] In 2005 there were around 7,000 'faith schools' in England, of which 6,955 were Christian, 36 Jewish, five Muslim and two Sikh (reported in the *Guardian*, 23 August 2005).

[11] Reported in the *Guardian*, 24 August 2006.

Summary

- In spite of the narrowness of mainstream debate on immigration, there is increasing challenge to the idea of controls from a range of individuals and organisations.
- Views about immigration control can be differentiated according to the extent to which they place the national interest above the interests of migrants, and the extent to which they focus on rights as opposed to the expected consequences of migration.
- In practice, national borders and the boundaries between those included and those excluded by immigration controls have changed throughout history.
- The arguments for 'Movement without Borders' encompass ethical, economic and social dimensions.
- The ethical arguments for controls contradict principles based on universal humanity.
- Evidence on which to judge the impact of migration is limited and one's general view of migration influences which facts are seen as relevant.
- The 'liberal paradox' raises a serious potential conflict between free movement and the need for boundaries around those eligible for social and political rights.
- Citizenship rights could be allocated on the basis of residence rather than nationality.
- Citizenship involves tensions between equality and difference, and between universalism and particular notions of national identity.
- The democratisation of citizenship would involve the removal of privileged status for certain national, ethnic or religious groups while allowing for diversity in the expression of identity.
- There is an urgent need for wider debate on immigration that challenges accepted 'common sense'.

Questions for discussion

- Is a world without borders practically feasible or morally justified? What would be the likely impact in the short and longer run?
- Should immigration policy be determined by general principles or by evidence of its effects?
- How could citizenship rights be assigned if anyone was free to enter the country and to take up employment?

Further reading

Cole, P. (2000) *Philosophies of exclusion: Liberal political theory and immigration*, Edinburgh: Edinburgh University Press.

Hayter, T. (2000) *Open borders: The case against immigration controls*, London: Pluto.

Pecoud, A. and de Guchteneire, P. (2005) *Migration without borders: An investigation into the free movement of people*, Paris: UNESCO Global Commission on International Migration.

Ruhs, M. and Chang, H. (2004) 'The ethics of labor and immigration policy', *International Organization*, vol 58, pp 69–102.

Spencer, S. (ed) (2003) *The politics of migration: Managing opportunity, conflict and change*, London: Political Quarterly.

Appendix

Further information for researching migration policy

1. Legislation

Policy documents, including Acts, Bills and White Papers, can be downloaded from the Immigration and Nationality Department of the Home Office, www.ind.homeoffice.gov.uk. The site also contains news briefings, immigration and statistics.

Acts can also be downloaded from: www.opsi.gov.uk/Acts

2. Commentary on policy and research

The following organisations' websites provide updates and commentary on new legislation and policy:

Immigration Law Practitioners' Association (ILPA) www.ilpa.org.uk
ILPA exists to promote and improve the giving of advice on immigration and asylum, through teaching and provision of high-quality resources and information. The website provides briefings on new proposals and submissions to public bodies, as well as policy papers on specific aspects of the law and its impact.

Information Centre about Asylum and Refugees (Icar) www.icar.org.uk
An independent information and research organisation based in the School of Social Sciences at City University, London, which aims to increase public understanding of asylum issues.

Institute for Public Policy Research (Ippr) www.ippr.org.uk
The 'leading progressive think tank' carries out research and lobbies for policy change in a number of policy areas, including 'migration and integration'. Produces fact files, publications and reports.

Joint Council for the Welfare of Immigrants (JCWI)
www.jcwi.org.uk
JCWI is an independent national voluntary organisation, campaigning for justice and combating racism in immigration and asylum law and policy. Produces publications, free briefings on new policy, policy papers and free legal advice on immigration matters. The *Handbook of immigration, nationality and refugee law* provides a useful guide to law for practitioners and others. Also lobbies and organises campaigns, for example on migrant workers' rights and regularisation.

Migration Watch www.migrationwatchuk.org
A 'voluntary, non political, body which is concerned about the present scale of immigration into the UK'. Lobbies for a reduction in migration and produces briefing papers on migration trends and commentary on policy.

Refugee Council www.refugeecouncil.org.uk
The largest refugee organisation, with regional offices across England and in Scotland and Wales. Campaigns and lobbies on refugee issues, provides services to asylum seekers and refugees. Produces briefings on new policy and carries out and commissions research. Publications can be downloaded from the website.

Refugee Action www.refugee-action.org.uk
An independent national charity that works with refugees to build new lives in the UK. Produces advice and information leaflets about aspects of immigration law.

3. Campaigns

Barbed Wire Britain www.barbedwirebritain.org.uk
Campaigns against detention, site includes information about campaigning activities and detainees' stories about the experience of detention.

Close Campsfield info@closecampsfield.org.uk
Long-running campaign for the closure of the Campsfield IRC at Oxford.

National Coalition of Anti-Deportation Campaigns (NCADC)
www.ncadc.org.uk
Provides information on individual campaigns against deportation and detention (current and past) and commentary on law and policy. Information can also be sent by email by subscribing to email list at the site.

4. Migration trends

a. International statistics

International Organization for Migration (IOM) www.iom.int
Produces World Migration Reports on migration trends in hard copy and downloadable.

United Nations Statistics Division www.unstats.un.org
Responsible for collecting and disseminating national data on international level through the *Demographic Yearbook* (for purchase).

United Nations High Commissioner for Refugees (UNHCR)
www.unhcr.org
Collects and compiles data on asylum seekers and refugees including asylum applications, refugee status determination, recognition rates, refugee populations and movements. Detailed data on global refugee trends downloadable.

b. European Union data

Eurostat http://epp.eurostat.ec.europa.eu
The statistical office of the European Commission, it collects and harmonises data from national data sets, available online. Detailed data sets for every EU country can be ordered from the Eurostat National Support Centres.

c. British statistics

Home Office Research Development and Statistics Directorate (RDS)
www.homeoffice.gov.uk/rds/immigration1.html
General Home Office statistics on immigration and asylum, including quarterly asylum statistics. More detailed data sets, such as NASS statistics at local level, are available on request.

References

Ackers, L. (1998) *Shifting spaces. Women, citizenship and migration within the European Union*, Bristol: The Policy Press.

Ager, A. (1999a) 'Perspectives on the refugee experience', in A. Ager (ed) *Refugees: perspectives on the experience of forced migration*, London: Continuum.

Ager, A. (ed) (1999b) *Refugees: Perspectives on the experience of forced migration*, London: Continuum.

Ahearn, F., Loughry, M. and Ager, A. (1999) 'The experience of refugee children',in A. Ager (ed) *Refugees: Perspectives on the experience of forced migration*, London: Continuum.

Ali, E. (1997) 'Gender relations and the Somali community', paper presented to annual conference of Women's Studies Network, June 1997.

Andall, J. (2000) *Gender, migration and domestic service: The politics of black women in Italy*, Aldershot: Ashgate.

Anderson, B. (1983) *Imagined communities*, London: Verso.

Anderson, B. (1997) 'Servants and slaves: Europe's domestic workers', *Race and Class*, vol 39, no 1, pp 37–49.

Anderson, B. (2001) 'Different roots in common ground: transnationalism and migrant domestic workers in London', *Journal of Ethnic and Migration Studies*, vol 27, no 4, pp 673–83.

Aneesh, A. (2000) 'Rethinking migration: high-skilled labor flows from India to the United States', Working paper 18, Rutgers University.

Ang, I. (1998) 'Migrations of Chineseness: ethnicity in the postmodern world', *Mots Pluriels*, no 7 (accessed through www.artsuwa.edu.au).

Anthias, F. (1983) 'Sexual divisions and ethnic adaptation', in A. Phizacklea (ed) *One way ticket*, London: Routledge and Kegan Paul.

Anthias, F. and Yuval Davis, N. (1992) *Racialized boundaries*, London: Routledge.

Appleyard, R. (1991) *International migration: Challenge for the nineties*, Geneva: IOM.

Association of Labour Providers (ALP) (2005) 'The workers registration scheme – The case for abolition', 25 May 2005, ALP Policy Papers, online at www.labourproviders.org.uk/

Audit Commission (2000a) *A new city: Supporting asylum seekers and refugees in London*, London: Audit Commission.

Audit Commission (2000b) *Another country: Implementing dispersal under the Immigration and Asylum Act 1999*, London: Audit Commission.

Aybak, T. (2004) 'Construction of the Natasha migration as a societal security in the Black Sea region', Harriman Institute, Columbia University, New York, 11 April.

Ayotte, W. (2000) *Separated children coming to Western Europe. Why they travel and how they arrive*, London: Save The Children.

Baines, E. (2004) *Vulnerable bodies: Gender, the UN and the global refugee crisis*, Aldershot: Ashgate.

Balibar, E. (1991) 'Es gibt keinen staat in Europa: racism and politics in Europe today', *New Left Review*, vol 186, pp 5–19.

Barbesino, P. (1998) 'Observing migration: the construction of statistics in a national monitoring system', in K. Koser and H. Lutz (eds) *The new migration in Europe: Social constructions and social realities*, Basingstoke: Macmillan.

Barnardo's, The Children's Society, NCH, NSPCC and Save the Children (undated) 'Room for improvement: a manifesto for children' (accessed April 2005 from www.nspcc.org.uk/Inform/PolicyAndPublicAffairs/Westminster/RoomForImprovement_ifega40840.html).

Barrett, M. and McIntosh, M. (1980) 'The family wage: some problems for socialists and feminists', *Capital and Class*, vol 11, pp 51–72.

Beaverstock, J.V. and Boardwell, J.T. (2000) 'Negotiating globalization, transnational corporations and global city financial centres in transient migration studies', *Applied Geography*, vol 20, no 3, pp 227–304.

Benhabib, S. (2004) 'The rights of others. Aliens, residents and citizens', CRASSH conference on Migrants, Nations and Citizenship, Cambridge, July 2004.

Bennett, F. (2006) (with Paul Dornan) *Fit for the future: Sixty years of support for children*, London: Child Poverty Action Group.

Benton, G. (2005) 'Chinatown UK v. colonial Hong Kong: an early exercise in transnational militancy and manipulation, 1967–1969', *Ethnic and Racial Studies*, vol 28, no 2, pp 331–47.

Bernardotti, M.A., Carchedi, F. and Ferone, B. (2005) *Schiavitu emergente: La tratta e lo sfruttamento delle donne nigeriane sul litorale domitio*, Rome: Ediesse.

Bhabha, J. and Finch, N. (2006) 'Seeking asylum alone', report for John and Catherine McArthur Foundation, London.

Bhattacharya, A. (1997) 'The public/private mirage: mapping homes undomesticating violence work in the South Asian Immigrant community', in J. Alexander and C. Mohanty (eds) *Feminist genealogies, colonial legacies, democratic futures*, London: Routledge, pp 308–29.

Black, R. and Koser, K. (eds) (1999) *The end of the refugee cycle? Refugee repatriation and reconstruction*, Oxford: Berghahn.

Blitz, B. (2003) 'Refugee returns in Croatia: contradictions and reform', *Politics*, vol 23, no 3, pp 181–91.

Blitz, B., Sales, R. and Marzano, L. (2005) 'Non voluntary return? The politics of refugee return to Afghanistan', *Political Studies*, vol 53, pp 182–200.

Bloch, A. (1999) 'Introduction', in A. Bloch and C. Levy (eds) *Refugees, citizenship and social policy in Europe*, Basingstoke: Macmillan.

Bloch, A. and Levy, C. (eds) (1999) *Refugees, citizenship and social policy in Europe*, Basingstoke: Macmillan.

Bloch, A. and Schuster, L. (2002) 'Asylum and welfare: contemporary debates', *Critical Social Policy*, vol 22, no 3, pp 393–414.

Bloch, A. and Schuster, L. (2005) 'At the extremes of exclusion: deportation, detention and dispersal', *Ethnic and Racial Studies*, vol 28, no 3, pp 491–512.

Borjas, G.J. (1989) 'Economic theory and international migration', *International Migration Review*, vol 23, no 3, pp 457–85.

Boswell, C. (2001) *Spreading the costs of asylum seekers: A critical assessment of dispersal policies in Germany and the UK*, London: Anglo-German Foundation for the Study of Industrial Society.

Botero, A., Lyon, F., Sepluveda, L. and Syrett, S. (2006) 'Refugees, new arrivals and enterprise', Centre for Enterprise and Economic Development Research (CEEDR), Middlesex University.

Boyd, M. (1989) 'Family and personal networks in international migration: recent developments and new agendas', *International Migration Review*, vol 23, pp 638–70.

Bralo, Z. (2000) *Routes project: London case study*. London: draft.

BMA (British Medical Association) (2002) *Asylum seekers: Meeting their health care needs*, London: BMA.

BMA (2004) *Asylum seekers and their health*, London: BMA.

Brubaker, R. (2004) 'Comments on "Modes of immigration politics in liberal democratic states"', *International Migration Review*, vol 29, no 4/122, pp 903–8.

Brubaker, R. (2005) 'The "diaspora" diaspora', *Ethnic and Racial Studies*, vol 28, pp 1-19.

Buijs, G. (ed) (1993) *Migrant women: Crossing boundaries and changing identities,* London: Berg.

Burchardt, T., Le Grand, J. and Piachaud, D. (2001) 'Degrees of exclusion: developing a dynamic, multidimensional measure', in J. Hills, J. Le Grand and D. Piachaud (eds) *Understanding social exclusion*, Oxford: Oxford University Press.

Burrell, K. (2006) *Moving lives: Narratives of nation and migration among Europeans in post-war Britain*, Aldershot: Ashgate.

Callamard, A. (1999) 'Refugee women: a gendered and political analysis of the refugee experience', in A. Ager (ed) *Refugees: Perspectives on the experience of forced migration*, London: Continuum.

Cantle, T. (2001) *Community cohesion*, Report of the Independent Review Team chaired by Ted Cantle, London: Home Office.

Carchedi, F., Picciolini, A., Mottura, G. and Campani, G. (eds) (2000) *I Colori della Notte*, Milan: Franco Angeli.

Carens, J. (undated) 'Immigration, democracy and citizenship' (University of Chicago, http://www.uchicago.edu/, accessed 10 March 2006).

Carey-Wood, J., Duke, K., Karn, V. and Marshall, T. (1995) *The settlement of refugees in Britain*, London: HMSO.

Castells, M. (1975) 'Immigrant workers and class struggles in advanced capitalism: the Western European experience', *Politics and Society*, vol 5, no 1, pp 33–66.

Castles, S. (2000) *Ethnicity and globalization*, London: Sage.

Castles, S. (2003) 'The new global politics and the emerging forced migration regime', paper presented to seminar, Institute for the Study of European Transformations and London European City of Immigration Group Seminar Series, 8 April 2003, London.

Castles, S. (2004a) 'The factors that make and unmake migration policies', *International Migration Review*, vol 38, no 3, pp 852–84.

Castles, S. (2004b) 'Why migration policies fail', *Ethnic and Racial Studies*, vol 27, no 2, pp 205–27.

Castles, S, Crawley, H. and Loughna, S. (2003) *States of conflict: causes and patterns of forced migration to the EU and policy responses*, London: Ippr.

Castles, S. and Davidson, A. (2000) *Citizenship and migration: Globalization and the politics of belonging*, Basingstoke: Macmillan.

Castles, S. and Kosack, G. (1973) *Immigrant workers and class structure in western Europe* (1st/2nd edn), Oxford: Oxford University Press.

Castles, S. and Loughna, S. (2003) 'Globalization, migration and asylum', in V. George and R. Page *Global social problems and global social policy*, Cambridge: Polity.

Castles, S. and Miller, M.J. (1993) *The age of migration* (1st edn), Basingstoke: Macmillan.

Castles, S. and Miller, M.J. (1998) *The age of migration* (2nd edn), Basingstoke: Macmillan.

Castles, S. and Miller, M.J. (2003) *The age of migration* (3rd edn), Basingstoke: Macmillan.

Cemlyn, S. and Briskman, L. (2003) 'Asylum, children's rights and social work', *Child and Family Social Work*, vol 8, pp 163–78.

Cesarani, D. and Fullbrook, M. (1996) 'Introduction', in D. Cesarani and M. Fullbrook (eds) *Citizenship, nationality and migration in Europe*, London: Routledge.

Chan, C.K., Bowpitt, G., Cole, B., Somerville, P., and Chen, J. (2004). *The UK Chinese people: Diversity and unmet needs,* Division of Social Work, Social Policy and Human Services, Nottingham Trent University.

Chatwin, M. (2001) 'The new law and procedure', in Immigration Law Practitioners' Association, *Asylum seekers: a guide to recent legislation*, London: ILPA/Resource Information Service.

Children's Society (2006) 'Briefing on the Queen's speech', 15 November 2006, www.childrenssociety.org.uk, accessed 29 December 2006.

Chimni, B. (2004) 'From resettlement to involuntary repatriation: towards a critical history of durable solutions to refugee problems', *Refugee Survey Quarterly*, vol 23, no 3, pp 55–73.

Clarke, J. and Newman, J. (1997) *The managerial state*, London: Sage.

Clarke, J. and Salt, J. (2003) 'Work permits and foreign labour in the UK: a statistical review', *Labour Market Trends*, November, pp 563–74.

Cohen, R. (1997) *Global diasporas: An introduction*, London: UCL Press.

Cohen, R. (2006) *Migration and its enemies: Global capital, migrant labour and the nation-state*, Aldershot: Ashgate.

Cohen, S. (2002) 'In and against the state of immigration controls: strategies for resistance', in S. Cohen, B. Humphries and E. Mynott (eds) *From immigration controls to welfare controls*, London: Routledge.

Cohen, S. (2003) *No one is illegal: Asylum and immigration control past and present*, Stoke on Trent: Trentham.

Cohen, S., Humphries, B. and Mynott, E. (eds) (2002) *From immigration controls to welfare controls*, London: Routledge.

Coker, J. (2001) 'Access to health, employment and education', in Immigration Law Practitioners' Association, *Asylum seekers: A guide to recent legislation*, London: ILPA/Resource Information Service.

Cole, P. (2000) *Philosophies of exclusion: Liberal political theory and immigration* Edinburgh: Edinburgh University Press.

Cole, P. (2005) 'Arrivals and departures: migration and human rights – the case of health care professionals', Paper presented to Conference on 'The Right to Migration', Madrid, organised by the European Research Training Network on Applied Global Ethics, November 2005.

Cole, P. (2007) 'Human rights and the national interest: migrants, health care and social justice', *Journal of Medical Ethics* (forthcoming).

Conradson, D. and Latham, A. (2005) 'Friendship, networks and transnationality in a world city: antipodean transmigrants in London', *Journal of Ethnic and Migration Studies*, vol 31, no 2, pp 287–305.

Crawley, H. (1997) *Women as asylum seekers: A legal handbook*, London: Immigration Law Practitioners' Association.

Crisp, J. (2003) 'Refugees and the global politics of asylum', *Political Quarterly*, vol 74, Supplement 1, pp 74–87.

Crisp, J. (2004), *The local integration and local settlement of refugees: a conceptual and historical analysis*, New Issues in Refugee Research, Working Paper 102, Evaluation and Policy Analysis Unit, UNHCR, Geneva.

CRONEM (Centre for Research on Nationalism, Ethnicity and Multiculturalism) (2006) 'Polish migrants survey results', Report of a survey commissioned by BBC *Newsnight*, University of Surrey.

Cunningham, S. and Tomlinson, J. (2005) '"Starve them out": does every child really matter? A commentary on Section 9 of the Asylum and Immigration (Treatment of Claimants, etc) Act, 2004', *Critical Social Policy*, vol 25, pp 253–75.

Curtis, L. (1984) *Nothing but the same old story*, London: Pluto.

D'Angelo, A. (2006) 'Le migrazioni polacche nell'Unione Europea dell'allargamento: flussi e caratteristiche', in K. Golemo, K. Kowlaska-Angelelli, F. Pittau and A. Ricci (eds) *Polonia: nuovo paese di frontiera*, Rome: Nuovo Anterem.

Dennis, J. (2002) *A case for change: How refugee children in England are missing out*, First finds from the monitoring project of the Refugee Children's Consortium London: Refugee Council, Save the Children, The Children's Society.

Donini, A. (2004) 'Taking sides: the Iraq crisis and the future of humanitarianism', *Forced Migration Review*, no 19, pp 38–40.

Duffield, M. and Waddell, N. (2004) 'Human security and global danger: exploring a governmental assemblage', Report of project financed by Economic and Social Science Research Council's (ESRC) New Security Challenges programme.

Duke, K. (1996) 'The resettlement experiences of refugees in the UK: main findings from an interview study', *New Community*, vol 22, no 3, pp 461–78.

Duke, K., Sales, R. and Gregory, J. (1999) 'Refugee settlement in Europe', in A. Bloch and C. Levy (eds) *Refugees, citizenship and social policy in Europe*, London: Macmillan.

Dummett, A. and Nicol, A. (1990) *Citizens, aliens and others: Nationality and immigration law*, London: Weidenfeld and Nicolson.

Dunkerley, D., Scourfield, J., Maegusuku-Hewett, T. and Smalley, N. (2006) 'The experience of frontline staff working with children seeking asylum', in C. Jones Finer (ed) *Migration, immigration and social policy*, Oxford: Blackwell.

Dunstan, R. (2006) 'Shaming destitution: NASS Section 4 support for asylum seekers who are temporarily unable to leave the country', Citizens' Advice Bureau (CAB) Evidence Briefing, June.

Duvell, F. (2004) 'Polish undocumented immigrants, regular high-skilled workers and entrepreneurs in the UK', Working Paper 54, Institute for Social Studies, Warsaw University.

Duvell, F. and Jordan, B. (2001) '"How low can you go?" Dilemmas of social work with asylum seekers in London', *Journal of Social Work Research and Evaluation*, vol 2., no 2, pp 189–205.

Duvell, F. and Jordan, B. (2003) 'Immigration control and the management of economic migration in the United Kingdom: organisational culture, implementation, enforcement and identity processes in public services', *Journal of Ethnic and Migration Studies*, vol 29, no 3, pp 299–336.

Evans, M. (1997) *Introducing contemporary feminist thought*, Cambridge: Polity Press.

Faist, T. (1995) 'Boundaries of welfare states: immigrants and social rights on the national and supranational level', in R. Miles and D. Thranhardt (eds) *Migration and European integration: The dynamics of inclusion and exclusion*, London: Pinter.

Fekete, L. (1997) 'Blackening the economy: the path to convergence', *Race and Class*, vol 39, no 1, pp 1–17.

Flynn, D. (2005) 'New borders, new management: the dilemmas of modern immigration policies', *Ethnic and Racial Studies*, vol 28, no 3, pp 463–90.

Frank, A.G. (1966) 'The development of underdevelopment', *Monthly Review*, vol 18, no 4, pp 17–31.

Freeman, A. and Kagarlitsky, B. (eds) (2004) *The politics of empire*, London: Pluto Press.

Freeman, G. (1995) 'Modes of immigration politics in liberal democratic states', *International Migration Review*, vol 29, no 4/122, pp 881–902.

Garapich, M.P. (2005) 'Soldiers and plumbers: immigration business and the impact of EU enlargement on Polish migrants', Paper presented to the international conference 'New Patterns of East West Migration in Europe,' Hamburg, 18–19 November.

Geddes, A. (2000) *Immigration and European integration: Towards fortress Europe?,* Manchester: Manchester University Press.

Gibney, M. (2001) 'The state of asylum: democratization, judicializaton and evolution of refugee policy in Europe', *New issues in refugee research*, Working Paper 50, Refugee Studies Centre, Oxford.

Glover, S., Gott, C., Loizillon, A., Portes, J., Price, R., Spencer, S., Srinivasan, V. and Willis, C. (2001) *Migration: An economic and social analysis*, RDS Occasional Paper 67, London: Home Office.

Goss, J. and Lindquist, B. (1995) 'Conceptualizing international labor migration: a structuration perspective', *International Migration Review*, vol 29, no 2, pp 317–51.

Gough, I. (1979) *The political economy of the welfare state*, London: Macmillan.

Gradstein, L. (2006) 'Rational choice, mandatory detention and asylum seekers', Unpublished DPsych thesis, Deakin University, Melbourne, Australia.

Grasmuck, S. and Pessar, P. (1991) *Between two islands: Dominican international migration*, Berkeley, CA: University of California Press.

Gray, B. (1996) 'The home of our mothers and our birthright for ages?: nation, diaspora and Irish women', in M. Maynard and J. Purvis (eds) *New frontiers in women's studies*, London: Taylor and Francis.

Gregory, J. (1987) *Sex, race and the law: Legislating for equality*, London: Sage.

Griffiths, D., Sigona, N., Zetter, R. and Sigona, D. (2005) *Refugee community organisations and dispersal: Networks, resources and social capital*, Bristol: The Policy Press.

Guild, E. (2000) 'The United Kingdom: Kosovar Albanian refugees', in J. van Selm (ed) *Kosovo's refugees in the European Union*, London: Pinter.

Gunder Frank, A. (1966) *The development of underdevelopment*, New York: Monthly Review Press.

Habermas, J. (1975) *Legitimation crisis*, Boston: Beacon.

Halfmann, J. (1998) 'Citizenship universalism and the risks of exclusion', *British Journal of Sociology*, vol 49, no 4, pp 513–33.

Hansen, R. (2003) 'Migration to Europe since 1945: its history and its lessons', *Political Quarterly*, vol 74, Supplement 1, pp 25–38.

Hargreaves, A. and Wihtol de Wenden, C. (1993) 'Guest editors' introduction', *New Community*, vol 20, no 1.

Harrell-Bond, B. (1999) 'The experience of refugees as recipients of aid', in A. Ager (ed) *Refugees: Perspectives on the experience of forced migration*, London: Continuum.

Harris, N. (1996) *The new untouchables: Immigration and the new world worker*, Harmondsworth: Penguin.

Harris, N. (2002) *Thinking the unthinkable: The immigration myth exposed*, New York: I.B. Tauris.

Harris, T. (2002) 'Afghanistan too "precarious" for returning refugees: UNHCR', Agence France Press.

Harrison, J. (2003), 'Boundary strategies: statecraft and imagined identities', Unpublished PhD thesis, Department of Sociology, University of Leicester.

Hayes, D. (2002) 'From aliens to asylum seekers: a history of immigration controls and welfare in Britain', in S. Cohen, B. Humphries and E. Mynott (eds) *From immigration controls to welfare controls*, London: Routledge.

Hayes, D. and Humphries, D. (eds) (2004) *Immigration control and social work*, London: Jessica Kingsley.

Hayter, T. (2000) *Open borders: The case against immigration controls*, London: Pluto.

Hek, R. (2002) 'Integration not segregation: young refugees in British schools', *Forced Migration Review*, vol 15, pp. 31–2.

Hek, R., Sales, R. and Hoggart, L. (2001) 'Supporting refugee and asylum seeking children: an examination of refugees' experience and the support structures that facilitate settlement in school', Unpublished report, Middlesex University.

Hewitt, R. (2005) *White backlash and the politics of multiculturalism*, Cambridge: Cambridge University Press.

Hickman, M.J. and Walter, B. (1997) *Discrimination and the Irish community in Britain*, London: CRE.

Hills, J., Le Grand, J. and Piachaud, D. (eds) (2001) *Understanding social exclusion*, Oxford: Oxford University Press.

Hills, J. and Stewart, K. (2005) *A more equal society? New Labour, poverty, inequality and exclusion*, Bristol: The Policy Press.

Hirst, P. and Thompson, G. (1999) *Globalization in question*, Cambridge: Polity Press.

Hobsbawm, E. (1964) *Labouring men*, London: Weidenfeld and Nicolson.

Hochschild, A. (2000) 'Global care chains and emotional surplus value', in W. Hutton and A. Giddens (eds) *On the edge: Living with global capitalism*, London: Jonathan Cape.

Hoggart, L., Sales, R., Raman, I. and Gunbey, A. (2000) 'Turkish-speaking mothers in Hackney: an investigation of needs and use of health provision and a trial of a volunteer visiting scheme for first-time mothers', Final report of a research and development project funded by NHS Executive Middlesex University Social Policy Research Centre.

Hollifield, J. (2004) 'The emerging migration state', *International Migration Review*, vol 38, no 3, pp 885–912.

Holmes, C. (1988) *John Bull's island: Immigration and British society, 1871–1971*, Basingstoke: Macmillan.

Holmes, C. (1991) *A tolerant country? Immigrants, refugees and minorities in Britain*, London: Faber and Faber.

Home Office (1998a) *Fairer, Faster and Firmer: A modern approach to immigration and asylum*, White Paper, Cm 4018, London: The Stationery Office.

Home Office (1998b) *Asylum Seekers Support: An information document setting out proposals for the new support scheme for asylum seekers in genuine need and inviting expressions of interest from potential support providers,* London: Immigration and Nationality Directorate.

Home Office (2001) Anti-terrorism, Crime and Security Act, London: HMSO.

Home Office (2002a) *Secure Borders, Safe Haven: Integration with diversity in Modern Britain*, White Paper, London: HMSO.

Home Office (2002b) Nationality, Immigration and Asylum Bill, London: HMSO.

Home Office (2004a) Asylum and Immigration (Treatment of Claimants, etc) Act, London: HMSO.

Home Office (2004b) *Life in the United Kingdom: A journey to citizenship*, London: HMSO.

Home Office (2005a) *Controlling our borders: Making migration work for Britain. Five year strategy for asylum and immigration*, London: Home Office.

Home Office (2005b) Immigration and Nationality Bill, London: HMSO.

Home Office (2006a) 'Accession monitoring report, May 2004–September 2006', Joint online report by Home Office, DWP, HM Revenue and Customs and ODPM, www.ind.homeoffice.gov.uk/aboutus/reports/accession_monitoring_report.

Home Office (2006b) *Fair, effective, transparent and trusted: Rebuilding confidence in our immigration system*, London: HMSO.

Home Office (2006c) *A points-based system: Making migration work for Britain*, London: HMSO.

Home Office (2006d) *Asylum figures*, London: HMSO.

Hondagneu-Sotelo, P. (1994) *Gendered transitions: Mexican experiences of immigration*, Berkeley, CA: University of California Press.

Humphries, D. (2002) 'Fair immigration controls – or none at all?', in S. Cohen, B. Humphries and E. Mynott (eds) *From immigration controls to welfare controls*, London: Routledge.

Hussain, Y. and Bagguley, P. (2005) 'Citizenship, ethnicity and identity: British Pakistanis after the 2001 "Riots"', *Sociology*, vol 39, no 3, pp 407–25.

Hynes, T. (2003) 'The issue of trust in research with refugees', UNHCR Working Papers, UNHCR Working Paper No 98, Evaluation and Policy Analysis Unit, Geneva: UNHCR.

Hynes, T. (2007) 'The dispersal policy and exclusion', Unpublished Phd thesis, Middlesex University.

IDOS (Dossier Statistico Immigrazione) (2003) *Contemporary immigration in Italy: current trends and future prospects*, Rome: Nuova Anterem.

IDOS (Dossier Statistico Immigrazione) (2004) *Dossier Statistico Immigrazione XIV rapporto*, Rome: Anterem.

IDOS (Dossier Statistico Immigrazione) (2006) *Dossier Statistico Immigrazione XVI rapporto*, Rome: Anterem.

Indra, D.M. (1987) 'Gender: a key dimension of the refugee experience', *Refuge*, vol 6, no 1, p 1.

Information Centre about Asylum and Refugees in the UK (ICAR) (2004) 'Media image, community impact: executive summary', Commission by Mayor of London, www.icar.org.uk.

International Organization for Migration (IOM) (1995) *Chinese migrants in Central and Eastern Europe: The cases of Czech Republic, Hungary and Romania*, Geneva: IOM.

International Organization for Migration (IOM) (2005) *World migration: costs and benefits of international migration*, IOM World Migration Report Series 3, Geneva: IOM.

Ippr (Institute for Public Policy Research) (2004) 'Labour migration to the UK: an Ippr fact file', 15 June.

Ippr (2006) *Irregular migration in the UK*, Ippr Factfile, London: Ippr.

Iredale, R. (1997) *Skills transfer, international migration and accreditation issues*, Wollongong: University of Wollongong Press.

Jessop, B. (1990) *State theory: Putting capitalist states in their place*, Cambridge: Polity.

Joint Council for the Welfare of Immigrants (JCWI) (1997) *Immigration, nationality and refugee law handbook*, London: JCWI.

Joint Council for the Welfare of Immigrants (JCWI) (2006) *Immigration, nationality and refugee law handbook*, London: JCWI.

Joly, D. (1996) *Haven or hell? Asylum policies and refugees in Europe*, Basingstoke: Macmillan.

Jones, C. (1977) *Immigration and social policy in Britain*, London: Tavistock.

Jordan, B. (2002) 'Migrant Polish workers in London: mobility, labour markets and the prospects for democratic development', Paper presented at conference, 'Beyond Transition: Development Perspectives and Dilemmas', Warsaw, April 2002.

Jordan, B. and Duvell, F. (2003) *Migration: the boundaries of equality and justice*, Cambridge: Polity.

Jubany, O., Naletto, G., Sales, R. and Wilpert, C. (2004) 'Skilled migrants in the labour market', Report of 'SMILING' project, European Union.

Kay, D. (1989) 'The politics of gender in exile: Chileans in Glasgow', in D. Joly and R. Cohen (eds) *Reluctant hosts: Europe and its refugees*, Aldershot: Avebury.

Kearns, G. (2004) 'The moral economy of migration', Paper presented to CRASSH conference on Migrants, Nations and Citizenship, Cambridge, July 2004.

Kelley, N. and Stevenson, J. (2006) *First do no harm: Denying healthcare to people whose asylum claims have failed*, London: Refugee Council.

Kepinska, E. (2004) 'Recent trends in international migration, Poland 2003', Institute for Social Studies, Warsaw University.

Kofman, E. (2005a) 'Citizenship, migration and the reassertion of national identity', *Citizenship Studies*, vol 9, no 5, pp 453–67.

Kofman, E. (2005b) 'Figures of the cosmopolitan: privileged nationals and national outsiders', *Innovation*, vol 18, no 1, pp 83–97.

Kofman, E. (2006) 'Gender, remittances and migration: Latin Americans and Caribbeans in Europe', Paper presented to Foro Internacional sobre el nexo entre ciencias sociales y politicas, UNESCO, February 2006.

Kofman, E., Lloyd, C. and Sales, R. (2002) 'Civic stratification, social exclusion and migrant trajectories in three European States', Final report of project funded by the ESRC One Europe or Several programme.

Kofman, E., Phizacklea, A., Raghuram, P. and Sales, R. (2000) *Gender and migration in Europe*, London: Routledge.

Kofman, E., Raghuram, P. and Merefield, M. (2005) *Gendered migrations: Towards gender sensitive policies in the UK*, Ippr Asylum and Migration Series Working Paper 5, London: Ippr.

Kofman, E. and Sales, R. (1996) 'The geography of gender and welfare in the new Europe', in M.D. Garcia Ramon and J. Monk (eds) *South and north: Women's work and daily lives in the European Community*, London: Routledge.

Kofman, E. and Sales, R. (1998) 'Migrant women and exclusion in Europe', *European Journal of Women's Studies*, vol 5, nos 3–4, pp 381–98.

Kohli, R. (2001) 'Social work with unaccompanied asylum seeking young people', *Forced Migration Review*, vol 12, no 1, pp 31–3.

Kohli, R. and Mather, R. (2003) 'Promoting psychosocial well-being in unaccompanied asylum seeking people in the United Kingdom', *Child and Family Social Work*, vol 8, no 3, pp 201–12.

Kos, A.M. and Derviskadic-Jovanovic, S. (1998) 'What can we do to support children who have been through war?', *Forced Migration Review*, vol 3, pp 4–7.

Koser, K. (2000) 'Return, readmission and reintegration: changing agendas, policy frameworks and operational programmes', in B. Ghosh (ed) *Return migration, journey of hope or despair?*, Geneva: International Organization for Migration.

Koser, K. and Lutz, H. (1998) 'The new migration in Europe: contexts, constructions and realities', in K. Koser and H. Lutz (eds) *The new migration in Europe: Social constructions and social realities*, Basingstoke: Macmillan.

Koser, K. and Pinkerton, C. (2002) 'Information dissemination to potential asylum seekers in countries of origin and/or transit', *Findings*, vol 220, London: Home Office.

Koslowski, R. (2002) 'Immigration, border control and aging societies in the European Union', *Brown Journal of World Affairs*, vol 8, no 2, pp 169–80.

Koslowski, R. (2004) 'Intersections of information technology and human mobility: globalization vs. homeland security', Paper delivered at ESRC/SSRC, 'Money and Migration after Globalization Colloquium', Oxford, 25–28 March.

Kunz, E.F. (1973) 'The refugee in flight: kinetic models and forms of displacement', *International Migration Review*, vol 7, Summer, pp 125–46.

Kymlicka, W. (2003) 'Immigration, citizenship, multiculturalism: exploring the links', *Political Quarterly*, vol 74, Supplement 1, pp 195–208.

Lane, M. (2004) 'Questioning state- and nation-centred perspectives on global migration', Paper presented at CRASSH conference on 'Migrants, Nations and Citizenship', Cambridge, July 2004.

Lee, M., Chan, A., Bradby, H. and Green, G. (2002) 'Chinese migrant women and families in Britain', *Women's Studies International Forum*, vol 25, no 6, pp 607–18.

Leibfried, S. (1993) 'Conceptualising European social policy; the EC as social actor', in L. Hantrais and S. Mangen (eds) *The policy making process and the social actors*, Cross-National Research Papers 3/1, Loughborough: European Research Centre.

Levitas, R. (1998) *The inclusive society: Social exclusion and New Labour*, Basingstoke: Macmillan.

Levitt, P., DeWind, J. and Vertovec, S. (2003) 'International perspectives on transnational migration: an introduction', *International Migration Review*, vol 37, no 3, pp 565–75.

Levitt, P. and Glick Schiller, N. (2004) 'Conceptualizing simultaneity: a transnational social field perspective on society', *International Migration Review*, vol 38, no 3, pp 1002–39.

Levy, C. (1999) 'European asylum and refugee policy after the Treaty of Amsterdam: the birth of a new regime?', in A. Bloch and C. Levy (eds) *Refugees, citizenship and social policy in Europe*, Basingstoke: Macmillan.

Lewis, M. (2005) *Asylum: Understanding public attitudes*, London: Ippr.

Lister, R. (1997) *Citizenship. Gender perspectives*, London: Macmillan.

London, L. (2000) *Whitehall and the Jews, 1933–48: British immigration policy, Jewish refugees and the Holocaust*, Cambridge: Cambridge University Press.

Lumley, R. (2003) *Children in detention*, Refugee Council Policy Paper, November, London: Refugee Council.

Lutz, H. (1993) 'In between or bridging cultural gaps? Migrant women from Turkey as mediators', *New Community*, vol 19, no 3, pp 485–94.

Ma Mung, E. (2002) 'Les Mutations des migrations Chinoises', *Ville-Ecole-Integration Enjeux*, vol 131, pp 129–45.

MacGregor, S. (1999) 'Welfare, neo-liberalism and new paternalism: three ways for social policy in late capitalist societies', *Capital and Class*, vol 67, pp 91–118.

Mahroum, S. (2000) 'Highly skilled globetrotters: mapping the international migration of human capital', *R & D Management*, vol 30, no 1, pp 23–31.

Marshall, T.H. (1950) *Citizenship and social class*, Cambridge: Cambridge University Press.

Massey, D.S., Arango, J., Hugo, G., Kouaouci, A., Pellegrino, A. and Taylor, J.E. (1993) 'Theories of international migration: a review and appraisal', *Population and Development Review*, vol 19, no 3, pp 431–66.

May, J.P. (1978) 'The Chinese in Britain, 1860–1914', in C. Holmes (ed) *Immigrants and minorities in British society*, London: George Allen and Unwin.

Mayor of London (2004a) *Offering more than they borrow: Refugee children in London*, London: Greater London Authority.

Mayor of London (2004b) *Safe and sound: asylum seekers in temporary accommodation*, London: Greater London Authority.

Meetoo, V. and Mirza, H. (2007) 'Lives at risk: multiculturalism, young women and "honour" killings', in B. Thom, R. Sales and J. Pearce (eds) *Growing up with risk*, Bristol: The Policy Press.

Meillassoux, C. (1981) *Maidens, meal and money*, Cambridge: Cambridge University Press.

Melzac, S. (1999) 'Work with refugees from political violence', in M. Lanyado and A. Horne (eds) *The handbook of child and adolescent psychotherapy*, London, Routledge.

Mesquita, J. and Gordon, M. (2005) *The international migration of health workers: A human rights analysis*, London: Medact, www.medact.org/content

Meyer, J-B. (2001) 'Network approach versus brain drain: lessons from the diaspora', *International Migration*, vol 39, no 5, pp 91–108.

Miller, D. (2004) 'Immigrants, nations and citizenship', paper presented to CRASSH conference on 'Migrants, Nations and Citizenship', Cambridge, 5–6 July.

Morokvasic, M. (1984) 'Birds of passage are also women', *International Migration Review*, vol 18, no 4, pp 886–907.

Morokvasic, M. (2004) 'Settled in mobility: engendering post-wall migration in Europe', *Feminist Review*, vol 77, pp 7–25.

Morris, J. (2003) 'Children on the edge of care', York: JRF, July 2003. (Later version available as pdf from Joseph Rowntree Foundation (JRF), www.jrf.org.uk)

Morris, L. (1997) 'A cluster of contradictions: the politics of migration in the EU', *Sociology*, vol 31, pp 241–59.

Morris, L. (2002) *Managing migration: Civic stratification and migrants' rights*, London: Routledge.

Morris, L. (2003) 'Managing contradiction: civic stratification and migrants' rights', *International Migration Review*, vol 37, pp 74–100.

Morrison, J. (2000) *The trafficking and smuggling of refugees: The end game in European asylum policy?*, Geneva: UNHCR.

Mynott, E. (2002) 'Nationalism, racism and immigration control: from anti-racism to anti-capitalism', in S. Cohen, B. Humphries and E. Mynott (eds) *From immigration controls to welfare controls*, London: Routledge.

National Aids Trust (2006) *Dispersal of asylum seekers living with HIV*, London: National Aids Trust.

Newman, J. (2001) *Modernising governance: New Labour, policy and society*, London: Sage.

Nienhuis, M. (2006) 'Eroding UK "privilege"', *JCWI Bulletin*, Spring, p 14.

Oakley, A. (1992) *Social support and motherhood*, Oxford: Blackwell.

OAU (Organisation of African Unity) (1969) *Convention governing the specific aspects of refugee problems in Africa*, available at: www.africa-union.org

O'Neill, M. and Spybey, T. (2003) 'Global refugees, exile, displacement and belonging: editors' introduction', *Sociology*, vol 37, no 1, pp 7–12.

Ouseley, H. (2005) 'Is it racist to target the bigot's vote?', *Guardian*, 26 April 2005.

Owers, A. (1994) 'The age of internal controls?', in S. Spencer (ed) *Strangers and citizens: A positive approach to migrants and refugees*, London: Rivers Oram Press.

Owers, A. (2006) *Report on an unannounced short follow-up inspection of Yarl's Wood Immigration Removal Centre*, London: HM Inspectorate of Prisons.

Papademetriou, D. (2003) 'Managing rapid and deep change in the newest age of migration', in S. Spencer (ed) *The politics of migration: Managing opportunity, conflict and change*, London: Political Quarterly.

Pateman, C. (1998) *The sexual contract*, Cambridge: Polity.

Paul, K. (1997) *Whitewashing British: Race and citizenship in the postwar era*, Ithaca, NY: Cornell University Press.

Pecoud, A. and de Guchteneire, P. (2005) *Migration without borders: An investigation into the free movement of people*, Paris: UNESCO Global Commission on International Migration.

Pellew, J. (1989) 'The Home Office and the Aliens Act, 1905', *Historical Journal*, vol 32, no 2, pp 369–85.

Pessar, P. and Mahler, S. (2003) 'Transnational migration: bringing gender in', *International Migration Review*, vol 37, no 3, pp 812–46.

Petrillo, A. (1999) 'Italy: farewell to the "Bel Paese"?', in R. Dale and M. Cole (eds) *European Union and migration labour*, Oxford: Berg.

Phillips, T. (2005) 'Preface', to M. Lewis, *Asylum: Understanding public attitudes*, London: Ippr.

Phizacklea, A. (1983) *One way ticket*, London: Routledge.

Phizacklea, A. (1988) 'Migration and globalization: a feminist perspective', in K. Koser and H. Lutz (eds) *The new migration in Europe: Social constructions and social realities*, Basingstoke: Macmillan, pp 21–38.

Phizacklea, A. and Miles, R. (1980) *Labour and racism*, London: Routledge.

Phizacklea, A. and Wolkowitz, C. (1995) *Homeworking women*, London: Sage.

Pieke, F. (2004) *Chinese globalization and migration to Europe*, Working Paper 94, March, San Diego, CA: Centre for Comparative Immigration Studies.

Poinsot, M. (1993) 'Competition for political legitimacy at local and national levels among young North Africans in France', *New Community*, vol 20, no 1, pp 59–77.

Portes, A. (1997) 'Immigration theory for a new century: some problems and opportunities', *International Migration Review,* vol 31, pp 799–827.

Portes, A. (2003) 'Conclusion: theoretical convergencies and empirical evidence in the study of immigrant transnationalism', *International Migration Review*, vol 37, no 3, pp 874–92.

Portes, A. (2004) 'A cross-Atlantic dialogue: the progress of research and theory in the study of international migration', *International Migration Review*, vol 38, no 3, pp 823–51.

Portes A., Guarnizo, L.E. and Landolt, P. (1999) 'The study of transnationalism: pitfalls and promise of an emergent research field', *Ethnic and Racial Studies*, vol 22, pp 218–37.

Principe, L. (1998) 'L'immagine mediatica dell'immigrato: dallo stereotipo all'integrazione ('The mediated image of the immigrant: from stereotype to integration'), Paper to the conference 'Coordinamento europeo per il diritto degli stranieri a vivere in famiglia' ('European coordination for the right of foreigners to family life'), Genoa, March.

Pugliese, E. (2000) 'L'Italia tra migrazioni internazionali e migrazione interne' ('Italy between international and internal migration'), in Agenzia Roma per la preparazione del Giubileo *Migrazioni. Scenari per il XXI secolo* Convengno internazionale (Agency for the organisation of the Jubilee, Rome, International Conference on *Migration, Scenarios for the twenty-first century*).

Raghuram, P. (2004) 'The difference that skills make: gender, family migration strategies and regulated labour markets', *Journal of Ethnic and Migration Studies*, vol 30, no 2, pp 303–21.

Raghuram, P. and Kofman, E. (2002) 'The state, skilled labour markets and immigration: the case of doctors in England', *Environment and Planning A*, vol 34, pp 2071–89.

Rawls, J. (1971) *Theory of justice*, Cambridge, MA: Harvard University Press.

Refugee Children's Consortium (2002) 'The Nationality, Immigration and Asylum Bill, second reading briefing', www.refugeecouncil.org.uk

Refugee Council (1996) *Women refugees*, London: Refugee Council.

Refugee Council (2003) *A joint statement on the withdrawal of asylum support for in-country applications*, London: Refugee Council.

Refugee Council (2004) 'The impact of Section 55 on the inter-agency partnership and the asylum seekers it supports', Refugee Council Briefing, www.refugeecouncil.org.uk, February.

Refugee Council (2005a) *Annual report for 2004–05*, London: Refugee Council.

Refugee Council (2005b) 'Asylum and Immigration Act 2004: an update', March.

Refugee Council (2006) *Unaccompanied children and the Dublin II regulation*, Refugee Council Briefing, November, London: Refugee Council.

Robinson, V. and Carey, M. (2000) 'Peopling skilled international migration: Indian doctors in the UK', *International Migration*, vol 38, no 1, pp 89–108.

Robinson, V., Andersson, R. and Musterd, S. (2003) *Spreading the 'burden'? A review of policies to disperse asylum seekers and refugees*, Bristol: The Policy Press.

Rosewarne, S. (2001) 'New world borders: globalisation, the new migration and rehoning the boundaries of the nation-state', *Overland*, no 164, Spring, pp 22–6.

Rossiter, A. (1991) 'Bringing the margins back into the centre: a review of aspects of Irish women's emigration', in A. Smyth (ed) *Irish women's studies reader*, Dublin: Attic Press.

Rowthorn, R. (2004) 'The economic impact of immigration', Civitas Online Report, April, /www.civitas.org.uk/

RSA (Royal Society of Arts) (2005) *Migration: A welcome opportunity – A new way forward by the RSA Migration Commission*, London: RSA.

Rubin, I.I. (1979) *A history of economic thought* (3rd edn), London: Ink Links.

Rudolph, H. (1996) 'The new *gastarbeiter* system in Germany', *New Community*, vol 22, no 2, pp 287–300.

Ruhs, M. and Chang, H. (2004) 'The ethics of labor and immigration policy', *International Organization*, vol 58, pp 69–102.

Rutter, J. (2003) *Working with refugee children*, York: Joseph Rowntree Foundation.

Ryan, L. (2007) Migrant women, social networks and motherhood: the experiences of Irish nurses in Britain, *Sociology* (forthcoming).

Saggar, S. (1992) *Race and politics in Britain*, London: Harvester.

Saggar, S. (2003) 'Immigration and the politics of public opinion', *Political Quarterly*, vol 74, Supplement 1.

Sales, R. (1997) *Women divided: Gender, religion and politics in Northern Ireland*, London: Routledge.

Sales, R. (2002a) 'Contemporary migration policy in Europe', in R. Sykes, C. Bochel and N. Ellison (eds) *Social Policy Review 14*, Bristol: The Policy Press.

Sales, R. (2002b) 'The deserving and the undeserving: refugees, asylum seekers and welfare in Britain', *Critical Social Policy*, vol 22, no 1, pp 456–78.

Sales, R. (2005) 'Secure borders, safe haven: a contradiction in terms', *Ethnic and Racial Studies*, vol 28, no 3, pp 445–62.

Sales, R. (2006) 'I polacchi in Europa: il caso di Londra', in K. Golemo, K. Kowlaska-Angelelli, F. Pittau and A. Ricci (eds) *Polonia: nuovo paese di di frontiera*, Rome: Nuovo Anterem.

Sales, R. (2007) 'In need of protection? Immigration policy and young refugees', in B. Thom, R. Sales and J. Pearce (eds) *Growing up with risk*, Bristol: The Policy Press.

Sales, R., Blitz, B. and Marzano, L. (2003) 'The Afghan community in the UK: professional capacity and views on return', report for Refugee Action and International Organization of Migration, London.

Sales, R. and Gregory, J. (1998) 'Refugee women in London: the experience of Somali women', *Refuge, Journal of the Centre for Refugee Studies*, vol 17, no 1, pp 16–20.

Sales, R. and Hek, R. (2004) 'Dilemmas of care and control: the work of an asylum team in a London borough', in D. Hayes and D. Humphries (eds) *Immigration control and social work*, London: Jessica Kingsley.

Sales, R. and Siara, B. (2006) 'Generations of Polish migrants in London', Paper presented to Conference on 'Transnational identities – cities unbound – migrations' redefined organised by Centre for Research on Nationalism, Ethnicity and Multiculturalism (CRONEM), University of Surrey and Centre for European Studies, Jagiellonian University, Kraków, October.

Sassen, S. (1991) *Global city: New York, London, Tokyo*, Princeton: Princeton University Press.

Schuster, L. and Solomos, J. (1999) 'The politics of refugee and asylum policies in Britain: historical patterns and contemporary realities', in A. Bloch and C. Levy (eds) *Refugees, citizenship and social policy in Europe*, Basingstoke: Macmillan.

Sciortino, G. (2000) 'Towards a political sociology of entry policies: conceptual problems and theoretical proposals', *Journal of Ethnic and Migration Studies*, vol 26, no 2, pp 213–28.

Seglow, J (2005) 'The ethics of immigration' *Political Studies Review* 3/3, pp 317-434.

Sen, A. (1980) *Poverty and famines: An essay on entitlement*, Oxford: Oxford University Press.

SEU (Social Exclusion Unit) (2004) *A better life for all*, London: Social Exclusion Unit.

Silove, D., Steel, Z. and Watters, C. (2000) 'Policies of deterrence and the mental health of asylum seekers', *Journal of the American Medical Association*, vol 284, no 5, pp 584–90.

Smith, A. (1976) *An inquiry into the nature and causes of the wealth of nations*, Oxford: Oxford University Press.

Sodersten, B. (1978) *International economics*, Basingstoke: Macmillan.

Solomos, J. (2003) *Race and racism in Britain*, Basingstoke: Palgrave Macmillan.

Somerville, W. (2006) 'Success and failure under Labour: problems of priorities and performance in migration policy', *JCWI Immigration Rights Project*, London: JCWI, www.jcwi.org.uk/archives/

Song, M. (2004) 'When the "global chain" does not lead to satisfaction all round: a comment on the Morecambe Bay tragedy', *Feminist Review*, no 77, pp 137–40.

Song, M. (2005) 'Global and local articulations of Asian identity', in C. Alexander and C. Knowles (eds) *Making race matter: Bodies, space and identity*, Basingstoke: Palgrave Macmillan.

Southall Black Sisters (SBS) (1997) 'The one year immigration rule. A stark choice: domestic violence or deportation?', *National Women's Network Newsletter*, vol 1, July/August.

Soysal, Y. (1994) *Limits of citizenship: Migrants and postnational membership in Europe*, Chicago, IL: University of Chicago Press.

Spencer, S. (ed) (1994) *Strangers and citizens: A positive approach to migrants and refugees*, London: Rivers Oram Press.

Spencer, S. (ed) (2003) *The politics of migration: Managing opportunity, conflict and change*, London: Political Quarterly.

Sriskandarajah, D. (2006) 'Pulling up the drawbridge will damage our economy', *Guardian*, 23 August.

Stanley, K. (2001) *Cold comfort: Young separated refugees in England*, London: Save the Children.

Stark, O. (1984) 'Migration decision-making: a review article', *Journal of Development Economics*, vol 14, pp 251–9.

Statham, P. (2003) 'Understanding anti-asylum rhetoric: restrictive politics of racist publics?', *Political Quarterly*, vol 74, Supplement 1, pp 163–77.

Stein, B. (1997) 'Refugee repatriation, return and refoulement during conflict', Paper presented to United States Agency for International Development, Promoting Democracy, Human Rights, and Reintegration in Post-conflict Societies, Washington, DC, 30–31 October.

Summerfield, H. (1993) 'Patterns of adaptation; Somali and Bangladeshi women in Britain', in G. Buijs (ed) *Migrant women: Crossing boundaries and changing identities*, Oxford: Berg.

Tacoli, C. (1999) 'Just like one of the family', in J. Gregory, R. Sales and A. Hegewisch (eds) *Women, work and equality: The challenge of equal pay in a deregulated market*, London: Macmillan.

Taylor, G. (2007) 'Health related quality of life for Congolese refugees in London and Paris', Unpublished PhD thesis, Middlesex University.

Tilki, M. (2003) 'Health beliefs of the Irish Community in London', Unpublished PhD thesis, Middlesex University.

Todaro, M. (1969) 'A model of labour migration and urban unemployment in less developed countries', *American Economic Review*, vol 59, pp 138–48.

Todaro, M. (1976) *Internal migration in developing countries*, Geneva: ILO.

Toft, M.D. (2000) 'Repatriation of refugees: a failing policy', Unpublished paper, John F. Kennedy School of Government, Harvard University.

Truong, T.D. (1996) 'Gender, international migration and social reproduction: implications for theory, policy, research and networking', *Asian and Pacific Migration Journal*, vol 5, no 1, pp 27–52.

Tuitt, P. (1999) 'The precarious safety of refugees', in A. Bloch and C. Levy (eds) *Refugees, citizenship and social policy in Europe*, Basingstoke: Macmillan.

Turton, D. (2003) 'Refugees, forced resettlers and "other forced migrants": towards a unitary study of forced migrants', UNHCR Working Paper 94, Oxford: Refugee Studies Centre, University of Oxford.

Turton, D. and Marsden, P. (2002) 'Taking refugees for a ride? the politics of refugee return to Afghanistan', Afghanistan Research and Evaluation Unit, www.areu.org.af/

UNESCO (2005) 'Information kit on UN Convention on Migrants' Rights 2003', Paris: UNESCO, p 7, www.unesco.org

UNHCR (1951) 'Geneva Convention relating to the status of refugees', Geneva: UNHCR (www.unhcr.org).

UNHCR (2004) 'Comments on the Asylum and Immigration (Treatment of Claimants, etc.) Act 2004', clause 2 draft guidance of June 2004, www.unhcr.org.uk, accessed 12 November 2006.

UNHCR (2006) *The state of the world refugees: Human displacement in the new millennium*, Geneva: UNHCR.

UNICEF UK (2004) 'Child trafficking', Position statement, 3 June (www.unicef.org/).

Vertovec, S. (2003) 'Migration and other modes of transnationalism: towards conceptual cross-fertilization', *International Migration Review*, vol 37, no 3, pp 641–65.

Vertovec, S. (2004) 'Migrant transnationalism and modes of transformation', *International Migration Review*, vol 38, no 3, pp 970–1001.

Vertovec, S. (2006) 'The emergence of super-diversity in Britain', Centre on Migration, Policy and Society (COMPAS) Working Paper 25.

Walby, S. (1990) 'Is citizenship gendered?', *Sociology*, vol 28, no 2, pp 379–95.

Wallace, C. (2002) 'Opening and closing borders: migration and mobility in East-Central Europe', *Journal of Ethnic and Migration Studies*, vol 28, no 4, pp 603–25.

Walzer, M. (1983) *Spheres of Justice*, New York: Basic Books.

Watters, C. (2001) 'Emerging paradigms in the mental health care of refugees', *Social Science and Medicine*, vol 52, pp 1709–18.

Waylen, P. (1986) 'Women and neoliberalism', in J. Evans, S.J. Hill, K. Hunt, E. Meehan, T. ten Tusscher, U. Vogel and G. Waylen (eds) *Feminism and political theory*, London: Sage.

Wong, L. (2003) 'Belonging and diaspora: the Chinese and the internet', *First Monday* (internet journal /www.firstmonday.org/), vol 8, no 4.

Yeates, N. (2004) 'A dialogue with "global care chain" analysis: nurse migration in the Irish context', *Feminist Review*, vol 77, pp 79–95.

Young, J. (2002) 'To these wet and windy shores: recent immigration policy in the UK', Paper presented at the Common Study programme in Critical Criminology, University of Athens, April.

Yuval Davis, N. (1997) 'Ethnicity, gender relations and multiculturalism', in P. Werbner and T. Modood (eds) *Debating cultural hybridity*, London: Zed.

Yuval Davis, N., Anthias, F. and Kofman, E. (2005) 'Secure borders and safe haven and the gendered politics of belonging: beyond social cohesion', *Ethnic and Racial Studies*, vol 28, no 3, pp 513–35.

Zarzosa, H.L. (1998) 'Internal exile, exile and return: a gendered view', *Journal of Refugee Studies*, vol 11, no 2, pp 189–99.

Zetter, R. and Pearl, M. (2000) 'The minority with the minority: refugee community-based organisations in the UK and the impact of restrictionism on asylum-seekers', *Journal of Ethnic and Migration Studies* vol 26, no 4, pp 675–97.

Zolberg, A., Suhrke, A. and Aguayo, S. (1989) *Escape from violence: Conflict and the refugee crisis in the developing world*, New York: Oxford University Press.

Index